PRAISE FOR
DAY BY DAY THROUGH THE BIBLE

"Twenty years ago, as a pastor, I met Allen and first learned of the Ezra Project. Allen's passion then and now, and the goal of this series of reflections, is to get you into the Word of God day by day. I share that passion. Read the Bible, study it, meditate on it, memorize it, pray it through, listen to it preached—and let it lead you to the God of the Bible."

— **Dr. Donald W. Sweeting,** *president,*
Colorado Christian University

"Instruction. Inspiration. Intercession. You'll experience all of these with *Day by Day Through the Bible: The Writings of Paul.* God communicated His wisdom through Paul, and now Allen J. Huth communicates it to you. Be instructed. Be inspired. And join Allen in a prayer of thanksgiving."

—**Dr. Woodrow Kroll,** *former president,*
Back to the Bible

"Allen Huth has spent years reading from God's Word and applying God's wisdom to his life. In *Day by Day Through the Bible,* Allen shares with us what God's Spirit has impressed upon his heart. As you read God's Word, and then read the wisdom Allen has received from God's Spirit through God's Word, your heart and soul will be fed in new ways – and you will find practical application of God's Word to your life."

—**John Snyder,** *lead pastor,*
Crossroads Community Church

"Reading the *Day by Day Through the Bible* series gets you excited to read the Word of God. I highly recommend this series for those who desire a fresh new way to see and hear from God in your daily devotion."

—David Love, *pastor,*
Calvary Castle Rock

"In *Day by Day Through the Bible,* Allen shares his personal journey through the Scriptures, and has challenged me to see *The Writings of Paul* in an entirely different light. He opened my heart and mind to the intimate call of God. I have a brand new exploratory manner of reading *The Writings of Paul.*"

—Denise Washington Blomberg,
AM91 Radio News Director

"You can really feel Allen's love for God's Word in these devotional lessons. His combination of real-life stories and practical applications make daily Bible reading fun and rewarding for anyone."

—Arlen Nordhagen, *entrepreneur, business owner,*
president of The Nord Foundation

"My favorite kind of book? The kind that explains insightful truths from scripture illustrated by relatable personal stories. Allen J. Huth has done that! He weaves threads from his well-worn Bible, his multiple journals, his extensive travels, and his experiences into a tapestry of lessons that will encourage you daily. I'll be quoting him many times!!"

—Robert J. Morgan, *best-selling gold-Illuminations,*
and gold-medallion winning author, speaker, Bible teacher

DAY *by* DAY SERIES

DAY *by* DAY
THROUGH THE
BIBLE

The Writings of Paul

ALLEN J. HUTH

MEDIA.COM

DAY *by* DAY
THROUGH THE
BIBLE

Published by
Illumify Media Global
www.IllumifyMedia.com
"Let's bring your book to life!"

Library of Congress Control Number: 2022907099

Paperback ISBN: 9781955043731

Typeset by Art Innovations (http://artinnovations.in/)
Cover design by Debbie Lewis

Printed in the United States of America

CONTENTS

FOREWORD

The Apostle Paul's journey was one uniquely reserved for him. Jesus appeared to the man known as Saul on the road to Damascus, telling him how he would suffer and calling him to share the good news of the gospel with the Gentiles. Saul's name was changed to Paul, and he immediately became effective at using the Old Testament to convince people of Christ. He spent three years in the wilderness, as God revealed the mystery of the gospel to him. God sends him on missionary journeys, planting churches throughout Asia Minor and into southern Europe.

Imagine the opportunity to eat dinner with Paul – what he could share with you as he reflected on his walk with the Lord! Paul's theme in that discussion likely would be reflected in his words as recorded in Philippians 3:8, *"Indeed, I count everything as loss because of the surpassing worth of knowing Christ Jesus my Lord. For his sake I have suffered the loss of all things and count them as rubbish, in order that I may gain Christ."*

Rather than having dinner with Paul, what might you learn if you walked day-by-day with Paul, learning from him and reflecting on what he learned and how it applies to your life? Through this workbook written by Allen J. Huth, you can do just that.

More than twenty years ago, Allen followed a call God placed on his heart, starting a nonprofit corporation known as the Ezra Project. The mission of the Ezra Project is stated very simply – "Connecting God's people to God's Word, by encouraging Christians to engage in the Bible daily." In pursuit of that mission, Allen has written *"Day by Day through the Bible: The Writings of Paul"*. Allen takes a chapter each day of the writings of Paul, sharing insight he gained in his life when he read from God's Word daily, and he takes you deeper into the meaning and impact these verses can have in your life.

My prayer for you, as you follow through the daily study, is God's Word will come alive in your life, your understanding of the mystery of the gospel will be strengthened, and you, too, will grow to a place of counting all things as rubbish when compared to the surpassing worth of knowing Christ Jesus as your Lord.

—Daniel J. Heighway
Executive Director
The Gideons International

PREFACE

The Writings of Paul is a workbook of daily devotions in the thirteen books and epistles attributed to Paul in the New Testament:

- Romans
- 1 and 2 Corinthians
- Galatians
- Ephesians
- Philippians
- Colossians
- 1 and 2 Thessalonians
- 1 and 2 Timothy
- Titus
- Philemon

Done day by day, it will cover eight-seven days. There is much to be gleaned from the writings of Paul, which make up the majority of the New Testament.

Comments on Bible passages, life applications, and prayers are based on the audio daily devotion, ADDBIBLE, a free app that can be heard daily on your smartphone or tablet. The scripture verses in the daily readings are drawn from the English Standard Version (ESV) unless otherwise noted.

ADDBIBLE was recorded using written records from thirty-five years of my personal Bible reading journals. I started reading the Bible at fifteen years old and started journaling my quiet times in 1983. I have been blessed *"exceedingly abundantly"* (Eph. 3:20) by what God has revealed to me in His Word.

I count it an awesome privilege to share insights from my personal journals including personal stories of how God's Word has specifically impacted my life and short prayers we can pray together, all in 10-15 minutes per day.

This workbook is one of a series of *Day by Day Through the Bible: The Writings of . . .* daily devotions featuring other Biblical authors like Solomon, John, the Minor Prophets, and more. Access them all by visiting ezraproject.net.

May God richly bless you as you enjoy a portion of God's Word each and every day.

Abiding in the Word,

*— **Allen J. Huth***
President
The Ezra Project

Thanks Gwynne Olson, Ezra Project Operations Manager, for your labor of love, pouring over every word, quote, and punctuation of the *Day by Day Through the Bible* series! Teamwork indeed!

ABOUT PAUL[1]

"*And the witnesses laid down their garments at the feet of a young man named Saul... And Saul approved of his execution... But Saul was ravaging the church, and entering house after house, he dragged off men and women and committed them to prison.*" (Acts 7:58, 8:1, 3). Those verses introduce the great apostle Paul in the holy scriptures.

He next appears on the road to Damascus in Acts 9:3-8:

Now as he went on his way, he approached Damascus, and suddenly a light from heaven shone around him. And falling to the ground, he heard a voice saying to him, "Saul, Saul, why are you persecuting me?" And he said, "Who are you, Lord?" And he said, "I am Jesus, whom you are persecuting. But rise and enter the city, and you will be told what you are to do." The men who were traveling with him stood speechless, hearing the voice but seeing no one. Saul rose from the ground, and although his eyes were opened, he saw nothing. So they led him by the hand and brought him into Damascus.

Jesus Himself confronted Saul and changed his life forever!

Paul the Apostle, originally named Saul of Tarsus, was born about 4 B.C. in Tarsus. Though not one of the original twelve disciples of Jesus, he became one of the leaders of the first generation of Christians. Some consider Paul to be the most important person after Jesus in the history of Christianity. His surviving letters have had enormous influence on subsequent Christianity and secure his place as one of the greatest religious leaders of all time.

Paul was a Greek-speaking Jew from Asia Minor. His birthplace, Tarsus, was a major city in eastern Cilicia, a region that had been made part of the Roman province

---

1   Much of About Paul was adapted from information found in Britannica.

of Syria by the time of Paul's adulthood. Although the exact date of his birth is unknown, he was active as a missionary in the 40s and 50s of the first century. From this, it may be inferred that he was born about the same time as Jesus, or a little later. He was converted to faith in Jesus Christ about 33 A.D., and he died, probably in Rome, about 62–64 A.D.

His trade, tent making, which he continued to practice after his conversion to Christianity, helps explain important aspects of his apostleship. He could travel with a few leather-working tools and set up shop anywhere. His letters were written in common Greek, rather than in elegant literary Greek, illustrating Paul was a common man who made his living with his own hands, not an aristocrat.

Until about the midpoint of his life, Paul was a member of the Pharisees. Pharisees believed in life after death, which was one of Paul's deepest convictions. Pharisees were very careful students of the Hebrew Bible, and Paul was able to quote extensively from the Greek translation. By his own account, Paul was the best Jew and the best Pharisee of his generation (Phil. 3:4–6; Gal. 1:13–14), though he claimed to be the least apostle of Christ (2 Cor. 11:22–3; 1 Cor. 15:9–10) and attributed his successes to the grace of God.

Paul spent much of the first half of his life persecuting the Christian movement, an activity to which he refers several times. Paul's persecutions involved traveling from synagogue to synagogue urging the punishment of Jews who accepted Jesus as the Messiah.

After his Damascus Road encounter with Jesus, he went into Arabia. He then returned to Damascus, and three years later he went to Jerusalem to become acquainted with the leading apostles there. Afterwards, he began his missionary trips to the west, preaching first in his native Syria and Cilicia. During the next twenty years, he established several churches in Asia Minor and at least three in Europe.

Of the twenty-seven books in the New Testament, thirteen are attributed to Paul, and approximately half of another, Acts, deals with Paul's life and works. Thus, about half of the New Testament stems from Paul and the people whom he influenced. Build your knowledge of Christianity and your faith in Jesus Christ as you dwell in *Day by Day Through the Bible: The Writings of Paul.*

SIXTEEN DAYS IN ROMANS

ROMANS 1

Without Excuse

Today, we begin the Book of Romans. Paul most likely wrote Romans from Corinth about 57 A.D. I call it the Ph.D. of the New Testament. Others call it the Christian Manifesto or the Constitution of Christianity. It is a high-level book of Christian thought.

The theme is the revelation of God's judging and saving righteousness in the gospel of Jesus Christ. Of all of Paul's writings, it is the fullest expression of Paul's theology, filled with lofty theological ideas and vocabulary.

Romans is the most complete teaching about God and our relationship to Him. What we will learn in Romans is summarized in my English Standard Version Study Bible introduction to the Book of Romans:

(Paul) addresses matters of interest for a church that includes both Jewish and Gentile Christians: (1) Can one be right with God through obeying the law? (2) What can be learned from Abraham, and is he the father of both Jewish and Gentile Christians? (3) What role does the law play with reference to sin? (4) What does the salvation of Gentiles indicate about the future of Israel as God's people? (5) Should Christians observe (Old Testament) food laws, and how should they relate to fellow believers on such matters? (p. 2151).

Dr. Woodrow Kroll is the former President of Back to the Bible. He put out an English Standard Version Bible, and in his introduction to Romans, he says, "Romans is a book to savor. To read slowly and carefully. Why? Because it presents an irrefutable argument for the world's need for a savior and the eternal plan of the sovereign God to draw needy sinners to that Savior. You'll probe the depth of the wisdom of God. This book will challenge your mind, strengthen your faith, and guide your Christian conduct."

That makes you want to jump into Romans right now, so please read or listen to Romans 1.

COMMENTS

In our devotions from the Book of Romans, I will use three of my personal Bible reading journals. One from the summer of 1994. The next from the summer of 2001, when I was reading both the Old and New Testaments. And the third from the fall of 2013, when I read Romans in about twenty days. I like to use my personal Bible reading journals from various decades. So here, we will have one from the '90s, the '00s, and the 0-teens. Let's get into Romans 1.

When I read Romans 1 in 1994, I was in Indianapolis at a Gideon International Convention. I wrote, "Paul was a prayer warrior, holding up those he had preached and witnessed to. He wanted to go to Rome, *'that I may impart some spiritual gift to you . . . that is, that I may be encouraged together with you while among you'* (vv. 11-12 NASB). Then he changes his focus from what he can do for them to what they can do for each other."

Next, I wrote, "Romans 1:16-32 is a great sermon for a non-believer. Don't be ashamed of the gospel. It is righteousness. There's also the wrath of God. All of us know about God from within and in creation, but we don't honor Him and give thanks, so our heart becomes darkened. We become fools. We worship the creature or creation, rather than the creator. And God lifts His hand of grace and gives us over to our degrading passions and our depraved minds to do those things which are not proper."

In 2001, I focused primarily on verse 18 (NASB), which says, *"For the wrath of God is revealed from heaven against all ungodliness and unrighteousness of men'*. We forget this characteristic of God. To say everybody's going to make it to heaven flies in the face of this verse."

In the fall of 2013, I actually read half of this chapter on one day and half on a second day. As I share the journal entry from 2013, I think it is amazing how sometimes it is very similar to what I read and wrote almost twenty years before and then sometimes very different. I think I capture the essence of this chapter in my 2013 journal.

I quoted verse 8, *"First, I thank my God through Jesus Christ for all of you, because your faith is proclaimed in all the world.'* Paul wants to go to Rome to *'impart to you some spiritual gift to strengthen you – that is, that we may be mutually encouraged by each other's faith'* (vv. 11-12). Paul had a calling in his life to preach the gospel to Gentiles, Greeks, and Barbarians; lost people.

"What is my obligation? To connect God's people to God's Word through the Ezra Project, and to get Christians back into their Bibles and see lost people come to Jesus through the distribution of His Word by my membership in The Gideons International. I am not ashamed of the gospel. It is the power of salvation. Lord, help me share it even more. I live by faith more so every day as I age and experience God."

I summarized the second half of Romans 1 by writing, "Paul gets right after it after his greeting and his expression of longing to visit Rome. He starts with the wrath of God directed to all who suppress the truth. What can be known about God's plan for people? God is evidenced in His creation, so every human being must have an instinctive awareness of God. People exchange the glory of God to worship idols, so God gives us over to the lust of our hearts because they exchanged the truth about God for a lie. We cannot exchange the truth of God if we don't know it. Homosexuality is not natural. One is not born in it, according to verses 26-27. The result of godlessness is sinful behavior."

DIGGING DEEPER

Right off the bat, Romans answers some of the most pressing questions we have in our day. First, what about people who "don't know" about Jesus? Let's see what Paul has to say about it:

For the wrath of God is revealed from heaven against all ungodliness and unrighteousness of men, who by their unrighteousness suppress the truth. For what can be known about God is plain to them, because God has shown it to them. For his invisible attributes, namely, his eternal power and divine nature, have been clearly perceived, ever since the creation of the world, in the things that have been made. So they are without excuse (vv. 18-20).

Those verses answer that question. Everybody knows about God. Even if it is only through His creation, everybody knows. But I believe, also, it is internal. God has put an awareness of Himself in every human life. He reminds us we are without excuse. Then he goes on to say, *"Claiming to be wise, they became fools, and exchanged the glory of the immortal God for images resembling mortal man and birds and animals and creeping things"* (vv. 22-23). In other words, human beings exchange the worship of the immortal God for the worship of manmade idols.

> Romans 1 answers the question, what about those who do not know Jesus?

God does not force us to worship Him. Paul goes on to say, *"Therefore God gave them up in the lusts of their hearts to impurity, to the dishonoring of their bodies among themselves, because they exchanged the truth about God for a lie and worshiped and served the creature rather than the Creator"* (vv. 24-25). Romans 1 answers the question, what about those who do not know Jesus? Everybody—God created everybody—to know Him through His own creation and an instinctive knowledge of God in each one of us.

The next question, which is sensitive in our culture today, probably always has been, is about homosexuality. Let's read what the Word of God says:

For this reason God gave them up to dishonorable passions. For their women exchanged natural relations for those that are contrary to nature; and the men likewise gave up natural relations with women and were consumed with passion for one another, men committing shameless acts with men and receiving in themselves the due penalty for their error (vv. 26-27).

No, I am not going to dwell on the issue of homosexuality. I think it is clear if you read the Word of God, the cultural argument that people are born this way, is just not a biblical position. I encourage you to grab your Bible and go back and look at Romans 1:26-27 yourself.

Romans 1 starts out with a bang. Paul gets right after it. He tells us, claiming to be wise, we become fools. And we exchanged the truth about God for a lie. Let's close Romans 1 with a prayer I wrote in my journal in 2013, "Forgiveness for exchanging truth for a lie, bring us back to biblical belief. Keep me from falling."

Prayer

Father, as we head down the road of the Book of Romans, we pray for wisdom, knowledge, and understanding in this book I call the Ph.D. of Christianity, others have called the Christian Manifesto, and others the Constitution of Christianity. Give us wisdom, knowledge, and understanding in Your Word. We pray for it and ask for it, in Jesus' name. Amen.

MY THOUGHTS

ROMANS 2

Judge Not

Romans 2 is about God's judgment. Do you pass judgment on others? Please read or listen to Romans 2.

COMMENTS

In 1992, when reading Romans 2, I realized it was a continuation of what we left off with in Romans 1. I wrote, "Don't judge one another." And then, "Very hard to do. God rightly judges those who practice the things of Romans 1."

Let's remind ourselves of how Romans 1 ended. Verses 29-31 said, *"They were filled with all manner of unrighteousness, evil, covetousness, malice. They are full of envy, murder, strife, deceit, maliciousness. They are gossips, slanderers, haters of God, insolent, haughty, boastful, inventors of evil, disobedient to parents, foolish, faithless, heartless, ruthless."* That is the list Paul is referring to in this first verse of chapter 2 when he says, *"For in passing judgment on another you condemn yourself, because you, the judge, practice the very same things."*

> Virtue is not what we demonstrate outwardly, but from our heart.

Your tendency, like mine, might be, wait a minute. I do not do those things. Well, let's look at a couple of those again. How about unrighteousness or covetousness? How about creating strife? Or what about gossiping? How about being boastful? What about disobedience to parents? I do not know about you, but I could find myself guilty of many of those practices.

Back to my journal entry, "God renders to every man according to his deeds. Wrath or glory, honor and peace; our choice, based upon how we live. God judges our doing, the secrets of men." I continued, "Not only know what's right, but we must do what is right. Virtue is not what we demonstrate outwardly, but from our heart."

In 2001, I had a one-line summary of Romans 2, "We are all caught up in sin, Jew or Gentile."

In 2013, I wrote, "Be careful when judging others that I don't practice the very same thing. And God's kindness is meant to lead people to repentance. We may be judged by works, but not saved by them, according to verses 6-11." Then I wrote, "Paul levels the playing field of Jews and Gentiles in verses 12-16. The law does not save. Behavior is the key. One can follow the precepts of the law, but never even know it exists. Yet, Jews, who have it and know the law, can be breaking it. Jews thought circumcision was a rite of passage, but Paul argues circumcision is a matter of the heart. Paul is saying being Jews or being Gentiles is not what matters. It's our actions."

DIGGING DEEPER

I want to focus on the issue of judging others in this chapter. I know as a young Christian, an immature Christian, I was pretty good at this. I thought I had the corner on righteousness. I thought I knew the difference between good and evil. And so, I was pretty good at judging others, Christian or non-Christian.

I remember a particular incident when we were in a young married class in our church and one of the couples was struggling and the guy told me he was going to divorce his wife. I told him he could not do that; divorce is not biblical. That may be true, but what right did I have to jump in the middle of his marriage and decide what he could and could not do? We were friends and they did end up getting divorced, and my judgmental spirit really hurt our friendship for many, many years.

He moved out-of-state, and by the grace of God we got reconnected somehow, and our friendship was restored. And I am much less judgmental.

Maybe you too have had a judgmental spirit. I remind us both of this verse in chapter 2, *"We know that the judgment of God rightly falls on those who practice such things"* (v. 2). As I have grown in my Christianity and matured in my faith, I figured out I am going to let God be the judge.

To wrap up the discussion on judging others, the end of verse 16 also says, *"God judges the secrets of men by Christ Jesus."* I can only see the outward appearance, the outward actions of somebody. I cannot judge their hearts. I cannot judge the secrets of men.

Prayer

Lord, I pray, confessing that yes, I have had a judgmental spirit much of my Christian life. Forgive me, Lord. Forgive me. And Lord help me to be way less judgmental now as I understand the Word and understand my faith in You much, much more.

I thank You that You do not judge just my outward stuff, but You know my heart. I also thank You for forgiving me when I fail You, either by judging someone else or by not living up to the Christian standards You want me to live by. But this chapter also reminds me I am not judged just by my works, I am judged by my trust and faith in Jesus Christ, who loves me and died for my sins. That is what is going to get me to heaven, not my deeds. Thank You, Jesus. Thank You for the gift of forgiveness at the cross. In Your name, we pray. Amen.

MY THOUGHTS

ROMANS 3

None Righteous, No, Not One

Today, we are in Romans 3, one of the most powerful chapters of scripture. Do you think people are basically good or basically evil? Please read or listen to Romans 3.

COMMENTS

In 2002, I read Romans 3 (NASB) on two different days, part one and part two. Here is a summary of what I wrote in my journal concerning Romans 3. "Jews were entrusted with the oracles of God. The Gideons are entrusted with the oracles of God today. *'Let God be found true, though every man be found a liar'* (v. 4). We don't sin to get grace, verse 8. We're all under sin, verse 9. *'None righteous, no, not one'* (v. 10 KJV). No one seeks God, referring to verses 10 and 11. *'There is none who does good, There is not even one'* (v. 12). *'No fear of God before their eyes'*" (v. 18).

And part two, from Romans 3:20 to the end, "The law is the definition of what is acceptable and what is not. It defines sin by saying do or don't do certain things. The law defines sin and it is clear by its definition, *'all have sinned and fall short of the glory of God'* (v. 23). Justification is a gift of grace, according to verse 24. Man is justified not by works, but by faith in the giver of the gift of grace."

In 2001, I wrote, "God is God over all. Not just Jews, but also Gentiles. *'There is none righteous, no, not one'* (v. 10 KJV). We are all sinners, therefore need salvation and a savior."

In 2013, I wrote, "Jews were entrusted with the Word of God according to verse 2; one unique blessing from God to Israel. God also remains faithful, though we may become unfaithful, according to verses 3 and 4. *'There is none righteous, no, not one'* (v. 10 KJV). Jew or Gentile, *'for all have sinned and fall short of the glory of God'* (v. 23). Sin is overcome, not by the law but *'through faith in Jesus Christ for all who believe'*, according to verse 22 and we *'are justified by his grace as a gift through the redemption that is in Christ Jesus'"* (v. 24).

As we go back through scripture, we see God chose a family through Abraham, Isaac, and Jacob. He started and created the nation of Israel. One of the privileges of the nation of Israel, the Jews, was being entrusted with the oracles of God, the Word of God itself. That, according to this chapter, is one of the advantages of being Jewish.

> **Do you think people are basically good or basically evil?**

Have the Jews always been faithful to or with the Word of God? Probably not. But regardless of what men do with the Word of God, the Word of God is the Word of God. Verse 4 says, *"Let God be true though every one were a liar"*. So God's Word, the oracles of God, the Word of God is true regardless of what men try to do it.

Then Paul makes a different argument. He says, *"What then? Are we Jews any better off? No, not at all. For we have already charged that all, both Jews and Greeks, are under sin"* (v. 9). So, though the Jews were entrusted with the Word of God, the oracles of God, it did not give them a special place. Paul levels the playing field, as I said, by calling all of us, Jews and Gentiles, sinners.

Paul then quotes something the Jews would be very familiar with, the Book of Psalms. He first quotes Psalm 14:1-3:

The fool says in his heart, "There is no God."
They are corrupt, they do abominable deeds;

there is none who does good.

The Lord looks down from heaven on the children of man,

to see if there are any who understand,

who seek after God.

They have all turned aside; together they have become corrupt;

there is none who does good,

not even one.

The same thing is written in Psalm 53:1-3:

The fool says in his heart, "There is no God."

They are corrupt, doing abominable iniquity;

there is none who does good.

God looks down from heaven

on the children of man

to see if there are any who understand,

who seek after God.

They have all fallen away;

together they have become corrupt;

there is none who does good,

not even one.

It is almost word for word in Psalm 14 and Psalm 53. Paul summarizes this whole argument in verse 23, where he says, *"for all have sinned and fall short of the glory of God".* That principle is so very important to understand. That is why I call this a powerful chapter of scripture.

Do you think people are basically good or basically evil? In our heart, we want to believe people are basically good. But this chapter makes it very clear *"There is none righteous, no, not one"* (v. 10 KJV). There is none who does good. We are all caught up in this thing called sin.

DIGGING DEEPER

One illustration of this is as a parent. If you are a parent, you have seen it. You never had to teach a child to do something wrong. It seems to come naturally. For example, you never had to teach a child to take a toy away from another child. You never had to teach your child to be selfish, but you always had to try to teach your child to share. I do not believe any parent ever taught his child to lie, it just comes naturally.

If we think about those with a world view, they might say, people are basically good, and all we have to do is educate them, and everything is going to be fine. But as we go through the Bible, we can get a biblical world view. Romans 3 is very clear. *"None is righteous, no, not one"* (v. 10). *"(N)o one does good, not even one"* (v. 12). *"(A)ll have sinned and fall short of the glory of God"* (v. 23).

Prayer

Father, we are glad Romans does not end here, it is only chapter 3, and You have a remedy for sin. You have a way of escape that we may endure our sinfulness, and we look forward to reading about it in the rest of Romans. Thank You, Jesus, for going to the cross at Calvary to pay the penalty for our sin, so we can be saved. Thank You. In Jesus' name, amen.

MY THOUGHTS

ROMANS 4

Righteousness

Romans 4 is about faith and righteousness. What is righteousness? How do we become righteous? Please read or listen to Romans 4.

COMMENTS

In 1992, when I read Romans 4, I made a note in my journal that it was my daughter's thirteenth birthday. I wrote, "I am now a father of three teenagers!" Maybe some of you can relate to that, even today. I summarized Romans 4 with just a couple of lines, "Righteousness is based in faith, not being Jewish." Secondly, "Abraham is father of all who believe, not just Jews."

> Belief in God is the key to why Abraham can be the father of both the Jews, the circumcised, and Gentiles, the uncircumcised.

In 2001, I was reading both Old Testament and New Testament each day, so I had some short summaries of the verses and chapters I was reading. On Romans 4, I wrote, "Belief is the beginning of righteousness, not religious ceremonies like circumcision. Believe in God. Trust in Him in life."

In 2013, I wrote, "Paul uses the father of the Jews as an example. Abraham was justified by faith, not by works or by circumcision, or by the law. Abraham believed

God before he was circumcised and before the law existed. Belief in God is the key to why Abraham can be the father of both the Jews, the circumcised, and Gentiles, the uncircumcised."

I finished the summary of chapter 4 with those great verses 20 and 21, *"No unbelief made him waver concerning the promise of God, but he grew strong in his faith as he gave glory to God, fully convinced that God was able to do what he had promised."* I wrote in my journal, "What a verse to live by!"

DIGGING DEEPER

I am not a theologian, nor a pastor. I am just a guy who reads the Bible every day and tries to figure out what it says. I think I get what Paul is doing in this chapter. He is making an argument to his Jewish audience that being Jewish, being circumcised, or being obedient to the law is not what God designed to save us from sin. He argues that Abraham, the father of the Jews, believed God and it was counted to him as righteousness before there was circumcision or the law of God brought down from Mount Sinai by Moses.

Verses 9 and 10 verify this, *"we say that faith was counted to Abraham as righteousness. How then was it counted to him? Was it before or after he had been circumcised? It was not after, but before he was circumcised."* Then verse 13, about the law, says, *"For the promise to Abraham and his offspring that he would be heir of the world did not come through the law but through the righteousness of faith."*

Because belief and righteousness before God are not based on being Jewish or based on the oracles of God, Abraham can be the father of faith, not just for the Jews, but also as verse 17 says, *"I have made you the father of many nations"*, which include the Gentiles, Paul's other audience.

Paul closes out his argument about Abraham in the last few verses of this chapter:

No unbelief made him waver concerning the promise of God, but he grew strong in his faith as he gave glory to God, fully convinced that God was able to do what he had promised. That is why his faith was "counted to him as righteousness." But the words "it was counted to him" were not written for his sake alone, but for ours also. It will be counted to us who believe in him who raised from the dead Jesus our Lord, who was delivered up for our trespasses and raised for our justification (vv. 20-24).

Paul links Abraham to faith in Jesus. What a great way to end this chapter.

Prayer

Lord, we thank You these words Paul just described were not just for Abraham. These words Paul wrote are not just for the Jews, but they are for us today. It all applies to us and we can be counted as righteous, those *"who believe in him who raised from the dead Jesus our Lord"* (v. 24). That is what gives us our justification. And we thank You that You are making it clear in the Book of Romans. Continue to teach us we are saved by faith, not by works, not by being good, but by believing in You. We give You the praise. In Jesus' name, amen.

MY THOUGHTS

ROMANS 5

Christ Died for Sinners

Romans 5 reminds us while we were sinners, Christ died for us. Where did sin come from? Please read or listen to Romans 5.

COMMENTS

Hallelujah! What a great chapter. I want to go back to my journal in 1994, as we look at Romans 5. I wrote in my journal, "Faith equals justification plus peace and grace according to verses 1 and 2." Then I wrote, "Exalt in our tribulations. Easy to say, hard to do." I continued, "God demonstrates His love toward us, and that while we were yet still sinners, Christ died for us. Hallelujah! Praise God! Thank You, Jesus!" I wrote, "Reconciled by His death, saved by His life. Exalt in God."

That was a pretty exciting journal entry in 1994 on the first half of Romans 5. I continued, "Sin has always been in the world. The law simply defined what it was. Sin passes through because of one transgression, it is inherited. We are born condemned. Forgiveness of that sin is from Jesus Christ. No other way out."

In 2001, I was reading Romans 5 on a Saturday. I was reading through the Old and New Testament, so I did read a part of Psalms that day, but I did not write any notes on Romans 5, probably because I read it, then went to my Gideon prayer meeting. I did write some notes on my Old Testament reading in Psalms, but nothing on Romans 5. So we move on to the next journal.

In 2013, on Romans 5, I wrote, "Justified by faith, we have peace with God. How? Through Jesus Christ. We also access grace through Jesus Christ, according to verses 1 and 2. No other way. Thanks to grace, we can rejoice in sufferings which produce endurance, character, and hope, according to verses 3-5." And I wrote, "Trinity." I like to write in my journal Trinity-sightings, so I wrote, "Trinity. God in verse 1, Jesus in verse 1, Holy Spirit in verse 5."

I continued, "5:8, great verse. We are saved by His blood. From what? *From the wrath of God*', according to verse 9." And, "Through Jesus, we are reconciled back to God, referring to verse 11. Sin came into the world through Adam. Death came because of sin, referring to verse 12. Sin brings condemnation, but grace brings justification, referring to verse 16 and *'eternal life through Jesus Christ our Lord'* (v. 21). It's all through Jesus. No one else. No other way."

DIGGING DEEPER

I wish I could master verses 3-5, *"Not only that, but we rejoice in our sufferings, knowing that suffering produces endurance, and endurance produces character, and character produces hope, and hope does not put us to shame, because God's love has been poured into our hearts through the Holy Spirit who has been given to us."*

I must say I am not very good at rejoicing in my sufferings, though I know it is what the scripture tells me to do: suffering produces endurance, endurance produces character, and character produces hope. I think it has been true in my life; through sufferings I have developed character over my many years of being a Christian, but this part still does not get easier for me. When something bad happens, or something is difficult, I have a hard time rejoicing, especially initially when these things happen in my life.

But that is a good reason to stay in the Word, right? Because when we read a verse like this, it reminds us when tough stuff comes, we are supposed to hold on and rejoice and understand God is still in control. He can work through things in our lives. When He does, it does produce endurance for the next time we suffer. It produces character and it produces hope because we have been through this before. So, I thank the Lord for this kind of verse, though it has been hard for me to master it in my own life.

> **When something bad happens, or something is difficult, I have a hard time rejoicing.**

We move on to verse 8, one of the power verses in the Bible, *"but God shows his love for us in that while we were still sinners, Christ died for us."* That is a hallelujah verse in my life and probably in yours. While I was in my sin, Christ knew it, and He still died for me. Hallelujah! Thank You, Jesus!

Verse 12 helps us understand how sin came into the world, *"Therefore, just as sin came into the world through one man, and death through sin, and so death spread to all men because all sinned".* This takes us back to the story in Genesis about Adam and Eve and that apple and the serpent. We remember Eve was the one tempted by the serpent and she was one that took the apple, and, therefore, she was the one that sinned. But this passage does not say sin came into the world through a woman, through Eve. It says it came into the world through one man, Adam. That might stir your thoughts today.

Let's not dwell on how sin came into the world. Let's dwell on how we get forgiveness from sin. Let's look to verse 17, *"For if, because of one man's trespass, death reigned through that one man, much more will those who receive the abundance of grace and the free gift of righteousness reign in life through the one man Jesus Christ."* Sin and death came through one man, Adam; but grace and righteousness, the free gift of forgiveness, comes through the one man, Jesus Christ. Again, hallelujah!

The conclusion of the matter is in the last verse of the chapter, *"so that, as sin reigned in death, grace also might reign through righteousness leading to eternal life through Jesus Christ our Lord"* (v. 21). That can take us all the way back to verse 1, *"Therefore, since we have been justified by faith, we have peace with God through our Lord Jesus Christ."*

Chapter 5 tells us how sin and death came into the world to all men. But chapter 5 also tells us through Jesus, through grace, and through faith, we can become justified and gain eternal life.

Prayer

Father, thank You for the reminders in this chapter, where sin comes from, where death comes from, but also where forgiveness comes from. We thank You that while we were yet sinners, You died for us. We also pray, Lord, if we are suffering right now, for any reason, You remind us to rejoice, even though it is difficult, because You are producing endurance, character, and hope through our suffering. Thanks for the reminder today, Jesus came with grace, love, and mercy for the forgiveness of our sins. We say a big hallelujah today. In Jesus' name, amen!

MY THOUGHTS

ROMANS 6

Does God Need to Forgive You?

Romans 6 is another one of these great chapters in Romans. Paul helps us understand sin. Do you have a casual attitude about sin? Please read or listen to Romans 6.

COMMENTS

In 1994, on Romans 6 (NASB), I wrote, "We can walk in newness of life. We can be dead to sin and alive in Christ Jesus. Lord, help me refrain from sin and accept Your grace when I do fail. We are creatures of sin, but through Jesus Christ, we can get out from under sin and live under grace. Verse 14, *'sin shall not be master over you'*. Verse 18, *'freed from sin'*" and continuing on verse 18, "Can become *'slaves of righteousness'*. Verse 22, become *'enslaved to God'*. Results? Sanctification. Eternal life."

In 2001, I had a short summary of Romans 6 (NKJV), but it is important. "Sin and freedom from it. I would like to believe verse 14, *'Sin shall not have dominion over you'*". I continued, "I fight sin and sinfulness every day." After reading the passage and writing that in my journal, I wrote my prayer, "For my battle with sin. Does anything really matter in life? Is it worth fighting and arguing about stuff or just letting everything go?" I wrote that question in 2001, a long time ago. I do not think I got an answer to it yet, though.

In 2013, I wrote, "As Christians, we *walk in newness of life*, according to verse 4. I thank God for this. I am not caught up in how I was born or stuff passed on through generations. I am a new creature in Christ. Old things pass away, all things become new, referring to 2 Corinthians 5:17."

I continued to write, "We are dead to sin, being raised in Christ, alive in Him. Yet, we need to control sin in our flesh and not fall into its passions. We must strive to turn away from sin toward righteousness in the Lord. Sin leads to death. But the free gift of forgiveness, grace, offers us eternal life in Christ Jesus our Lord. Thank You, Jesus."

DIGGING DEEPER

In this chapter, Paul asks his audience a question, and he frames it two different ways. He asks the question in verses 1 and 2, and then he asks it again in verse 15. In verses 1 and 2, he says, *"Are we to continue in sin that grace may abound? By no means!"* In verse 15, he says, *"What then? Are we to sin because we are not under law but under grace? By no means!"*

Sometimes Christians and sometimes non-Christians take sin casually. Because we live under grace and forgiveness, sometimes we have an attitude that, hey, if I sin it is okay because God has to forgive me. That is the very attitude Paul is warning against in this chapter.

> Because we live under grace and forgiveness, sometimes we have an attitude that, hey, if I sin it is okay because God has to forgive me.

As Christians, we cannot have a casual attitude towards sin. Just because we are under grace, does not mean we can have a casual attitude toward our sin. And just because we are not under the law anymore, does not mean we can have a casual attitude toward sin. Paul warns us in verse 12, we have to fight against this. He says, *"Let not sin therefore reign in your mortal body, to make you obey its passions."* Sin is passionate and we want, so often, to obey its luring.

Paul gives us the answer in verses 17 and 18, *"But thanks be to God, that you who were once slaves of sin have become obedient from the heart to the standard of teaching to which you were committed, and, having been set free from sin, have become slaves of righteousness."* He goes on to say, *"I am speaking in human terms, because of your natural limitations. For just as you once presented your members as slaves to impurity and to lawlessness leading to more lawlessness, so now present your members as slaves to righteousness leading to sanctification"* (v. 19).

How do we get out from under this thing called sin? We go to the Bible. We understand the scriptures, the standard of teaching. Paul refers to *"the standard of teaching to which we must commit ourselves"* (v. 17).

Though we enjoy the forgiveness of sin and the grace of God, we still must fight off the luring, the passions, of sin. Verse 22 says, *"But now that you have been set free from sin and have become slaves of God, the fruit you get leads to sanctification and its end, eternal life."* Then this great verse, Romans 6:23 says, *"For the wages of sin is death, but the free gift of God is eternal life in Christ Jesus our Lord."* That is a power verse in scripture. *"For the wages of sin is death, but the free gift of God is eternal life"* (v. 23). How? *"In Christ Jesus our Lord"* (v. 23).

Prayer

Father, thank You for providing a way of escape from sin. Thank You for a way out of death. Thank You for the free gift of eternal life through Jesus Christ our Lord. Hallelujah!

None of us need to be caught up in sin, though it is a battle. You tell us in this chapter it is our obligation to fight it. We do not have to lose to the battle of sin thanks to Your forgiveness. We thank You, too, that we do not have to be bound by generational sin, or sins from our past, we can be forgiven and become new creatures in Christ. Old things pass away, and all things become new.

Jesus, You free us from the clutches of sin and death. Because of that, I pray I never have a casual attitude toward sin. Help me to become a slave to You. A slave to righteousness. In Your name, we pray. Amen.

MY THOUGHTS

ROMANS 7

The Battle Rages Within

Today brings us to Romans 7. Do you hear voices? Who are they? Where are they coming from? Please read or listen to Romans 7.

COMMENTS

It is going to be fun to untangle this chapter. Let's go back to my journal in 1994, after reading chapter 7 (NASB), "Our old husband, Mr. Law, has died, and we can marry a new husband, Jesus Christ. Mr. Law defines sin. Jesus frees us from sin. The law was not sin. It defined it. Sin causes death, not the law." Then I quoted, *"'evil is present in me'* (v. 21), sin nature." Then verse 22, *"'the law of God in the inner man,'* spiritual nature. Different laws in my body wage war against the law of my mind." Quoting verse 25. *"On the one hand, I myself with my mind am serving the law of God, but on the other, with my flesh the law of sin."*

I continued to write, "The spiritual warfare defined in Paul is evident in me. Often I don't, or can't, do what I want or know is right, rather I succumb to my sin nature. I am thankful, though, that I have spiritual warfare within me. If I wasn't a Christian, I would only have a sin nature telling me what to do."

In 2001, I wrote, "The law defines sin. I have the same battle Paul did in verses 15-25. So often, I find myself saying or doing sinful things even when I know better. The war goes on. How can I sin less and act more Christ-like?"

In 2013, I wrote, "So Christ replaces the law like a new husband replaces a dead husband. We are released from the law and serve in a new way of the Spirit and not the old way of the written code. The law defines sin, yet no one could live up to the letter of the law. And as we sin, we are subject to death. So, in a sense, the law led to death. Really, sin leads to death, but we wouldn't know what sin is without the law defining it."

> **The war goes on. How can I sin less and act more Christ-like?**

On those verses, starting with 15, I wrote, "Conflict. Desiring to serve God, yet warring with our flesh, Paul describes it well from a personal perspective. I have the same fight, and I'm often amazed how I fall to my sin nature in my flesh even after over forty years of being a Christian. I know better, but I do it anyway. Oh, wretched man that I am, who delivers me from this internal struggle? Jesus, Jesus, Jesus. Thank You for forgiveness and the Holy Spirit. Thank You for living in me, for speaking to me, and guiding my steps away from sin toward God. I try, but when I fail, at least I can be forgiven."

DIGGING DEEPER

Let's focus on verses 15-20:

For I do not understand my own actions. For I do not do what I want, but I do the very thing I hate. Now if I do what I do not want, I agree with the law, that it is good. So now it is no longer I who do it, but sin that dwells within me. For I know that nothing good dwells in me, that is, in my flesh. For I have the desire to do what is right, but not the ability to carry it out. For I do not do the good I want, but the evil I do not want is what I keep on doing. Now if I do what I do not want, it is no longer I who do it, but sin that dwells within me.

What voices do I hear? The voice of the Holy Spirit? The voice of the flesh? Or the sin nature? This is the battle we all face. We want to do what is good. We want to do what is right, but we find ourselves continually failing. I know for me, I wonder why? I even think after forty years or more of being a Christian, I should not be fighting this battle anymore.

And as Christians we quote, *"greater is he that is in you, than he that is in the world"* (1 John 4:4 KJV). Yes, I believe the Holy Spirit lives in me. As I wrote in one of those journals, I am so thankful for that because He battles the sin nature within me. Without Him, I would only be subject to the sin nature. So thank You, Holy Spirit, for fighting the battle against my sin nature within me.

As much as I want to believe good and bad cannot exist in the same place, especially in me, I think we know better. The battles rage within us on a regular basis. I realize it in me, verse 24, *"Wretched man that I am! Who will deliver me from this body of death?"* Thanks be to God, through Jesus Christ our Lord.

Prayer

Jesus, though I know this battle rages within me, I thank You for sending us the Holy Spirit, our helper, my helper, who convicts me of my sin and leads me to righteousness through You. Without You, Holy Spirit, I would be absolutely lost in my sin nature.

Jesus, thank You for dying on the cross for my sins, rising from the dead, and sending Your Holy Spirit as a lifeline so I can battle my sin nature. Holy Spirit, do Your work in me. Fight off the voices of the flesh, the voices of my sin nature. May I hear Your voice more and more loud and clear in my own life. In Jesus' name, we pray. Amen.

MY THOUGHTS

ROMANS 8

What Can Separate Us from the Love of God?

Today, we reach the halfway point of the Book of Romans. We are in chapter 8, about condemnation and the love of God. Are you condemned or loved by God? Please read or listen to Romans 8.

COMMENTS

The opening verse of this chapter (NASB) says, *"There is therefore now no condemnation for those who are in Christ Jesus."* In 1994, I began my journal with this question, "No condemnation for those in Christ? What does that mean? The law condemned us because it defined our sin and we are guilty of sinning. But in Christ, our sin, though it continues, is forgiven, therefore, no condemnation? No eternal condemnation. But Jesus is not pleased with the life of sin or continuation of sin."

Then I referred to verse 7, *"the mind set on the flesh is hostile toward God; for it does not subject itself to the law of God, for it is not even able to do so"*. I concluded my journal entry with, "That's what's wrong now with many in our country. *'Those in the flesh cannot please God'"* (v. 8). Then I wrote, "Life according to the flesh or according to the spirit? By the flesh equals death. By the spirit equals life."

I look down in this journal a couple of days later. It was a Sunday, and I noticed I made a note in my journal that I checked out a book on Romans at our church. This was 1994 and I looked at the book where I checked it out, and it said I had read it back in 1981. My name was still on the card. So, I said when we started Romans, I thought it was the Ph.D. of Christianity. At

> "No condemnation to those who are in Christ Jesus" (Rom. 8:1). That's conditional.

least twice I read a book on Romans while reading Romans, so it helped me understand what this book is really all about.

In 2001, I had a little bit different take on this chapter (NASB) when I wrote, *"'no condemnation to those who are in Christ Jesus'* (v. 1). That's conditional. There is condemnation to those not in Christ Jesus. We must live in the Spirit to be free from the bondage of sin." Then I quoted verse 28, *"And we know that . . . all things work together for good to those who love God, to those who are called according to His purpose."* Again, I wrote, "Conditional. Two conditions, love God and called. I want to be called according to His purpose."

In 2013, I wrote, *"'no condemnation for those who are in Christ Jesus'* (v. 1). Not a blanket statement for all. A conditional statement for those in Christ. Those not in Christ are condemned. Those in Christ set their minds on the things of the Spirit, no longer on the things of the flesh." Quoting verse 8, *"'Those who are in the flesh cannot please God.'* We *'are not in the flesh . . . if in fact the Spirit of God dwells in you'"* (v. 9). And, *"the Spirit . . . who raised Jesus from the dead'* (v. 11) is the same Spirit who dwells in me. *'For if you live according to the flesh, you will die, but if by the Spirit . . . you will live'* (v. 13). Those who receive the Spirit are adopted sons, joint heirs with Jesus, children of God. Hallelujah!"

DIGGING DEEPER

Whatever we suffer on earth is nothing compared to the glory of heaven. Creation was not created in sin but ended up there because of Adam's sin. It too, like us, will be restored to a sinless nature. In our sinful state, though, we accept God's redemptive work on the cross. We still fail, so we get access to the Holy Spirit to help us in our weaknesses, our sinful state.

For those who love God and are called according to His purpose, all things work out, referring to verse 28. So if God is in control, and all things work together for good, who or what can be against us? Thanks to our standing in Christ, *"who can be against us?"* (v. 31). *"Who shall bring a charge against God's elect?"* (v. 33). *"Who is to condemn?"* (v. 34). *"Who shall separate us from the love of Christ?"* (v. 35). Nothing, no one, no how. Wow! Thank You, Jesus.

I finish this great chapter with the prayer I wrote in my journal in 2013 after reading Romans 8.

Prayer

"Nothing can separate me from Your love. I accept though I cannot comprehend. I love You for loving me. Help me understand the truths and walk in confidence in You. All things work together for good in my life because You are in control. Thank You, Jesus." In Your name, we pray. Amen.

MY THOUGHTS

ROMANS 9

Why the Jews?

Today, we begin the second half of Romans. Is Israel special to God? If so, why? Can you be special too? Please read or listen to Romans 9.

COMMENTS

I am going to start with my 2013 journal on Romans 9. "Paul is in anguish for the lost, particularly his own people. Israel is special to God, *'They are Israelites, and to them belong the adoption, the glory, the covenants, the giving of the law, the worship, and the promises. To them belong the patriarchs, and from their race, according to the flesh, is the Christ, who is God over all'* (vv. 4-5). Truly Jews are special to God."

I continued in my journal, "He entrusted them with His Word and through them, the birth of His Son. God has a *'purpose of election'* in verse 11. He chooses who He wants to accomplish His purposes. He also has mercy and compassion on whom He chooses, according to verse 15, and hardens whom He chooses, according to verse 18. We have no standing to question God, verse 20."

Let me stop the journal and read those verses, *"But who are you, O man, to answer back to God? Will what is molded say to its molder, 'Why have you made me like this?' Has the potter no right over the clay, to make out of the same lump one vessel for honorable use and another for dishonorable use?"* (vv. 20-21). I have heard some Christians say, "When I get to heaven, I have a few questions for God." Good luck with that!

I continued in my journal, "He has provided a way for both Jew and Gentile to be saved. By faith, according to verses 30-32."

Back in 1994, I wrote this about Romans 9, "Being Jewish is not enough to save. Never was. Abraham had two sons. One was selected. Isaac had twins from the same father and mother, but God still made a sovereign selection. Only some of Abraham's seed was selected based upon God's promises, not on their heritage."

God is a God of selection.

I continued to write, "God's Word did not fail. The Jews failed because they did not act in faith towards righteousness. Belief is the issue, not birth rite. God is sovereign to choose and spare those He will. Paul points out here that if the Jews got what they deserved, they would be history. But God spared some while leading some Gentiles to righteousness by faith."

So, God is a God of selection. He was and He is. He chose Abraham, Isaac, and Jacob to father the nation of Israel. He chose Israel to give the law, the Word of God, and the promises and He chose their race to be the family of the Messiah, Jesus Christ.

Verses 15 and 16 remind us, *"For he says to Moses, 'I will have mercy on whom I have mercy, and I will have compassion on whom I have compassion.' So then it depends not on human will or exertion, but on God, who has mercy."* And verse 18 says, *"So then he has mercy on whomever he wills, and he hardens whomever he wills."*

DIGGING DEEPER

Our practical application from this chapter is: God is sovereign, we are not.

> ## *Prayer*
>
> Lord, thank You for Your mercy on me and thank You for having compassion on me. In Your name, I pray. Amen.

MY THOUGHTS

ROMANS 10

The Romans Road

Romans 10 is another one of these great, fantastic chapters in the Book of Romans. Have you ever had a chance to share your faith, but did not know how? Please read or listen to Romans 10.

COMMENTS

I want to start Romans 10 (NASB) with my journal in 2001 because I wrote, "A great chapter of scripture!" I quoted verse 2, *"zeal for God, but not in accordance with knowledge."* Then I wrote about verse 3, "Ignorant of God's righteousness, seeking to establish their own righteousness have not submitted to the righteousness of God." I also wrote in my journal, "Answers. Verse 8, *'The Word is near you, in your mouth and in your heart'.* Verse 9, confess Jesus. Verse 13, call on Him."

In 1994, I summarized Romans 10, very shortly, with these words, "Jews failed to believe, though the message was there all along. They could have believed, called upon the Lord, and been saved." That statement probably does not just apply to Jews today, does it? The message of salvation, right here in Romans, has been here now thousands of years and yet people still do not believe.

In 2013, I wrote, "Verse 1 could be a theme for me, not because of my position on the Executive Committee of The Gideons International, but it has been a prayer of mine for years to be a soul-winner. Lord, hear my prayer." Stepping away from the journal for a moment, let's read Romans 10:1, *"Brothers, my heart's desire and prayer to God for them is that they may be saved."*

Back to my 2013 journal. "Many have a zeal for God, but not according to the knowledge of the truth of God. Zeal should be based on the Word of God, which is near us, in our mouth and in our hearts. Jesus is the way to salvation. Paul is opening the gospel to Jews and Gentiles based on faith, not the Mosaic Law. Everyone can be saved. The summary statement: *'So faith comes from hearing, and hearing through the Word of Christ'"* (v. 17).

DIGGING DEEPER

We have been cruising through the Book of Romans for several days now. This chapter reminds me of something you may have heard of called The Romans Road. The Romans Road is a collection of verses one can use to lead someone to saving faith in Jesus Christ. Though The Romans Road starts with John 3:16, all the other verses are in the Book of Romans. I would like to go over The Romans Road today.

If you ever get a chance or want a chance to share the gospel with someone, The Romans Road is a great tool to use. We begin with the first verse, the one that is the most famous verse in all the Bible, John 3:16. You share this with someone. *"For God so loved the world, that he gave his only Son, that whoever believes in him should not perish but have eternal life."* Then you can ask, "Do you believe God loves you?"

> **If you ever get a chance or want a chance to share the gospel with someone, The Romans Road is a great tool to use.**

The next verse follows right along. It is Romans 5:8, one we went over a few days ago, *"but God shows his love for us in that while we were still sinners, Christ died for us."* You can share, "Yes, God loves you. He loves you so much He died for you."

The next verse on The Romans Road is Romans 3:23, *"for all have sinned and fall short of the glory of God".* You can ask the person, "Do you believe that you are a sinner? Have you ever done anything wrong? This verse tells us we all have sinned."

And the next verse is Romans 6:23. It tells us the consequences of sin. It says, *"For the wages of sin is death, but the gift of God is eternal life in Christ Jesus our Lord."* The consequence of being sinners is death. But praise God He has a remedy for sin through Jesus Christ our Lord.

The next two verses of The Romans Road are right here in this chapter, Romans 10:9-10 tell us how we can receive the free gift of eternal life through Jesus Christ, *"if you confess with your mouth that Jesus is Lord and believe in your heart that God raised him from the dead, you will be saved. For with the heart one believes and is justified, and with the mouth one confesses and is saved."* To receive the remedy for sin, that gift from Jesus Christ, we have to confess with our mouth and believe in our heart and we will be saved.

The last verse on The Romans Road is Romans 10:13, *"For everyone who calls on the name of the Lord will be saved."* That is The Romans Road and it can be used to walk someone through the plan of salvation. When you get to the end, all you need to do is ask, "Do you want to do that? Do you want to pray and receive Jesus as your Lord and Savior?"

The Lord reminds us in this chapter, *"How beautiful are the feet of those who preach the good news"* (v. 15). In other words, those of us who get the chance to share the gospel with someone. It is a beautiful thing. It is a special opportunity God gives us.

Then that wonderful verse, verse 17, says, *"So faith comes from hearing, and hearing through the word of Christ."* When you get a chance to share, will everyone accept the Lord? No, this chapter tells us that. Verse 16 says, *"But they have not all obeyed the gospel. For Isaiah says, 'Lord, who has believed what he has heard from us?'"* No, not everyone will receive the gospel of Jesus Christ. But it is our privilege, our opportunity, to share something like The Romans Road with those around us.

Prayer

Lord, give me the chance, give me the opportunity, to share the gospel, The Romans Road, with someone in my family, or a friend, or a colleague. And Lord, give me the boldness to pray through this and do this as You open the doors of opportunity.

As this chapter reminds me, *"The word is near you, in your mouth and in your heart"* (v. 8). Lord, use my mouth and my heart to share You with someone, maybe even today. We ask it, in Jesus' name, amen.

MY THOUGHTS

ROMANS 11

Grafted In

In Romans 11, Paul explains Jews and Gentiles. Are you Jewish? Are you Gentile? Have you been grafted in? Please read or listen to Romans 11.

COMMENTS

To put chapter 11 in context, it helps to go back to the last few verses of chapter 10. Let's do so, starting with verse 18 of chapter 10:

> But I ask, have they not heard? Indeed they have, for
> "Their voice has gone out to all the earth,
> and their words to the ends of the world."
> But I ask, did Israel not understand? First Moses says,
> "I will make you jealous of those who are not a nation;
> with a foolish nation I will make you angry."
> Then Isaiah is so bold as to say,
> "I have been found by those who did not seek me;
> I have shown myself to those who did not ask for me."
> But of Israel he says, "All day long I have held out my hands to a disobedient
> and contrary people" (vv. 18-21).

Paul is finishing chapter 10 by saying, "Has Israel heard? Have they rejected the gospel?" He begins chapter 11 by saying, *"I ask, then, has God rejected his people? By no means!"* He says in verse 2, *"God has not rejected his people whom he foreknew"*. Then and now, God always keeps a remnant of the nation of Israel. That is His promise.

Now let's look at verse 11, *"So I ask, did they stumble in order that they might fall? By no means! Rather, through their trespass salvation has come to the Gentiles, so as to make Israel jealous."* It is beneficial to the Gentiles that the Jews mishandled the message of salvation because it allowed the message to be shared

> **It is beneficial to the Gentiles that the Jews mishandled the message of salvation because it allowed the message to be shared with them.**

with them. True, some Jews rejected God, His law, His prophets, and even Jesus the Messiah; and those branches have been broken off. But the good news is because they did, Gentiles are now given the opportunity to hear the message of salvation and be grafted in.

But then Paul warns, do not get too cocky. If God broke off some of the natural branches, the Jews, if you do not stand firm in your faith, He will break you off as well, *"For if God did not spare the natural branches, neither will he spare you"* (v. 21).

DIGGING DEEPER

What are the practical applications we can get out of this chapter? First, be thankful if you have ever heard the gospel, the plan of salvation. Secondly, do not reject it; embrace it. Thirdly, stand firm in your faith in Jesus Christ. Fourth, the chapter concludes with another great application in verses 33-36:

> *Oh, the depth of the riches and wisdom and knowledge of God! How unsearchable are his judgments and how inscrutable his ways!*
> *"For who has known the mind of the Lord,*
> *or who has been his counselor?"*

"Or who has given a gift to him
  that he might be repaid?"
For from him and through him and to him are all things. To him be glory
forever. Amen.

Though I may not understand all of Romans or even this chapter, I certainly can understand God's ways are higher than my ways. His thoughts are higher than my thoughts. Praise God! It ought to be that way because He is God and we are His creation.

Prayer

Lord, I just thank You that somehow, someway, You provided a way of salvation. From the beginning of time, You knew what You were going to do. You delivered the message through the Jewish people then You opened it up to the whole world.

I am thankful at one point in my life, at age fifteen, the gospel was revealed to me and I did not reject it. I accepted it. My prayer today is anybody who has not heard the message of salvation will get a Bible and listen or read about Your love, Your forgiveness, Your grace, and Your mercy and accept, not reject, Your offer of salvation.

And for all of us who have, may we stand firm in You. *"For from him and through him and to him are all things. To him be glory forever. Amen"* (v. 36).

MY THOUGHTS

ROMANS 12

Our Reasonable Service

Romans 12 challenges us to live for Christ. Paul lists several spiritual gifts to help us do so. Do you know your spiritual gifts? Are you using them in your reasonable service to the Lord? Please read or listen to Romans 12.

COMMENTS

We are going to start today with a wonderful journal entry from 1994. It was my thirty-ninth birthday and guess where I was? Maui, Hawaii! My journal entry said, "Left at 8:30 in the morning for Los Angeles and then on to Hawaii. Going for a business conference but went early. We had dinner at our hotel, the Maui Intercontinental, out on the patio watching the sun drop into the Pacific Ocean. Gorgeous, beautiful! What a birthday! What a blessing!" And, of course, very special because I was with Terry, my helpmate, my wife.

The next day, when I actually did read Romans 12 (NASB), I had this journal entry. "Up before the sun came up in Maui, because of time difference of four to five hours, sitting out on the patio looking out over the ocean through the palm trees as the sky begins to lighten. The mist burned away and the sky turns pink with a new day. It's easy to praise God in such a setting as this."

On that patio, I read Romans 12 and focused on these things, "Great words. How to act. Such as: *'cling to what is good'* (v. 9), honor one another, referring to verse 10, *'devoted to prayer'* (v. 12), practice hospitality, referring to verse 13, bless and curse not, referring to verse 14, don't be haughty, referring to verse 16, *'Respect what is right'* (v. 17), *'be at peace with all men'* (v. 18), *'overcome evil with good'"* (v. 21). Next to it, I wrote, "O, to live here." I presume I meant in Romans 12, not in Maui! But, I mean, it was a difficult choice, wasn't it? But what great words in Romans 12, how to live this Christian life.

In 2001, when I read Romans 12 (NKJV), I highlighted one verse, verse 6. *"Having then gifts differing according to the grace that is given to us, let us use them"* and I underlined *"let us use them"*.

In 2013, I had more to write about Roman 12, starting with verse 1, "I hope I have done this. I have given my life to God for His use." Then verse 2, "I have also tried to do this, not *'conformed to this world, but be transformed by the renewal of your mind'* every day in the Word of God. Verse 3, remain humble."

Then I wrote about gifting. "I think I have prophecy and leadership. I should lead with zeal." And, *"'If possible'* means I may not be at peace with everyone, but I try to be on my part." That is verse 18. I continued, "Behavior is important as Christians. Be humble, verse 3. Have sober judgment, genuine love, verse 9. Honor, verse 10. Hope, patience, verse 12. Help people in need, hospitality, verse 13. Bless others, verse 14. Live in harmony, verse 16. Peaceful, verse 18. Overcome evil with good, verse 21."

DIGGING DEEPER

In various years, I wrote a laundry list of things we can do as Christians to live out this Christian life. Let's go back through this wonderful chapter together.

Verse 1 is one of the power verses in scripture, *"I appeal to you therefore, brothers, by the mercies of God, to present your bodies as a living sacrifice, holy and acceptable to God, which is your spiritual worship."* In your Bible, it might say, "which is your reasonable service."

For all Jesus has done for us, what do we have to offer back to Him? We have ourselves. That is what this verse says, *"present your bodies as a living sacrifice, holy and acceptable to God, which is your spiritual worship (reasonable service)"* (v. 1). It is not too much to ask from God to give our lives back to Him. He is the one who breathed life in us in the first place.

> For all Jesus has done for us, what do we have to offer back to Him?

Verse 2, *"Do not be conformed to this world, but be transformed by the renewal of your mind".* For most of us this is difficult. We would love not to be conformed to this world. We would love to be transformed by the renewing of our mind. I mentioned in my journal, the way to do so is to stay in His Word. It makes sense, what we fill our mind with is what we will be, it is what we think about. It is who we become. So let's renew our mind by staying in God's Word daily.

Verse 3 says, *"not to think of himself more highly than he ought to think".* In this Christian life, it is important to remain humble. Staying in His Word and staying close to the Lord keeps us humble.

Next, Paul laundry lists a bunch of spiritual gifts. As one body, we all have different gifts, and he mentions several of them. As I go through these, think which ones may be your spiritual gifts. He mentions prophecy, service, teaching, exhortation, leading, mercy, and giving or generosity.

I mentioned in my journal, I thought I had the gifts of prophecy and leadership. That does not mean prophesy meaning being prophetic. Prophecy to me means one who speaks truth, who shares things other people do not want to share. When you think about the prophets, they had to give God's message to people, even though it was uncomfortable. I think that is what prophecy means. It is a gift of discernment and communication.

Which of these spiritual gifts touches you the most? Which one do you think God has endowed you with? Regardless of our gifts, verses 9 and 10 say, *"Let love be genuine. . . . Love one another with brotherly affection."* As Christians, we should be loving, we should be examples of love. The verse goes on to say, *"Outdo one another in showing honor"* (v. 10). As Christians, we are to honor all people.

Verse 11 says, *"be fervent in spirit, serve the Lord."* Are you doing that? Are you serving the Lord? Verse 12 tells us to *"be patient in tribulation".* Whoa! That one is a little tough for me. I hope I can get better at being patient when things are not going well. And the verse tells me how, *"Rejoice in hope"* and *"be constant in prayer."* Those two things would help me be more patient in tribulation.

Verse 16 says, *"Live in harmony with one another"*. Am I the cause of harmony or discontent in various relationships in my life? The verse also tells me, *"Never be wise in your own sight."* That goes back to remaining humble.

The last few verses remind us to live peaceably with everybody. Although we are tempted, we do not have to get even with people, we do not have to always be right with people, because *"Vengeance is mine, . . . says the Lord"* (v. 19). I heard a pastor recently say, "I can be right or I can be happy. I choose to be happy." As difficult as it is, leave revenge to the Lord.

The chapter ends with this verse, *"Do not be overcome by evil, but overcome evil with good"* (v. 21). There are many, many principles to live by in this chapter and I encourage you to listen again or get your Bible out and read this chapter and select one of those characteristics God would like you to focus on and make that your application today.

Prayer

Lord, for me, it is to help me be genuine in love. To love one another with brotherly affection. Help me be more loving as a Christian and less judgmental. And by exercising love, live peaceably with others. Lord, you know I am thinking about some particular relationships right now. So help me express love in the midst of some challenging relationships and by doing so, help me live in harmony with one another. In your name, I pray. Amen.

MY THOUGHTS

ROMANS 13

Submitting to Authority

Romans 13 is about submitting to authority, something many people struggle with. Are Christians to submit to all government authority? Are we to pay taxes? Please read or listen to Romans 13.

COMMENTS

Yesterday, I shared that I read Romans 12 in Maui, Hawaii. We were still in Hawaii, so we might as well take another tour trip through Maui. My journal entry says, "Drove to Hana yesterday in our convertible." Wow, how cool was that. We rented a convertible in Hawaii. So, "Drove to Hana yesterday in our convertible, it was spectacular. A twelve-hour trip through rain forest, waterfalls, desert, mountains, lava, black sand beaches, flowers. Very, very pretty."

Before heading out on the road to Hana, I had my quiet time with the Lord when I read Romans 13 and wrote, "How to live in society. Be subject to governing authorities. Do what is good. Pay taxes. Love one another. Love is fulfilment of the law. Behave properly. Make no provision for the lusts of the flesh." That was my summary of Romans 13 in Maui, Hawaii, 1994.

In 2001, I focused on a different aspect of Romans 13 (NKJV), verse 7, and wrote, *"Render therefore to all their due: . . . honor to whom honor."* And, "It is okay to honor people. Some may believe a standing ovation for a person is wrong. I think this passage says it's okay to honor people."

In 2013, I took a different take on this chapter, probably the more famous part of this chapter, when I wrote, "According to verse 1, does God select political leadership in every country? People say God must have wanted 'Obama' or 'Bush' or whoever to be president. I don't think this verse says that. Israel wanted a king. God didn't. He gave them one because it is what they wanted. If we elect 'Bush' or 'Obama', we get what we want. God may or may not want them. "Yet, He is not surprised by who we elect and they are not there without His allowance."

I continued, "Government is for our good. Without it, there's conflict or anarchy, not good. We are to pay our taxes, according to verse 6, and pay respect and honor to those in authority over us. The chapter continues, love one another. Love fulfills the law. Put on Jesus. Make no provision for the flesh. Refuse the flesh. Check it and take in Jesus."

Let's go back to the first couple of verses of chapter 13. *"For there is no authority except from God, and those that exist have been instituted by God"* (v. 1). That is controversial, sometimes, in Christianity, so I appreciate the footnote in my English Standard Version Study Bible:

> This passage addresses the responsibility of Christians to governing authorities. They are to be "subject to" (which generally means to obey) the government because it has been ordained by God. Paul is speaking here of the general principle of submission to government. Several other passages show that God approves of Christians disobeying government, but only when obedience to government would mean disobeying God. There were even times when God raised up leaders to rebel against the government and deliver his people from evil rulers (p. 2179).

My English Standard Version Study Bible footnotes continue with some notes on verse 1 itself, "It is true that those governing authorities that exist have been instituted by God, but sometimes God gives good authorities as a blessing, and sometimes he institutes evil rulers as a means of trial or judgment. These earthly 'authorities' will ultimately be superseded by the rule of Christ" (pp. 2179-2180).

Do I believe in living under the authority of the government? Absolutely. Do I believe God ordains or selects every president of the United States or the leaders of every country? Absolutely not. As I mentioned in my journal, Israel wanted a king. God did not want Israel to have a king, but God gave them the desire

> Do I believe God ordains or selects every president of the United States or the leaders of every country? Absolutely not.

of their heart. If the political system, regardless of which country, offers us a couple of candidates and we select from one of those candidates, does their election mean that was what God wanted? I do not believe so. I think often, God gives us the desire of our hearts in our elected leadership.

For example, I believe God would always put people in leadership who would follow Him and His laws. But that is not the case in many countries and many places on earth. So what is my responsibility as a Christian? Generally, it is exactly what this verse tells us. *"Let every person be subject to the governing authorities"* (v. 1). Verse 3 says, *"Then do what is good, and you will receive his approval"*. As long as I am behaving under the authority of the government, I should be just fine. However, verse 4 says, *"But if you do wrong, be afraid, for he does not bear the sword in vain."*

There are a few verses in here I wish all of our politicians would abide by. For example, verse 4, *"for he is God's servant for your good."* I wish all of our politicians were God's servants. Verse 6 says, *"for the authorities are ministers of God."* O, how I would love that to be true.

And this chapter tells Christians to pay our taxes. Verses 6 and 7, *"For because of this you also pay taxes, for the authorities are ministers of God, attending to this very thing. Pay to all what is owed to them: taxes to whom taxes are owed, revenue to whom revenue is owed, respect to whom respect is owed, honor to whom honor is owed."*

DIGGING DEEPER

Our life application from Romans 13 is to be subject to the governing authorities as long as they are not overtly disobeying God; and joyfully pay our taxes. Well, maybe not joyfully, but pay our taxes. And even go so far as to respect those in authority over us.

On a happier note, verse 9 gives us the golden rule, *"You shall love your neighbor as yourself."* Or do unto others as you would want done unto you. By loving others, we fulfill the law of Christ.

The chapter closes with a few other instructions, *"cast off the works of darkness and put on the armor of light"* (v. 12). And finally, *"But put on the Lord Jesus Christ, and make no provision for the flesh"* (v. 14).

Prayer

Lord, help me understand from this chapter, You do put people in authority over us. You allow everyone a leadership position wherever they are. But that does not mean everyone is Your choice. But it is our responsibility to respect authority, to be subject to authority, to pay our taxes, and to keep law and order in our country and in our lands.

Our job is to love our neighbor as ourselves; to love one another. And to put on the Lord Jesus Christ and deflect the desires of the flesh. Lord, it is easy to read, but it is hard to do. Strengthen us to do these very things and be a testimony for You. In Your name, we pray. Amen.

MY THOUGHTS

ROMANS 14

Biblical Eating and Drinking

Today, we are in Romans 14, only three chapters left in this great Book of Romans. Does the Bible tell us what we can eat and drink? Please read or listen to Romans 14.

COMMENTS

In 1994, remember, we were in Maui, Hawaii when I wrote in my journal, "Got up this morning to go to the Volcano Haleakala, ten thousand feet above sea level. Very pretty drive and a nice look at the inside of a dormant volcano. Real pretty. We're having a great time."

Even vacationing in Maui does not keep me from reading the scriptures each and every day. How about you? Is it harder for you on vacation to stay in the Word of God? It is my habit, has been for many decades, to spend a little bit of time with the Lord each and every morning regardless of where I am and regardless of what I am doing. I hope these *Day by Day Through the Bible* devotions are convincing you to do the same. Regardless of what day it is or regardless of whether you are going on vacation or going to work, start your day or end your day in the Word of God.

On that day, before we visited the volcano, I wrote, "Paul does not restrict diet or days. He leaves these issues open to the believer. *'Let each (man) be . . . convinced in his own mind'* (v. 5 NKJV) and live for the Lord."

In 2001, I had a different take on Romans 14 when I wrote, *"For none of us lives to himself, and no one of dies to himself"* (v. 7 NKJV). Then, "I hear this opposite argument often. What I do is private. It doesn't affect others, like abortion or sexual consent among two adults. Nothing is done in isolation. People observe, they find out, then they consider similar behavior. I agree with God's Word. No one lives to himself. What people do or don't do always affects someone else. We must be careful how our decisions and actions affect others."

What do you think about that? Do you agree whatever we do is not private? It always gets out and affects the lives of other people? Do you agree nothing we do is in isolation? Do people observe, find out, and consider

> **What people do or don't do always affects someone else.**

similar behavior? What kind of behavior are you modeling? If people watch what you do, do people see Christianity and do they see you modeling Christianity and want to be one? As I wrote in my journal, "What people do or don't do always affects someone else."

In 2013, I had another different take on Romans 14, "There is room in Christianity for some diversity, for example, food or days. Judaism had become a religion of many laws and rules, maybe to an extreme. And Paul is trying not to repeat legalism in Christianity. Today, this discussion would be about drinking. Verses 13, 17, and 19 give us our answer. Don't judge others who do or don't. Walk in love. Pursue peace and mutual understanding in our behavior. Don't cause a brother to stumble over such issues."

DIGGING DEEPER

Let's go back and look at verses 13, 17, and 19. Verse 13 says, *"Therefore let us not pass judgment on one another any longer, but rather decide never to put a stumbling block or hindrance in the way of a brother."* Verse 17 says, *"For the kingdom of God is not a matter of eating and drinking but of righteousness and peace and joy in the Holy*

Spirit." And verse 19 says, *"So then let us pursue what makes for peace and for mutual upbuilding."*

I have probably mentioned before in these devotions, in my early Christian life I had a pretty judgmental spirit. I probably still do today. But I have matured and I am trying to grow through this. Staying close to the Word of God helps me, especially passages like these. Regarding the do's and don'ts of Christianity, I think these verses are very, very helpful.

Like verse 5, which says, *"Each one should be fully convinced in his own mind."* And verse 12 tells us, *"each of us will give an account of himself to God."* Verse 14 helps us clarify it even more, *"I know and am persuaded in the Lord Jesus that nothing is unclean in itself, but it is unclean for anyone who thinks it unclean."* So, if you are strongly persuaded that Christians should not drink, then do not drink. But be careful about your judgment of others who do. Verse 20 says, *"Do not, for the sake of food, destroy the work of God".* We could modify that today and say, do not for the sake of drinking, destroy the work of God.

Let's summarize with a couple of verses. Verse 8 says, *"For if we live, we live to the Lord, and if we die, we die to the Lord. So then, whether we live or whether we die, we are the Lord's."* Is your behavior of the Lord?

And the last verse of the chapter tells us, *"For whatever does not proceed from faith is sin."* Does your behavior proceed from your faith? Does it proceed from your sense of living to the Lord, knowing all of us will give an account of our behavior to God Himself and not to one another?

Prayer

Lord, we thank You for freedom, freedom in Christ. Freedom to choose. Freedom to choose how we eat, how we drink, what day we want to worship and we thank You we live in the Lord. As we do, Lord, we are reminded by this chapter, we will all give an account of our behavior to You. Every knee will bow and every tongue confess before You. My prayer, Lord, is help my behavior line up with my beliefs. Help me where I need help and I will thank You for it. In Jesus' name, amen.

MY THOUGHTS

Why Read the Bible?

Today, we are in the second to the last chapter of the Book of Romans. How is life going for you? Do you need instruction, endurance, and encouragement from time to time? Please read or listen to Romans 15.

COMMENTS

In 1994, you might remember, we were in Maui, Hawaii and I wrote this in my journal as we were getting ready to leave, "Walked with Terry one more time around the coast because we were leaving that day." That was our first trip to Hawaii and Hawaii is a hard place to leave, but it is always good to come home.

I read Romans 15 and wrote, "Please your neighbor." And, "Be of the same mind with one another. Accept one another." And lastly, "The Romans were good. Paul's priority was to preach in new areas. He wanted to spread the gospel."

In 2001, I had some similar thoughts as 1994, "Help others above our selfish needs. Easy to say, hard to live. Paul's purpose was to preach, not where Christ was named, but to those who had not heard."

In 2013, I wrote, "Strong Christians have an obligation to help the weak by teaching them, setting examples for them like Jesus did. Strong and weak accept and help each other. Jesus came through the Jews, but the Gentiles were always part of the family." Then, "Paul knew his calling, do I? He also succeeded in his calling, do

I?" I wrote, "I hope I can say this as I begin traveling again for the Gideons." And I quoted verse 29, *"I know that when I come to you I will come in the fullness of the blessing of Christ."*

DIGGING DEEPER

I want us to consider Romans 15, by looking at verse 4, which says, *"For whatever was written in former days was written for our instruction, that through endurance and through the encouragement of the Scriptures we might have hope."*

These devotions are brought to you by the Ezra Project which was started in 2002 with one purpose, to connect God's people to God's Word. It is my sincere belief this is one of the greatest needs in the Christian church today, for Christians to come back to the daily habit of being in the scriptures. This verse reminds us why. It says, *"whatever was written in former days was written for our instruction . . . and through the encouragement of the Scriptures we might have hope"* (v. 4). Living in a secular world today, we need godly instruction. And where do we get it? We get it in the scriptures.

We also need encouragement. And we need hope. This verse tells us we also get that in the scriptures, but look at the little phrase in the middle. It says, *"that through endurance"* (v. 4), which means we must keep on, we must stay in the scriptures, we must keep going. We need to make it a habit to stay in God's Word on a daily basis.

> **We need to make it a habit to stay in God's Word on a daily basis.**

That is my encouragement to you. Endure. Stay in the scriptures. *"For whatever was written in former days was written for our instruction, that through endurance and through the encouragement of the Scriptures we might have hope"* (v. 4). Then verse 13 says, *"May the God of hope fill you with all joy and peace in believing, so that by the power of the Holy Spirit you may abound in hope."* If you need some hope today, find it in the Word of God. And when you do, you will experience joy and peace in believing and have the power of the Holy Spirit within you.

Prayer

Lord, we thank You so much for Your Word. We thank You it gives us instruction, it gives us encouragement, and it gives us hope. Holy Spirit, we ask You to keep us in Your Word because we need instruction, we need encouragement, and we need hope. As we stay in Your Word, Holy Spirit grant us Your peace and Your joy. In the name of Jesus, we pray. Amen.

MY THOUGHTS

ROMANS 16

Paul and People

Today, we finish our wonderful journey through the Book of Romans. We arrive at the last chapter and read Paul's greetings to various people, though he never visited Rome. Ministry is about people. Who are you ministering to? Please read or listen to Romans 16.

COMMENTS

In 1994, we were now home from Maui, Hawaii. I am back in my home reading Romans 16, when I wrote, "Paul greets a lot of people in Rome, a place he had never been. People must have traveled around more than we think. Or Paul was simply well aware of 'the church' all over, including a faraway place like Rome. Praise God for the network of His church communicating with and helping each other, now all over the world." I continued to write, "My long walk through Romans comes to an end. Praise God for the depth of understanding scripture affords, to contemplate its meaning. Thanks to those who have studied and written about its contents and to the Holy Spirit who reveals truth."

In 2001, my last journal entry on the Book of Romans was, "Paul names many to greet. What would my list be of people, Christians, saints, to greet? How many are willing to risk their lives for the building of the kingdom of God or the spreading of the gospel?" Those were my concluding remarks in 2001.

Let's look at 2013. My last entry in the Book of Romans was, "People matter. Paul greets many, commends them and recognizes their contribution to him, the church, or to each other." Then I quoted all the descriptions he made in this chapter toward these people: *"our sister'* (v. 1), *'my fellow workers'* (v. 3), *'the first convert to Christ'* (v. 5), *'my kinsman'* (v. 7), *'my beloved'* (v. 8), *'approved in Christ'* (v. 10), *'chosen in the Lord'"* (v. 13). Then I wrote, "How would someone describe me? How would I refer to some of my friends?"

I continued writing, "We are to watch out for those who cause divisions, who create obstacles contrary to traditional biblical doctrine, according to verse 17. And be wise as to what is good and innocent and as what is evil." I finished my journal entry in 2013 with this, "Jesus is able to strengthen me through the gospel, preaching of Jesus Christ and the Word of God. He deserves the glory."

DIGGING DEEPER

What adjectives would you use to describe the Christians around you? What adjectives would they use to describe you as a Christian in their eyes?

Chapter 16 is about people. Who are the key people in your life? What adjectives would you use to describe the Christians around you? Maybe more importantly, what adjectives would they use to describe you as a Christian in their eyes?

Paul was well-connected with the church of his day. Are you? Are you well-connected with a body of believers, with a church? If so, praise the Lord! If not, may I encourage you to get yourself into a body of believers. Find a good Bible-believing, Bible-teaching church and fellowship with fellow believers like Paul does here in Romans 16.

Paul then makes an appeal to them and to us, *"I appeal to you, brothers, to watch out for those who cause divisions and create obstacles contrary to the doctrine that you have been taught; avoid them. For such persons do not serve our Lord Christ, but their own appetites, and by smooth talk and flattery they deceive the hearts of the naive"* (vv. 17-18). Then and now, there are many who are out to deceive us with smooth-talking flattery. One means of protection from the deception of smooth-talking flattery is to stay in the Word of God.

Prayer

Paul closes with a wonderful doxology, the final verses of Romans 16. I will close with them as well:

Now to him who is able to strengthen you according to my gospel and the preaching of Jesus Christ, according to the revelation of the mystery that was kept secret for long ages but has now been disclosed and through the prophetic writings has been made known to all nations, according to the command of the eternal God, to bring about the obedience of faith— to the only wise God be glory forevermore through Jesus Christ! Amen (vv. 25-27).

MY THOUGHTS

SIXTEEN DAYS IN 1 CORINTHIANS

1 CORINTHIANS 1

Power or Foolishness?

Today, we begin our journey through 1 Corinthians. The Apostle Paul is the author of both 1 and 2 Corinthians. He wrote 1 Corinthians from Ephesus in about 53-55 A.D., and then 2 Corinthians from Macedonia around 55 to 56 A.D.

Paul established the church at Corinth in southern Greece, aided by two new-found friends from Rome, Priscilla and Aquila. Like Paul, they were Jews and tentmakers. They spent eighteen months in Corinth in the early '50s establishing the church.

Paul moved on to Ephesus, where he wrote this letter back to the church at Corinth. Paul wanted the church at Corinth to work together to advance the gospel. What was preventing unity was arrogance and one-upmanship. They were divided over misunderstandings about social snobbery and sexual immorality. They were confused about marriage, divorce, participation in pagan religions, order in their own worship services, and even the bodily resurrection of Christians.

Spiritual arrogance often stems from a lack of understanding of the holiness of God and His requirement of such holiness from His people.

The letter of 1 Corinthians is very relevant today. These same issues still plague our churches: relationship between Christians and pagan cultures; division within churches; church practices like the Lord's Supper and the use of spiritual gifts. The letter also deals with personal matters like sex, marriage, celibacy, and virtues like love.

There are two "firsts" in 1 Corinthians. The first "first" is the first announcement of our bodily resurrection. We will find that in 1 Corinthians 15:51-52. The second "first" in 1 Corinthians is the first recording of the church celebrating the Lord's Supper. We will find that in 11:23-26.

There are sixteen chapters in 1 Corinthians, and we will take them one a day. Please read or listen to 1 Corinthians 1.

COMMENTS

I selected three of my personal Bible reading journals to help us through 1 Corinthians. The first journal will be 1994, then ten years later, in 2004, and then eleven years later, in 2015. I try to select journals from different decades. Selecting various journals also represents different ages for me; thirty-nine years old in 1994, forty-nine years old in 2004, and a whopping sixty-years old in 2015. By selecting journals from various decades, it gives us perspective on how the Word of God speaks to us differently as we read scripture throughout our lifetime.

I begin with my journal in 1994 on 1 Corinthians 1 (NASB). I quoted verses that meant something to me as I read this chapter, *"the testimony concerning Christ was confirmed in you'* (v. 6). Help it be the case in me. Give me a renewed spirit of humility and integrity." I continued, *"God is faithful, through whom you were called into fellowship with His Son, Jesus Christ our Lord"* (v. 9). The next verse I referred to was, *"For the word of the cross is foolishness to those who are perishing, but to us who are being saved it is the power of God"* (v. 18).

Next, I commented on verse 22, "Verse 22 is true today. People ask for signs and wisdom and God gives both. But people do not want to give God the credit or the glory." Next, I quoted verse 25, *"the foolishness of God is wiser than men, and the weakness of God is stronger than men"*. I finished 1 Corinthians 1 with, *"no man may boast before God"* (v. 29).

In my journals, I also tend to write some prayers, and after reading 1 Corinthians 1, I wrote, "Help me with humility. Cause me to be careful and not to be prideful, not to be boastful."

In 2004, I was reading the Bible chronologically. To get through the whole Bible in one year, I had to read more than one chapter at a time. I read 1 Corinthians 1-4 and did refer to a few verses in chapter 1. I wrote in my journal, "Paul writes with such elegance." I quoted verse 25, *"the foolishness of God is wiser than men"*. Next, I quoted verse 18, *"the word of the cross is foolishness to those who are perishing, but to us who are being saved it is the power of God"*.

> **The foolishness of God is wiser than men.**
> **1 Cor. 1:25**

In 2015, after reading 1 Corinthians 1, I wrote, "Called. Like Paul, I sense God's call on my life, Gideons and the Ezra Project." Then I wrote about verse 9, "God is faithful" and verses 10-13, "No denominations." About verse 18, I wrote, "The cross is folly to unbelievers, but power to us who believe." About verses 22 and 23, I wrote, "Rather than suggest wisdom, preach Christ crucified." I continued, "God is wiser and stronger than men, referring to verse 25." And lastly, about verses 29-31, "We have nothing to boast about. Our life, our strength, wisdom, everything comes from Him."

My note on prayer after 1 Corinthians 1 was, "The power of the cross in my life. Also no boasting, and using the gifting You give me in the right way."

DIGGING DEEPER

Let's look at a couple of power verses in this chapter. Verses 7-9 drew my attention, *"you are not lacking in any (spiritual) gift, as you wait for the revealing of our Lord Jesus Christ, who will sustain you to the end, guiltless in the day of our Lord Jesus Christ. God is faithful, by whom you were called into the fellowship of his Son, Jesus Christ our Lord."* According to those verses, we lack no spiritual gift, and God will sustain us to the end. He is faithful. That gives me hope. Does it give you hope?

Then Paul gets to the crux of the matter of why he is writing this letter, *"I appeal to you, brothers, by the name of our Lord Jesus Christ, that all of you agree, and that there be no divisions among you, but that you be united in the same mind and the same judgment"* (v. 10). Remember in the book introduction, the point of this letter was to get the Corinthians to agree and move forward in spreading the gospel.

Next, another power verse, *"For the word of the cross is folly to those who are perishing, but to us who are being saved it is the power of God"* (v. 18). What a contrast. To those who do not believe, it is foolishness, but to those of us who believe, it is the power of God. Paul goes on in verses 23 and 24 to remind us, *"(B)ut we preach Christ crucified, a stumbling block to Jews and folly to Gentiles, but to those who are called, both Jews and Greeks, Christ the power of God and the wisdom of God."*

Then and now the cross divides people. To those of us who believe, it represents the power of Jesus Christ. But to the unbelieving world, it is just foolishness. What does Paul tell us to do? Preach Christ crucified.

Paul closes out chapter 1 by reminding us:

brothers: not many of you were wise according to worldly standards, not many were powerful, not many were of noble birth. But God chose what is foolish in the world to shame the wise; God chose what is weak in the world to shame the strong; God chose what is low and despised in the world, even things that are not, to bring to nothing things that are, so that no human being might boast in the presence of God. And because of him you are in Christ Jesus (vv. 26-30).

That is a good start to 1 Corinthians.

Prayer

Father, we ask, like Paul, that we would all agree there would be no divisions among us; the Christian church would be united in the same mind in You. We pray in thanks that the power of the Word of the cross is power to us. And we pray You would use us with that power to enlighten those who think it is foolishness.

These words remind me it is not Paul's eloquence or my own eloquence that is going to convince somebody. It is preaching Christ crucified. Father, give me the strength; give me the wisdom to point people to You. Change their foolishness into saving faith in Jesus Christ, our Lord and Savior. Amen.

MY THOUGHTS

1 CORINTHIANS 2

The Mind of Christ

1 Corinthians 2 is a short chapter, only sixteen verses. Do you know how to share your faith? Do you have the mind of Christ? Please read or listen to 1 Corinthians 2.

COMMENTS

"Oh, I wish it were so that I could have the mind of Christ." That is what I wrote in my journal in 1994 after reading this chapter (NASB). Then I wrote, "Stay focused! *'Know nothing except Jesus Christ, and Him crucified'* (v. 2). Faith rests on the power of God, referring to verse 5."

In 2004, I read 1 Corinthians 1-4 on the same day, and highlighted a couple of thoughts in chapter 2, "Paul taught not with fancy words, but in demonstration of the Spirit and of power. He boldly proclaims, *'We have the mind of Christ'* (v. 16). Wow!"

In 2015, I read 1 Corinthians 2 and 3 on the same day, and wrote, "Paul did not persuade people to become Christians. He demonstrated the Spirit and power of God by faith. In witnessing, this is important. I will not convince someone to become a Christian. Only the Holy Spirit can do that. I provide witness and testify of my own salvation and watch the Holy Spirit do the work, not the wisdom of men." Then I wrote, "I long to have the mind of Christ. I pray for it often, especially related to Gideon discussions and the Ezra Project."

DIGGING DEEPER

Paul opens chapter 2 with a persuasive argument, though he says he did not come proclaiming with great speech, lofty speech, or great wisdom, he does articulate his point very, very well. He says, I *"did not come proclaiming to you the testimony of God with lofty speech or wisdom"* (v. 1). He goes on to say, *"And I was with you in weakness and in fear and much trembling, and my speech and my message were not in plausible words of wisdom, but in demonstration of the Spirit and of power, so that your faith might not rest in the wisdom of men but in the power of God"* (vv. 3-5).

As I wrote in one of my journals, that is so important. It is not our eloquence that is going to convince someone to come to saving faith in Christ. It is the power of God. It is the Holy Spirit's job to draw them into faith in Christ. I am so thankful it is not on my eloquent words that eternity depends for someone's life. The great Apostle Paul argues this principle very well. Paul is clear about what we do share with people.

He continues, *"Yet among the mature we do impart wisdom, although it is not a wisdom of this age or of the rulers of this age . . . we impart a secret and hidden wisdom of God, which God decreed before the ages for our glory"* (vv. 6-7). Then he quotes Isaiah 64:4 in verse 9 *"as it is written, 'What no eye has seen, nor ear heard, nor the heart of man imagined, what God has prepared for those who love him.'"*

> What no eye has seen, nor ear heard, nor the heart of man imagined, what God has prepared for those who love him.
> Isa. 64:4

He continues in verse 10, *"these things God has revealed to us through the Spirit. For the Spirit searches everything, even the depths of God."*

So we can share with people from a spiritual perspective, the wisdom God gives us, as we open our mouth and proclaim testimony for Him. Here is a great verse to remember, verse 11, *"For who knows a person's thoughts except the spirit of that person, which is in him? So also no one comprehends the thoughts of God except the Spirit of God."*

Paul continues, *"And we impart this in words not taught by human wisdom but taught by the Spirit, interpreting spiritual truths to those who are spiritual. The natural person does not accept the things of the Spirit of God, for they are folly to him, and he is not able to understand them because they are spiritually discerned"* (vv. 13-14).

What do I get out of all this? God calls us to be witnesses, there is no question about that in scripture. But we have to be discerning. If God has not prepared the heart of the person we are sharing with, it will be folly to them. What we have to share is spiritual. If they are not spiritually prepared, they cannot receive it.

So, if you get in a conversation with someone, and it appears they are rejecting everything, it is best to stop and wait for a better time. That is why prayer is so important as we intend to share spiritually with someone. Pray the Spirit draws them. Pray the Spirit opens their heart to the things that are spiritual. Paul finishes this chapter with this incredible statement, *"But we have the mind of Christ"* (v. 16).

Prayer

O, I want that Lord. O, I pray for that. Father, help me have the mind of Christ. I cannot even comprehend what that statement means, Lord, but You said it here in Your Word that we can have the mind of Christ, so we pray it so. We ask humbly You impart to us the mind of Christ so we can be ambassadors for You, witnesses for You, so we can speak spiritually on Your behalf to those who need to hear spiritual truth. Father, by faith, we ask for the mind of Christ. In Jesus' name, we pray. Amen.

MY THOUGHTS

1 CORINTHIANS 3

Milk or Meat?

In 1 Corinthians 3, Paul challenges the Corinthians, and us, to grow in Christ. Are you growing into a holy temple for the Lord? Please read or listen to 1 Corinthians 3.

COMMENTS

Chapter 3 follows that great verse ending chapter 2, *"we have the mind of Christ"* (1 Cor. 2:16). If we go back to that verse and then start with chapter 3, it makes a little more sense. So the last verse in chapter 2 was, *"But we have the mind of Christ."* Chapter 3 starts, *"But I, brothers, could not address you as spiritual people, but as people of the flesh, as infants in Christ. I fed you with milk, not solid food, for you were not ready for it"* (vv. 1-2).

How about you? Are you still being fed with milk spiritually or are you ready for solid food? How long have you been a Christian? How would Paul describe you and your Christianity? Would he call you a spiritual person? Would he call you people of the flesh? Would he call you still an infant in Christ? Do you take your Christianity seriously? Do you long to grow, to mature, in your faith in Jesus?

That was the point Paul was making to the Corinthians. It is the same point he is making to us. It is time to get beyond the elementary principles of Christianity. It is time to move on to deeper spiritual things. But Paul tells the Corinthians, "But you are not ready." Are you ready?

Paul said to the Corinthians, *"For you are still of the flesh. For while there is jealousy and strife among you, are you not of the flesh and behaving only in a human way?"* (v. 3). How about you? Are you still of the flesh? Are you still dealing with petty issues of Christianity? Still behaving only in a human way?

One way of looking at the argument Paul is making is what we have made of denominations in Christianity. That is kind of what Paul is referring to here. He says to the Corinthians, some of you say, "I follow Paul", some of you say, "I follow Apollos." And Paul is telling them, "Forget about it." He says in verses 6 and 7, *"I planted, Apollos watered, but God gave the growth. So neither he who plants nor he who waters is anything, but only God who gives the growth."* Are you stuck on milk or are you ready to move on to solid food, the deeper things of Christianity found in the Word of God?

Paul goes on to say, the foundation of faith is Jesus Christ. Is He your foundation of your Christianity? If so, that is the foundation we build on, our foundation in Christ and Christ alone. But the foundation is only the foundation. We must build. We must build on

> **Do you not know that you are God's temple and that God's Spirit dwells in you?**
>
> 1 Cor. 3:16

our faith. In verse 16, Paul says, *"Do you not know that you are God's temple and that God's Spirit dwells in you?"* Are you a temple built on the foundation of Jesus Christ? Does God's Spirit dwell in you?

Paul goes on to tell us, *"For God's temple is holy, and you are that temple"* (v. 17). Are you a holy representation of God and of Jesus Christ? Have you built an honoring, glorious, beautiful temple that houses the Holy Spirit built on your foundation of Jesus Christ in your life?

Paul finishes the chapter by saying, *"and you are Christ's, and Christ is God's"* (v. 23). Are you Christ's? If so, you belong to God. If not, if you are not Christ's, what is your foundation? I encourage you to consider Christ, to let Jesus Christ become your foundation and build a holy temple acceptable to God, which is your reasonable sacrifice.

Go back to the book introduction when we said the point Paul was making to the Corinthians is to not be divisive. Do not divide yourselves over this doctrine or that doctrine but grow in the foundation of Jesus. It was an important message to the Corinthian church, and it is an important message to each one of us today.

DIGGING DEEPER

Let's close 1 Corinthians 3 by going back to verses 6-9, where Paul said, *"I planted, Apollos watered, but God gave the growth. So neither he who plants nor he who waters is anything, but only God who gives the growth. He who plants and he who waters are one, and each will receive his wages according to his labor. For we are God's fellow workers. You are God's field, God's building."*

May we build on a solid foundation, Jesus Christ. And may we become God's building, a temple, that can house the Holy Spirit and effectively serve and worship Jesus by being a holy temple, God's temple, here on earth. Again, verses 16 and 17, *"Do you not know that you are God's temple and that God's Spirit dwells in you?. . . For God's temple is holy, and you are that temple."*

Prayer

Father, remind us today, it does not matter where or how we got started into this faith called Christianity. What matters is You caused the increase, You caused the growth. We are thankful You grow us into a temple that the Holy Spirit can dwell in here on earth.

Lord, You want us to be a holy temple, a temple reflecting You. But we are flawed human beings, Lord, so help us. Help us set aside jealousy, strife, works of the flesh, our own human behavior, and allow Your Holy Spirit to grow a beautiful temple, a holy temple, dedicated to You. Use me as a temple for You. In Jesus' name, we pray. Amen.

MY THOUGHTS

1 CORINTHIANS 4

Spiritual Arrogance

In 1 Corinthians 4, Paul calls out the Corinthians for spiritual arrogance. Do you remember your spiritual roots? Have you become spiritually arrogant? Please read or listen to 1 Corinthians 4.

COMMENTS

In 1994, after reading this chapter, I wrote, "Jesus examines each one of us," referring to verse 4. Let's step aside from that journal entry and read verse 4, *"For I am not aware of anything against myself, but I am not thereby acquitted. It is the Lord who judges me."* Going back to the journal, I did say, "Jesus examines each one of us," based on that verse. "Arrogance has no place in the body of Christ." Then I wrote, "Paul wrote, *'we have become as the scum of the world'"* (v. 13 NASB).

In 2004, I was reading chronologically, so I was reading more than one chapter a day. On the day I read 1 Corinthians 1-4, I did not have an entry on this chapter in my journal.

In 2015, I read 1 Corinthians 4 and 5, and most of my journal is on chapter 4, "It is required of stewards that they be found trustworthy. What a weighty responsibility. God has given me stewardship over my home, my family, the Ezra Project, and as International Treasurer of The Gideons International. May I be found trustworthy."

I continued, "We must be good stewards because it is the Lord who judges me, according to verse 4. He discloses the purposes of the heart, according to verse 5. In my role of stewardship, I cannot go beyond what is written in scripture." That's verse 6. "I need to realize that whatever gifting I have, whatever talents and abilities I think I have, I have nothing I have not received from the Lord, according to verse 7. And how should I respond to adversity? *'When reviled, we bless; when persecuted, we endure; when slandered, we entreat'* (vv. 12-13). Lord, help me do that. I don't think I can really say, *'be imitators of me',* like Paul says in verse 16, but Christians need to live in such a way that people see and want to be one."

DIGGING DEEPER

Let's dwell on a few points made in my journal in 2015. The first point was about verse 2, *"Moreover, it is required of stewards that they be found trustworthy."* I mentioned I believe God has given me stewardship over my family, my home, the Ezra Project, and as a volunteer in The Gideons International serving on the Executive Committee. What has God given you stewardship over? Whatever your list is, He has asked us to be trustworthy. In fact, He goes beyond asking us, He demands it. This verse says it is required of stewards to be found trustworthy. A little later, Paul reminds us the Lord judges us. So, whatever He has given us stewardship over, He wants us to be trustworthy, and He judges us accordingly.

Verse 5 reminds me the Lord discloses the purpose of my heart. I relate that to being trustworthy in whatever stewardship God has given me. He knows my heart. He knows your heart. Are you trustworthy over the things God has given you stewardship over?

> **Moreover, it is required of stewards that they be found trustworthy.**
>
> **1 Cor. 4:2**

Next, Paul asks us, what do you have that you did not receive? Relating this to stewardship, whatever God has placed you a steward over, He has given it to you. You received it from Him. Paul goes on and asks us a question, *"If then you received it, why do you boast as if you did not receive it?"* (v. 7).

Going back to my journal entry, remember, I wrote, "I need to realize that whatever gifting I have, whatever talents and abilities I think I have, I have nothing I have not received from the Lord." I think that is worth pondering today. Whatever gifting you have, whatever talents you have, whatever God has given you stewardship over, you received from Him. Give Him the praise, and the glory, and the honor for whatever gifting you have, and whatever responsibility you have over something or someone else.

Did you catch the sarcasm from Paul? It is amazing Paul is so sarcastic as he writes to the Corinthians when he says:

> *Already you have all you want! Already you have become rich! Without us you have become kings! And would that you did reign, so that we might share the rule with you! For I think that God has exhibited us apostles as last of all, like men sentenced to death, because we have become a spectacle to the world, to angels, and to men. We are fools for Christ's sake, but you are wise in Christ. We are weak, but you are strong. You are held in honor, but we in disrepute. To the present hour we hunger and thirst, we are poorly dressed and buffeted and homeless, and we labor, working with our own hands. When reviled, we bless; when persecuted, we endure; when slandered, we entreat. We have become, and are still, like the scum of the world, the refuse of all things* (vv. 8-13).

Paul is lighting up the Corinthians! He is saying, you really think you are something and I am nothing. Then Paul reminds them, *"For though you have countless guides in Christ, you do not have many fathers. For I became your father in Christ Jesus through the gospel"* (v. 15). What he is saying is he is the one that founded the church. He is the one that brought Christianity to the Corinthians. And now, they seem to be following the beat of a different drummer. That is why he says that phrase, *"be imitators of me"* (v. 16). In other words, go back to the real gospel. Forget all the false teaching you learned.

He says as much in verse 17, *"That is why I sent you Timothy, my beloved and faithful child in the Lord, to remind you of my ways in Christ, as I teach them everywhere in every church."* What Paul is saying is, "Don't get so uppity, Corinthians. Don't get so arrogant acting like you know more than I know. I have been doing this for a long time, and you are new at this. Come back to my teachings. Imitate me. Come back to where we started."

In summary, I think the lesson is clear. It is clear to the Corinthians, and it is clear to us. Whatever we have, we have received from the Lord, and He will hold us accountable. Let's not get spiritually arrogant, let's not be spiritually uppity. Let's remember, it is the Lord who judges us and He will disclose the purpose of our hearts.

Prayer

Father, help us guard our hearts against spiritual arrogance. You remind us in this chapter, whatever we have, we have received from You. We thank You for the gifts, talents, and abilities You have bestowed upon us. We are reminded, You hold us accountable. You want to find us trustworthy. May it be so in each one of us. And Lord, where we need to repent, we repent today. We say we are sorry for taking for granted the gifts You have given us. We ask You to forgive us if You have not found us trustworthy in the stewardship You have given us. Scripture helps us course correct. We pray we can get back on track so You can find us trustworthy servants of Yours. Find us faithful, Lord. Amen.

MY THOUGHTS

1 CORINTHIANS 5

Sexual Immorality in the Church

In 1 Corinthians 5, Paul reveals what he knows about immoral sexual tolerance in the Corinthian church. He instructs them to clean it up. Are you in, or tempted by, an immoral sexual relationship? Please read or listen to 1 Corinthians 5.

COMMENTS

My journal entry in 1994 is the only one that really deals with the subjects in this chapter (NASB). I wrote, "The church cannot tolerate open immorality. It will spread like cancer among the body. *'Clean out the old leaven'* (v. 7). Don't associate with immoral people, referring to verse 9. Not with *'any so-called brother if he is an immoral person'* (v. 11). Judge those within the church, referring to verse 12. *'Remove the wicked man from among yourselves'*" (v. 13).

In 2004, I was reading the Bible chronologically, so I was reading more than one chapter at a time. On this day, I read 1 Corinthians 5-8. I did have a couple of lines referring to chapter 5, "We must recognize willful sin within the body and not tolerate it. It can destroy the church." I went on to chapter 6 and quoted verse 20, *"For you have been bought with a price: therefore glorify God in your body."* I finished with, "Be careful how we live so we don't cause others to stumble."

In 2015, I read 1 Corinthians 4 and 5 on the same day, and my entry was all about chapter 4, with nothing about chapter 5.

DIGGING DEEPER

In the first four chapters of 1 Corinthians, Paul covered the arrogance of the church and some of the divisiveness based on who was following whom. Now, he lets the Corinthian church know he is aware of some of their sexual immorality. Paul has some pretty harsh words for tolerance of sexual immorality in the church. *"When you are assembled in the name of the Lord Jesus and my spirit is present, with the power of our Lord Jesus, you are to deliver this man to Satan for the destruction of the flesh, so that his spirit may be saved in the day of the Lord"* (vv. 4-5).

Then and now, Paul is saying we cannot tolerate sexual immorality within the body of Christ. He uses the illustration of leaven in a lump of bread, *"Do you not know that a little leaven leavens the whole lump? Cleanse out the old leaven that you may be a new lump"* (vv. 6-7). He is saying to them and to us, "We have to deal with sins like this within the church or it can spread."

Paul concludes this chapter by saying:

> But now I am writing to you not to associate with anyone who bears the name of brother if he is guilty of sexual immorality or greed, or is an idolater, reviler, drunkard, or swindler—not even to eat with such a one. For what have I to do with judging outsiders? Is it not those inside the church whom you are to judge? God judges those outside. *"Purge the evil person from among you"* (vv. 11-13).

Purge the evil person from among you.

1 Cor. 5:13

These sound like harsh words from Paul to the church at Corinth. What would he think of our churches today? Remember, his point earlier in the chapter was to discipline sexual immorality so the person could be restored. Isn't that true as parents? We discipline our children. Not to punish them eternally, but to restore them to correct behavior. That is the love side of this message in this chapter. Paul is telling the

Corinthians, he is telling us, when you know something is going wrong within the body of Christ, deal with it, so that it will not spread, and the person can be restored to faith.

Does your church handle obvious sinful behavior in such a way? Do you have a discipline manual or a discipline procedure to handle such things? I personally have never been in church leadership, so I have never handled a discipline case within a church. But I have been involved in the disciplinary matters of The Gideons International, a ministry. The Gideons International has a discipline manual. I have been involved in personal and corporate discipline of our membership. These matters are never easy to deal with, but 1 Corinthians 5 tells us we need to do so.

There is certainly a corporate application to this chapter, whether you are in a church or a ministry, sexual immorality cannot be tolerated. But there is also a personal application. If you are currently involved in a sexually immoral relationship, stop. Go back to the last chapter, 3:16-17, *"Do you not know that you are God's temple and that God's Spirit dwells in you? If anyone destroys God's temple, God will destroy him. For God's temple is holy, and you are that temple."* If you are caught up in sexual immorality at the moment, repent. Confess your sin to the Lord, who is faithful and just to forgive us our sins and cleanse us from all unrighteousness. Repentance means to turn from sin. Forgiveness means we are cleansed in the blood of Jesus.

Prayer

Thank You, Lord, that You give us a way of escape from sinful, immoral behavior. Thank You for being a God who hears our prayers, forgives us, and cleanses us. In the name of Jesus, we pray. Amen.

MY THOUGHTS

1 CORINTHIANS 6

Flee Sexual Immorality

1 Corinthians 6 is a continuation of chapter 5 concerning sexual immorality. It is also a famous chapter about whether Christians can take each other to court. What do you think? Please read or listen to 1 Corinthians 6.

COMMENTS

Sometimes the chapter breaks are inconvenient, so let's go back to the end of chapter 5 to connect it to the beginning of chapter 6. The end of chapter 5 says:

I wrote to you in my letter not to associate with sexually immoral people— not at all meaning the sexually immoral of this world, or the greedy and swindlers, or idolaters, since then you would need to go out of the world. But now I am writing to you not to associate with anyone who bears the name of brother if he is guilty of sexual immorality or greed, or is an idolater, reviler, drunkard, or swindler—not even to eat with such a one. For what have I to do with judging outsiders? Is it not those inside the church whom you are to judge? God judges those outside. "Purge the evil person from among you" (vv. 9-13).

Let's continue right on with the beginning of 6:

When one of you has a grievance against another, does he dare go to law before the unrighteous instead of the saints? Or do you not know that the saints will judge the world? And if the world is to be judged by you, are you incompetent to try trivial cases? Do you not know that we are to judge angels? How much more, then, matters pertaining to this life! So if you have such cases, why do you lay them before those who have no standing in the church? I say this to your shame. Can it be that there is no one among you wise enough to settle a dispute between the brothers, but brother goes to law against brother, and that before unbelievers? To have lawsuits at all with one another is already a defeat for you. Why not rather suffer wrong? Why not rather be defrauded? But you yourselves wrong and defraud—even your own brothers! (vv. 1-8)

Connecting these two passages makes sense. Paul finished chapter 5 by saying, *"Is it not those inside the church whom you are to judge? God judges those outside. 'Purge the evil person from among you'"* (vv. 12-13). In the beginning of chapter 6, he is saying, "But you do not do that. You would rather take matters inside the church outside the church and basically have pagans judge you than to deal with these things inside the church."

Verse 4 says, *"So if you have such cases, why do you lay them before those who have no standing in the church?"* Verse 5 says, *"Can it be that there is no one among you wise enough to settle a dispute between the brothers".* So, as a continuation of the end of chapter 5, Paul is saying, "Deal with sexual immorality within the church. And not only sexual immorality but other sinful behavior."

The first eight verses of chapter 6 have been used many times to say Christians ought not sue one another in a court of law. I have personally seen and been involved where Christians have disputed one another and some have not taken their matters to court and others have. I think it is clear to say, that as best we can, we ought to solve our issues within the walls of the church.

In 1994, after this chapter, I wrote, "Do not sue. Be wronged." Then, "Homosexuals are included in the list of those who will not inherit the kingdom of God." I continued, "Be biblically correct, not politically correct. All things are lawful, but not profitable. Don't be mastered by anything. Glorify God in your body."

Let's go on to verses 9-11. The scripture says:

Or do you not know that the unrighteous will not inherit the kingdom of God? Do not be deceived: neither the sexually immoral, nor idolaters, nor adulterers, nor men who practice homosexuality, nor thieves, nor the greedy, nor drunkards, nor revilers, nor swindlers will inherit the kingdom of God. And such were some of you. But you were washed, you were sanctified, you were justified in the name of the Lord Jesus Christ and by the Spirit of our God.

DIGGING DEEPER

There is a long list of people who will not inherit the kingdom of God. But then, Paul gives the out, *"And such were some of you. But you (can be) washed, you (can be) sanctified, you (can be) justified in the name of the Lord Jesus Christ and by the Spirit of our God"* (v. 11).

Aren't you glad we love a God who loves us and forgives us for our mistakes, for our failures? Paul continues his theme about sexual immorality, when he writes, *"The body is not meant for sexual immorality, but for the Lord, and the Lord for the body"* (v. 13). He continues, *"Do you not know that your bodies are members of Christ? Shall I then take the members of Christ and make them members of a*

> You are not your own, for you were bought with a price. So glorify God in your body.
>
> 1 Cor. 6:19-20

prostitute? Never! Or do you not know that he who is joined to a prostitute becomes one body with her? For, as it is written, "The two will become one flesh" (vv. 15-16).

Paul continues, *"Flee from sexual immorality. Every other sin a person commits is outside the body, but the sexually immoral person sins against his own body. Or do you not know that your body is a temple of the Holy Spirit within you, whom you have from God? You are not your own, for you were bought with a price. So glorify God in your body"* (vv. 18-20).

Is sexual sin worse than any other sin? No. Is it different than other sin? Yes. As Paul writes, *"Every other sin a person commits is outside the body, but the sexually immoral person sins against his own body"* (v. 18).

Prayer

Lord, I have no idea how many are struggling with this issue of sexual immorality. Whether some are struggling with this issue right now, or have in the past, we are thankful You give us hope through Your Word. If it is a past failure, it can be forgiven. Maybe it already has been. If you are in a current sexually immoral relationship, stop, and it can be forgiven. Verse 11 says, *"And such were some of you. But you were washed, you were sanctified, you were justified in the name of the Lord Jesus Christ and by the Spirit of our God."* That is hope. That is forgiveness. That is love.

Father, help us turn from our ways of behavior and help us understand the last verse in this chapter, *"So glorify God in your body"* (v. 20). Thank You that You forgive our pasts. May we correct our behavior as we live for You in our futures. In Jesus' name, we pray. Amen.

MY THOUGHTS

1 CORINTHIANS 7

Single or Married?

1 Corinthians 7 covers principles of singleness and marriage. Are you single and satisfied? Are you married and distracted from serving the Lord? Please read or listen to 1 Corinthians 7.

COMMENTS

Paul begins chapter 7 with the phrase, *"Now concerning the matters about which you wrote"*. The Corinthians asked Paul to comment on certain issues and this is one of them. The beginning of chapter 7 follows the end of chapter 6, where Paul had already been saying, *"The body is not meant for sexual immorality"* (6:13). *"Flee from sexual immorality. Every other sin a person commits is outside the body, but the sexually immoral person sins against his own body"* (6:18). Then he said, *"your body is a temple of the Holy Spirit"* (6:19). Now, as a continuation, really not a chapter break, he says, *"It is good for a man not to have sexual relations with a woman"* (v. 1).

The beginning of chapter 7 really continues chapter 6, but it also inserts that phrase again in verse 1, *"Now concerning the matters about which you wrote"*. So this was an issue the Corinthians were concerned about. Paul clarifies it in verse 2, *"But because of the temptation to sexual immorality, each man should have his own wife and each woman her own husband."*

In 2015, in my journal, I wrote about this paragraph, "Unpopular today, but biblical truth. Sex outside of marriage is prohibited, according to verses 1 and 2." I also wrote, "Married or single, both can be blessed by God." We will talk about that in a moment.

Going back to my journal in 1994, on the first few verses of chapter 7 (NASB), I wrote, "Husband and wife should satisfy each other sexually, so there is no reason to look outside the marriage." I wrote again, "Being single is okay." Then I quoted verse 20, *"Each man must remain in that condition in which he was called."* And verse 17, *"the Lord has assigned to each one, as God has called each, in this manner let him walk".*

Going back to the first few verses of chapter 7, Paul makes it pretty clear, sexual relations belong inside the marriage. Anything outside the marriage is basically prohibited by God. Paul goes on to say, *"I wish that all were as I myself am"* (v. 7), meaning single. Then he says, "However, if you cannot remain single because you burn with passion, it is better to be married so sexual activity remains in a marital relationship."

How many single people want to be married? And how many married people, after they got married, liked being single better? Paul tells us in verse 32, *"I want you to be free from anxieties."* If you have anxieties about

> **I want you to be free from anxieties.**
>
> 1 Cor. 7:32

getting married, maybe you should not get married. If you have anxieties as a married couple, maybe you should not have gotten married. But he says, *"The unmarried man is anxious about the things of the Lord, how to please the Lord. But the married man is anxious about worldly things, how to please his wife. . . . the unmarried or betrothed woman is anxious about the things of the Lord, how to be holy in body and spirit. But the married woman is anxious about worldly things, how to please her husband"* (vv. 32-34).

I continued to write in my journal in 1994, "Unmarried Paul alerts us that marriage brings on certain trouble in this life. He argues that singles are better able to focus on the things of God." I put, "Maybe" in my journal. "Singles may also be distracted with sex, finding a mate, etc. God ordained marriage. I happen to like it. Does it constrain ministry? At times. Would I be doing more single? Maybe."

Let's go back to Paul's advice. He says in verse 27, *"Are you bound to a wife? Do not seek to be free. Are you free from a wife? Do not seek a wife."* Then go back up to verse 24, *"So . . . in whatever condition each was called, there let him remain with God."* That has to do with being slaves or free, but I think it also has to do with being called to be married or to be single. Those who are single can serve the Lord. And those who are married can also serve the Lord.

DIGGING DEEPER

What is the application in chapter 7 of 1 Corinthians? Going back to the very beginning of the chapter, it is to keep sexual relationships within marriages. That is biblical. Sex outside of marriage is unrighteousness.

Secondly, whether you are single or you are married, either way, serve the Lord. If you are single and you can serve the Lord without a passion for being married, amen! And if you are married, do not let the distractions of the world keep you from serving the Lord.

Prayer

Father, we thank You for those who are single and serve You wholeheartedly. Bless them, Lord. Keep them faithful to You. And, Lord, we thank You for those who are married that serve their families and serve You. Keep them faithful, as well.

Thank You for using both single people and married people to build Your kingdom here on earth. We give You thanks and praise. In Jesus' name, amen.

MY THOUGHTS

1 CORINTHIANS 8

Should Christians Drink?

1 Corinthians 8 addresses eating and drinking. It is a short chapter, only thirteen verses. Drinking is controversial among Christians, like eating meat sacrificed to idols was to Corinthians. Is it permissible for Christians to drink? Please read or listen to 1 Corinthians 8.

COMMENTS

Chapter 8 starts out like chapter 7 did. It starts out with Paul's words saying, *"Now concerning"*, which means this was another matter the Corinthians wrote to Paul about. This time it is about food offered to idols. We do not have this matter today in our Christianity, but we have behaviors or matters very much like it. So let's look at my journals to see what I mean.

In 1994, on 1 Corinthians 8, I wrote, "Knowledge makes arrogant." Then, "There is but one God." I continued, "Take care, lest this liberty of yours somehow becomes a stumbling block to the weak, referring to verse 9. This is the key. We need to watch what we do, even though we are free to drink, eat, smoke. Does it hinder the weak? If we weaken someone by our actions, we sin against Christ."

In 2015, I was reading more than one chapter a day, so I read 1 Corinthians 8 and 9 on this day. I did write some things concerning chapter 8, "Love builds up.

Knowledge puffs up. Idols are not real, therefore, they have no power. And finally, what we eat as Christians really doesn't matter unless it weakens someone else. So drinking or not drinking alcohol is not Christian. It's a matter of creating a stumbling block for others."

I mentioned earlier, we may not be faced with the issue of eating meat sacrificed to idols, but we do have similar things in our Christianity we argue about. We discuss whether or not we should do certain behaviors, and I think Paul gives us some great advice here.

Let's look at the opening verses of this chapter, and not necessarily related to food worshiped to idols, but to us in our possession of knowledge. *"(W)e know that 'all of us possess knowledge.' This 'knowledge' puffs up, but love builds up. If anyone imagines that he knows something, he does not yet know as he ought to know. But if anyone loves God, he is known by God"* (vv. 1-3). All of us possess knowledge. We all do possess some level of knowledge. But is it puffing us up? Is it building us up? Is it creating some kind of arrogance in our spiritual life? Verse 2 is actually kind of funny, *"If anyone imagines that he knows something, he does not yet know as he ought to know."* These verses really tell us to be very careful about our spiritual arrogance.

Paul gives us the answer. He says, *"'knowledge' puffs up, but love builds up"* (v. 1). *"But if anyone loves God, he is known by God"* (v. 3). Yes, it is good to be thankful for the knowledge we have been gifted with, but let's not let it puff us up. Let us not become spiritually arrogant.

> **"Knowledge" puffs up, but love builds up.**
> 1 Cor. 8:1

Next, Paul talks about idols. I have had the opportunity to travel the world and see people worshiping idols. They have a zeal for God without knowledge. Paul says as much in verse 7, *"However, not all possess this knowledge."* What knowledge? *"(T)hat 'an idol has no real existence'"* (v. 4). If an idol has no existence, what difference does it make whether food is sacrificed to idols or not? I think that is the crux of Paul's argument here. Paul is saying, "What we eat or what we do not eat is not the issue. What we think about what we eat or do not eat is not really the issue either. It is what others think about what we are doing.

DIGGING DEEPER

Let's change the word "food" to "drinking". For example, in verses 8 and 9, instead of "food" put "drinking". It would say, (Drinking) *"will not commend us to God. We are no worse off if we do not (drink), and no better off if we do. But take care that this right of yours does not somehow become a stumbling block to the weak."* Let's jump down to verse 13 where Paul concludes the matter. Again substitute "drinking" for "food", *"Therefore, if (drinking) makes my brother stumble, I will never (drink), lest I make my brother stumble."*

Paul is more concerned with our behavior causing a weak brother to stumble than the behavior itself. Paul says it this way in verse 12, *"Thus, sinning against your brothers and wounding their conscience when it is weak, you sin against Christ."*

It is not a matter of what we think about our knowledge on these issues, it is a matter of how it affects those who watch our Christian behavior. People are more important than our behavior. Paul is willing to modify his behavior so that a brother would not stumble. Are we? Regardless of what we think about the matter of whether Christians should drink or not drink if it causes a brother to stumble, are we willing to give it up?

I conclude the matter as Paul did in verse 13, again substituting "drinking" for "food," and saying, *"Therefore, if (drinking) makes my brother stumble, I will never (drink), lest I make my brother stumble."*

Prayer

Father, we do not read scripture just for the sake of knowledge. Knowledge, as we are told at the beginning of this chapter, can puff us up. We read scripture so we can gain knowledge so it can modify our behavior. Paul was willing to modify his behavior so a brother would not stumble. Holy Spirit, cause me to think about these things from 1 Corinthians 8. Lord, help me decide whether I need to modify my behavior so I do not cause a brother to stumble. Thank You for Your Word that challenges how we live our lives. We give You thanks for it. In Jesus' name, amen.

MY THOUGHTS

1 CORINTHIANS 9

Compelled

In 1 Corinthians 9, we see Paul's compulsion to preach the gospel, as if he has no choice. Are you compelled? Are you running to win? Please read or listen to 1 Corinthians 9.

COMMENTS

I have some interesting journal entries on 1 Corinthians 9, so let's begin with my journal in 1994. I wrote, "Paul talks about himself in this chapter, but also about principles. We can expect fruit from our labors, according to verses 7 and 10." And, "Am I under compulsion for what I do?" The next thing I wrote is, "What? Woe to me if I do not speak." And then, "Appeal to your audience, verses 19-22. Play to win, verse 24. Run with aim, verse 26. Know where you are going." That is an interesting list of insights from a thirty-nine-year-old in 1994.

In 2004, I was in Breckenridge, Colorado over Thanksgiving weekend when I read 1 Corinthians 9-11 and wrote in my journal, "Paul could not not preach the gospel." I quoted verse 16, *"'I am under compulsion; for woe is me if I do not preach the gospel.'* He did all things for the sake of the gospel, according to verse 23. And he worked hard at it to win. I am compelled to share the Word of God. Paid or unpaid, with one-hundred or one, with those I have never met and those I have known my whole life. Through Gideons, Ezra, or my personal life, it comes out of me. It has to and it will. Thank You, Jesus, for compulsion."

In 2015, I wrote, *"those who proclaim the gospel should get their living by the gospel"*, according to verse 14." Then I quoted verse 11, *"If we have sown spiritual things among you, is it too much if we reap material things from you?"* It is biblical to pay preachers, pastors, rabbis, etc. Even us at the Ezra Project." Then I wrote, "Preachers should be called, compelled, to preach the gospel according to verses 15 and 16. Those who preach the gospel are entrusted with stewardship of it. Paul, as some today, chose to preach free of charge." I finished my journal entry in 2015 with this, "The body is a tool to preach Christ. Use it wisely."

Paul begins chapter 9 by defending himself as an apostle. Look at this amazing statement in verse 1. *"Have I not seen Jesus our Lord?"* It is a reminder to them and us that Paul did not get his gospel from Peter, John, or any of the apostles. He got it directly from Jesus Himself. Then Paul gets into the principles of this chapter. In verse 11, he says to them, *"If we have sown spiritual things among you, is it too much if we reap material things from you?"* And *"the Lord commanded that those who proclaim the gospel should get their living by the gospel"* (v. 14).

Should we financially support pastors, preachers, rabbis, priests? Absolutely. It is a scriptural principle to do so. But Paul says to the Corinthians, "I never exercised the right to do this." He says, *"Nevertheless, we have not made use of this right, but we endure anything rather than put an obstacle in the way of the gospel of Christ"* (v. 12). He says again, *"But I have made no use of any of these rights, nor am I writing these things to secure any such provision. For I would rather die than have anyone deprive me of my ground for boasting. For if I preach the gospel, that gives me no ground for boasting. For necessity is laid upon me. Woe to me if I do not preach the gospel!"* (vv. 15-16).

As I wrote in one of my journals, "Certainly some preachers, pastors, priests must be paid to proclaim the good news and others can do it freely." There are plenty of bi-vocational pastors out there, meaning they work and they also are a pastor of a church. That is what Paul did as a tentmaker. Paul understood the call on his life to preach the gospel. He said it was a necessity. *"Woe to me if I do not preach the gospel!"*

(v. 16). Surely most pastors, most priests, most preachers, believe they are called by God to preach the gospel, to be pastors of churches.

Paul is so sold out to the gospel. He says, "I am a servant of the gospel." In verses 22 and 23, he says, *"I have become all things to all people, that by all means I might save some. I do it all for the sake of the gospel, that I may share with them in its blessings."* Oh, to have preachers, pastors, and priests like Paul today. Sold out to preaching and sharing the gospel.

> I have become all things to all people, that by all means I might save some. I do it all for the sake of the gospel.
>
> 1 Cor. 9:22-23

Paul closes with this great illustration as an athlete, *"all the runners run, but only one receives the prize?"* (v. 24). *"Every athlete exercises self-control in all things"* (v. 25). He says, *"So I do not run aimlessly; I do not box as one beating the air. But I discipline my body and keep it under control, lest after preaching to others I myself should be disqualified"* (vv. 26-27). Paul sees his calling—preaching the gospel—like an athlete running a race to win. It takes discipline. It takes specific aim. It takes disciplining himself physically, keeping his body under control, to do that which God has called him to do.

DIGGING DEEPER

How about you? Are you compelled to do something by God? Is there something God is asking you to do that you cannot not do it? That was the Apostle Paul. Is it you? That was the argument Paul was making to the Corinthians. I am called to be an apostle. I gave you the gospel I got from Jesus. Hear me out. And though I had every right for financial benefit from this, I did not exercise that right. I gave it to you free of charge. That is the deep, deep commitment of the Apostle Paul. Do you have that type of deep, deep commitment to whatever God has compelled you to do?

Prayer

Lord, we thank You for calling the Apostle Paul. We thank You for his deep, deep commitment to sharing the gospel. So deep that thousands of years later we are reading his letters today. May we examine our hearts. What are we deeply committed to? What have You compelled us to do?

Whatever it is, Lord, help us commit to it, help us run the race with one goal in mind and that is to win the prize for You. Lord, reveal Your calling on my life to me and help me run the race with endurance that I might give You the prize when it is all over. We give You the praise for that. In Jesus' name, amen.

MY THOUGHTS

1 CORINTHIANS 10

Withstanding Temptation

In 1 Corinthians 10, Paul admonishes us not to test God. He also reminds us our feet cannot be planted in Him and in the world. Where are your feet planted? Please read or listen to 1 Corinthians 10.

COMMENTS

In my personal Bible reading journal 2015, I read 1 Corinthians 10 and 11 on the same day, and wrote, "Paul certainly thinks Christ was around in the Old Testament, referring to verse 4." Let's step aside from the journal for a moment and look at that verse. To put verse 4 in context, we have to start at the beginning of the chapter. Let's read the beginning of chapter 10, *"(For I want you to know) brothers, that our fathers were all under the cloud, and all passed through the sea, and all were baptized into Moses in the cloud and in the sea, and all ate the same spiritual food, and all drank the same spiritual drink. For they drank from the spiritual Rock that followed them, and the Rock was Christ"* (vv. 1-4). In the English Standard Version Study Bible, "Rock" is capitalized. That is why in my journal, I referred to the fact Paul thought Christ was around in the Old Testament.

I went on in my journal to write, "Don't put Christ to the test, referring to verse 9. This is a principle I learned early in my Christian life, and it sticks with me, even to this day." What I mean is, I do not believe in testing God in my Christianity. Some people say, "If You do this, I will do that." "God, if You answer this prayer, then I will do such-and-such." I have not done that in my Christian life. I do not believe in putting God to the test. I believe in trust, and walking in faith, and believing God that He will take care of me.

Next in my journal in 2015, I referred to verse 13. It is one of the first verses I memorized; still so valuable to me today, *"No temptation has overtaken you that is not common to man. God is faithful, and he will not let you be tempted beyond your ability, but with the temptation he will also provide the way of escape, that you may be able to endure it.'* What a promise! What a power verse in scripture. God will not tempt us beyond our ability to endure. And He provides the way of escape so we may be able to endure any temptation that comes our way. I have believed that verse all my Christian life. I am

> No temptation has overtaken you that is not common to man. God is faithful, and he will not let you be tempted beyond your ability, but with the temptation he will also provide the way of escape, that you may be able to endure it.
>
> 1 Cor. 10:13

so thankful God will not tempt me beyond what I am capable of handling. That gives me great comfort; I hope it also comforts you. When you get a chance, look up in your Bible, 1 Corinthians 10:13. Think about it and maybe even memorize it like I have.

In 1994, I read 1 Corinthians 10, the first thirteen verses on a particular day and wrote, "Let us not: crave evil things, be idolaters, act immorally, try the Lord, grumble, think we stand."

DIGGING DEEPER

I would like to take a few minutes to look at the "nots" in this chapter. Verse 5 says, *"God was not pleased"* with the people. Verse 6 says, *"Now these things took place as examples for us"*. Here in this chapter are several things we are not to do:

- Verse 6, we are not to desire evil as they did.

- Verse 7, we are not to be idolaters as some of them were.

- Verse 8, we are not to indulge in sexual immorality as some of them did.

- Verse 9, we are not to put Christ to the test as some of them did.

- Verse 10, we are not to grumble as some of them did.

- Verse 12, we are not to think we stand lest we fall.

What happened to them because they did those things? God was not pleased with them, and they were destroyed. Paul writes to us about this and tells us, *"Now these things happened to them as an example, but they were written down for our instruction"* (v. 11).

In 1 Corinthians 10, we have been instructed on six things we are not to do. We are not to desire evil. We are not to be idolaters. We are not to indulge in sexual immorality. We are not to put Christ to the test. We are not to grumble. And we are not to think highly of ourselves lest we fall.

Right after that in verses 14-21, Paul makes the case we cannot follow Christ and keep our feet in the world. In other words, you cannot have it both ways. Referring to idol worship and food sacrificed to idols, Paul says, *"I imply that what pagans sacrifice they offer to demons and not to God. I do not want you to be participants with demons. You cannot drink the cup of the Lord and the cup of demons. You cannot partake of the table of the Lord and the table of demons"* (vv. 20-21).

It is the same for us today. We cannot have our feet in Christianity and in the world at the same time. It did not work for the Corinthians. It will not work for us. Paul concludes the matter in the last couple of verses of this chapter, *"So, whether you eat or drink, or whatever you do, do all to the glory of God. Give no offense to Jews or to Greeks or to the church of God, just as I try to please everyone in everything I do, not seeking my own advantage, but that of many, that they may be saved"* (vv. 31-33). Paul's message to the Corinthians is the same message to us today. *"(W)hatever you do, do all to the glory of God"* (v. 31).

Prayer

Lord, get my feet out of the world and plant my feet on You and You alone, the Rock of Christ, as referred to in this chapter. Thank You for this great promise in verse 13, *"No temptation has overtaken you that is not common to man."* Thank You for being faithful, and not letting me be tempted beyond my ability, but with the temptation, providing the way of escape that I may be able to endure the temptation. What a promise! I thank You for it.

Thank You for not tempting me beyond what I can endure. And Lord, I hope my response is, whatever I do, I do all to the glory of You, so someone around me might be saved. I bless You, I praise You, I thank You. In the name of Jesus, amen.

MY THOUGHTS

1 CORINTHIANS 11

Headship

In 1 Corinthians 11, Paul covers creative order and the Lord's Supper. Do you believe the head of every man is Christ, the head of every wife is her husband, and the head of Christ is God, or two out of three? Please read or listen to 1 Corinthians 11.

COMMENTS

Chapter 11 starts out with quite a verse. Paul says, *"Be imitators of me, as I am of Christ."* The verse connects better with the end of chapter 10, so let's go back to those verses at the end of chapter 10 and hook this verse to it. Chapter 10:31-11:1 say, *"So, whether you eat or drink, or whatever you do, do all to the glory of God. Give no offense to Jews or to Greeks or to the church of God, just as I try to please everyone in everything I do, not seeking my own advantage, but that of many, that they may be saved. Be imitators of me, as I am of Christ."*

Remember yesterday was about doing all to the glory of God. Paul was saying, "That is what I try to do." Here he continues, "So do what I try to do."

I summarized 1 Corinthians 11 in my journal in 2015, with a couple of entries, "Can I say by the way I live my life, *'Be imitators of me'?*" (v. 1). And I wrote about spiritual authority relating to verse 3. Then lastly, the Lord's Supper, verses 23-26.

In 1994, I just focused on the spiritual authority aspects of this chapter. I actually drew a little diagram.

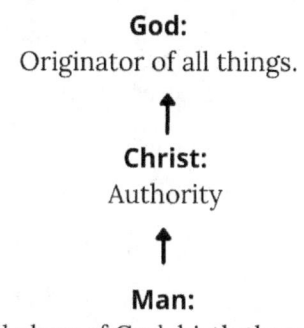

God:
Originator of all things.

Christ:
Authority

↑

Man:
Image and glory of God, birth through woman.

↑

Woman:
Glory of man, created for man's sake.
Originates from man.

DIGGING DEEPER

As we look at chapter 11:2-16, this may not fit our popular culture, but it is the Word of God. Paul says to the Corinthians and he says to us today, *"maintain the traditions"* (v. 2). And in verse 3, he writes, *"But I want you to understand that the head of every man is Christ, the head of a wife is her husband, and the head of Christ is God."*

We move to verse 8, *"For man was not made from woman, but woman from man. Neither was man created for woman, but woman for man."* And verses 11 and 12 say, *"Nevertheless, in the Lord woman is not independent of man nor man of woman; for as woman was made from man, so man is now born of woman."* I will let the words speak for themselves and not elaborate on my own thoughts about this passage. But I would like to quote a piece out of my English Standard Version Study Bible footnote on verse 3, **"The head of Christ is God** indicates that within the Trinity the Father has a role of authority of leadership with respect to the Son, though they are equal in deity and attributes. Paul applies this truth about the Trinity to the relationship of husband and wife. In marriage, as in the Trinity, there is equality in being and value but difference in roles" (p. 2206).

> But I want you to understand that the head of every man is Christ, the head of a wife is her husband, and the head of Christ is God.
>
> 1 Cor. 11:3

What I find interesting in the footnote is even in the Trinity, the Father has a role of authority and leadership and not once in Jesus' life did I ever see Him try to take over the leadership or authority of His Father.

The rest of the chapter is about the Lord's Supper. The Corinthians either had a misunderstanding or were having a hard time implementing aspects of the Lord's Supper. Paul clarifies it here for them and for us. In just about any church where communion is celebrated, you have probably heard verses 23-26 quoted:

> *For I received from the Lord what I also delivered to you, that the Lord Jesus on the night when he was betrayed took bread, and when he had given thanks, he broke it, and said, "This is my body, which is for you. Do this in remembrance of me." In the same way also he took the cup, after supper, saying, "This cup is the new covenant in my blood. Do this, as often as you drink it, in remembrance of me." For as often as you eat this bread and drink the cup, you proclaim the Lord's death until he comes.*

I praise the Lord for the outline of how the church is to celebrate communion. Verse 27 is sometimes quoted when referenced to communion services and it is an important verse for us to consider today. It says, *"Whoever, therefore, eats the bread or drinks the cup of the Lord in an unworthy manner will be guilty concerning the body and blood of the Lord."* Paul was covering this issue because some of the Corinthians were having communion in an unworthy manner. Paul goes on to say, *"Let a person examine himself, then, and so eat of the bread and drink of the cup"* (v. 28).

Prayer

Lord, we thank You that in this chapter, You give us a clear line of authority. *"(T)he head of every man is Christ, the head of a wife is her husband, and the head of Christ is God"* (v. 3).

We thank You for communion, the Last Supper, and clear instructions as to how we are to celebrate it. *"For as often as you eat this bread and drink the cup, you proclaim the Lord's death until he comes"* (v. 26). Again, we thank You for the clarity of Your Word even when it rubs against the culture of our day. Help us be people of the Word, not people of the world. In the name of Jesus, we pray. Amen.

MY THOUGHTS

1 CORINTHIANS 12

Spiritual Gifts

1 Corinthians 12 deals with spiritual gifts. Do you know yours? Please read or listen to 1 Corinthians 12.

COMMENTS

In 1994, I wrote, "Spiritual gifts are distributed throughout the body of Christ. Though we may not all possess the same gifts, we are one in the Trinity: Spirit, Lord, God. There is need for diversity in the body of Christ."

Ten years later in 2004, I read 1 Corinthians 12-14 in one day, and wrote related to this chapter, "God gifts us and puts us in the body of Christ just as He desired, referring to verse 18. Of the gifts listed in 8-10, I would say I have faith."

Eleven years later, in 2015, I read 1 Corinthians 12 and 13 together, and wrote about chapter 12, "One God, one Spirit, one Lord. God distributes spiritual gifts. We don't earn them, or we don't make them happen. I didn't realize wisdom and knowledge are two different spiritual gifts. I hope I have them both. The body of Christ needs all the gifts."

Before we get into the spiritual gifts, let's look at a very, very important phrase at the beginning of this chapter. Verse 3 says, *"Therefore I want you to understand that no one speaking in the Spirit of God ever says 'Jesus is accursed!' and no one can say 'Jesus is Lord' except in the Holy Spirit."* I would like to share my footnote on this verse from my English Standard Version Study Bible:

> Because of their background in pagan worship services, some Corinthians may have had concerns about speech gifts empowered by the Holy Spirit in the church. Paul first assures them that **no one speaking in the Spirit of God ever says, "Jesus is accursed!"** (and therefore they should not worry that Christians who speak in tongues might be uttering blasphemous things), and also **that no one can say** in genuine faith that **"Jesus is Lord" except in the Holy Spirit** (and therefore all who genuinely profess faith in Christ have the Holy Spirit within them, and none should be excluded, for they all have valuable gifts for the benefit of the church) (p. 2209).

The key is, *"no one can say 'Jesus is Lord' except in the Holy Spirit"* (v. 3).

Now to the gifts of the Spirit. There are actually two different lists in this chapter, so let's cover those. The first list is in verses 8-10. The second list is in verse 28. The first list has nine gifts. The second list has eight gifts. The gifts are not all the same in each list. Let's look at the first list from verses 8-10. The gifts are wisdom, knowledge, faith, healing, the working of miracles, prophecy, the ability to distinguish between spirits, various kinds of tongues, and the interpretation of tongues. Nine spiritual gifts. In verse 28, the gifts are apostles, prophets, teachers, miracles, healing, helping, administrating, and various kinds of tongues.

What is the point of spiritual gifts? What is the value of spiritual gifts? Verse 7 says, *"To each is given the manifestation of the Spirit for the common good."* Another reason for spiritual gifts is stated in verses 5 and 6, *"and there are varieties of service, but the same Lord; and there are varieties of activities, but it is the same God who empowers them all in everyone."*

> To each is given the manifestation of the Spirit for the common good.
>
> 1 Cor. 12:7

So spiritual gifts are for the common good, they are for service, they are for activity in the body of Christ. Verse 11 says, *"All these are empowered by one and the same Spirit, who apportions to each one individually as he wills."* Does every Christian have the same gift? No. Each one is given gifts individually. Verses 29 and 30 even clarify it more, *"Are all apostles? Are all prophets? Are all teachers? Do all work miracles? Do all possess gifts of healing? Do all speak with tongues? Do all interpret?"* By Paul asking the questions, the answer is obviously "no" to each one of those. And then he uses the illustration of the body to make it very clear each of us has individual spiritual gifts. We are all part of the body, but we are all different parts of the body.

If I have a spiritual gift, I should be offering it to the body and I should not be coveting someone else's spiritual gift. In other words, if I am a foot, I cannot wish I was a hand. As part of the body of Christ, it is our responsibility to know our gifts, to understand what our gifting is and to contribute it to the body of Christ.

DIGGING DEEPER

If you know your spiritual gifts, praise the Lord. I hope you are using them to the furtherance of the kingdom of God. But if you do not know your spiritual gifts, if you do not understand what any of this means, there are organizations that test for spiritual gifting. You may want to ask your church if they know of an organization like that. I thank the Lord He offers the church so many different spiritual gifts. I am also thankful to the Lord for the gifting He has given me that I can offer to the kingdom of God.

Your practical application from 1 Corinthians 12 may be to either understand your spiritual gifts or re-evaluate whether you are contributing them to the furtherance of the kingdom of God here on earth.

Prayer

Lord, I want to start my prayer at the end of this devotion by saying if someone cannot say, "Jesus is Lord," then they do not have the Holy Spirit. I pray now the Holy Spirit would empower them, come into their lives in such a way that they confess their sins, offer themselves to You, and can for the very first time say, "Jesus is Lord," because they now have the Holy Spirit.

The second part of my prayer is to thank You for the spiritual gifts Your Holy Spirit blesses the church with. Will you help us, Lord, function as one body, all using our individual gifting to further Your kingdom here on earth? Surely if we do that, You would be well pleased.

You close this chapter by saying, *"But earnestly desire the higher gifts"* (v. 31). We look forward to discovering them in the next chapter. In Your name, we pray. Amen.

MY THOUGHTS

1 CORINTHIANS 13

The Love Chapter

1 Corinthians 13 is well known as the Love Chapter. Is your definition of love based on the Bible or Hollywood? What is your love quotient? Please read or listen to the thirteen verses of 1 Corinthians 13.

COMMENTS

Concerning the Love Chapter, in 1994, I wrote, "Love is not provoked, does not seek its own." Then, "We only know in part." I finished with, "I need faith, hope, and love operating in my life daily, but mostly love."

In 2004, I wrote, "Love does not take into account a wrong suffered. I do, so I need to let things go, not get hurt when wronged. I have more faith and hope than love. I need to keep working on this."

In 2015, I wrote, "Love does not insist on its own way. We can only manifest any or all of these gifts partially because we are flawed, sinful human beings. Help me love."

What sets up the love chapter? We have to go back to the final few verses of chapter 12 where Paul was describing spiritual gifts. Let's go back to chapter 12:27-31 to set up chapter 13:

Now you are the body of Christ and individually members of it. And God has appointed in the church first apostles, second prophets, third teachers, then miracles, then gifts of healing, helping, administrating, and various kinds of tongues. Are all apostles? Are all prophets? Are all teachers? Do all work miracles? Do all possess gifts of healing? Do all speak with tongues? Do all interpret? But earnestly desire the higher gifts. And I will show you a still more excellent way.

Paul described various gifts, but then he said, *"But earnestly desire the higher gifts . . . a still more excellent way"* (v. 31). That is what leads us into the Love Chapter. As he begins chapter 13, he refers back to some of those other gifts. That is why he says:

If I speak in the tongues of men and of angels, but have not love, I am a noisy gong or a clanging cymbal. And if I have prophetic powers, and understand all mysteries and all knowledge, and if I have all faith, so as to remove mountains, but have not love, I am nothing. If I give away all I have, and if I deliver up my body to be burned, but have not love, I gain nothing (vv. 1-3).

Paul is referring back to that list of gifts in chapter 12. Then he turns to those higher gifts. The more excellent way as he defines love in verses 4-8, *"Love is patient and kind; love does not envy or boast; it is not arrogant or rude. It does not insist on its own way; it is not irritable or resentful; it does not rejoice at wrongdoing, but rejoices with the truth. Love bears all things, believes all things, hopes all things, endures all things. Love never ends."*

In verses 4-8, I count sixteen aspects Paul uses to define love. As we go over those sixteen, think about them and rate yourself on a scale 1 to 5 on these aspects of love. We are going to

> Love is patient and kind; love does not envy or boast; it is not arrogant or rude. It does not insist on its own way; it is not irritable or resentful; it does not rejoice at wrongdoing, but rejoices with the truth. Love bears all things, believes all things, hopes all things, endures all things. Love never ends.
>
> 1 Cor. 13:7-8

come up with your love quotient. As you re-read them, think between 1 and 5, five being the highest and one being the lowest, rate yourself. Let's see what your love quotient is. Love is:

patient   _____

kind   _____

does not envy   _____

does not boast   _____

is not arrogant   _____

is not rude   _____

does not insist on its own way   _____

is not irritable   _____

is not resentful   _____

does not rejoice at wrongdoing   _____

rejoices with the truth   _____

bears all things   _____

believes all things   _____

hopes all things   _____

endures all things   _____

never ends   _____

Those were the sixteen aspects of love. I hope you scaled yourself from 1 to 5. I did. The maximum love score would be 80 (16 x 5). I did not get anywhere close to eighty. My love quotient is sixty. My highest numbers were "love does not rejoice at wrongdoing", and "rejoices with the truth", and "hopes all things". I think I do pretty good at those three. My lowest score was "love does not insist on its own way." I gave myself a two.

After you score yourself, you might have your spouse or a really good friend, score you on the same scale to see if your perspective of your love quotient and your significant other's perspective of your love quotient is the same.

DIGGING DEEPER

1 Corinthians 13 is a great chapter on love, but there is another chapter on love I want to refer to, 1 John 4. In 1 John 4 between verses 7 and 19, there are wonderful definitions of love. To compliment what we are learning in 1 Corinthians 13, let's look at 1 John 4:7-12:

Beloved, let us love one another, for love is from God, and whoever loves has been born of God and knows God. Anyone who does not love does not know God, because God is love. In this the love of God was made manifest among us, that God sent his only Son into the world, so that we might live through him. In this is love, not that we have loved God but that he loved us and sent his Son to be the propitiation for our sins. Beloved, if God so loved us, we also ought to love one another. No one has ever seen God; if we love one another, God abides in us and his love is perfected in us.

Then jump down to verse 18, *"There is no fear in love, but perfect love casts out fear."* And lastly, verse 19, *"We love because he first loved us."* When we add 1 John 4 to 1 Corinthians 13, we get a pretty comprehensive view of love as defined in scripture.

By the way, if you wish to share this devotion with others, send them to ezraproject.net, Club 365. Members of Club 365 get access to all *Day by Day Through the Bible* devotions anytime, anywhere, so members can take the love quotient survey with a spouse or with someone else. To learn how to become a member of Club 365, visit ezraprojet.net, or the ADDBIBLE app.

After Paul defines love, he goes back to those spiritual gifts as he closes out chapter 13, *"As for prophecies, they will pass away; as for tongues, they will cease; as for knowledge, it will pass away"* (v. 8). Paul sandwiches the love chapter between the chapters on spiritual gifts.

Then he talks about a level of maturity when he says, *"When I was a child, I spoke like a child, I thought like a child, I reasoned like a child. When I became a man,*

I gave up childish ways" (v. 11). He is saying to the Corinthians, "Don't argue about the spiritual gifts. Focus on the higher gifts, the more excellent way." He finishes with, *"So now faith, hope, and love abide, these three; but the greatest of these is love"* (v. 13).

I did not score very well on the love quotient. I did not score very well on love in my journals either. If you remember, I wrote each year, I need to work on this. Ten, twenty, thirty years have gone by and I still need to work on love and being more loving. Maybe you do too, so let's pray.

Prayer

Father, we thank You for spiritual gifts. We thank You for the gifts You give us, but then You tell us there is a more excellent way and that is faith, hope, and love. And the greatest of these is love, so help us, Lord, if our love quotient is not as high as we would like it to be. Remind us to focus on some of these sixteen aspects of love, work on some of them, and become more loving toward others.

Lord, we also thank You for Your expression of love in 1 John 4. You say, *"God is love"* (1 John 4:8). You demonstrated Your love toward us by sending Your Son to die for us, the ultimate gift of love. *"For God so loved the world, that He gave his only begotten Son"* (John 3:16 KJV). Though we are flawed, sinful human beings, help us to love like You love. Stretch us to love You better and love our fellow man better. We ask this, in Jesus' name, amen.

MY THOUGHTS

1 CORINTHIANS 14

Tongues

I n 1 Corinthians 14, Paul shares about the gift of tongues. Do you speak with your tongue, with forked tongue, or in tongues? Please read or listen to 1 Corinthians 14.

COMMENTS

The subject of tongues is probably one of the most controversial issues in the New Testament and in churches today. Let's see what I have written in my journals over three decades about 1 Corinthians 14.

In 1994, I wrote, "Pursue love. Spiritual gifts should edify, exhort, and console. Tongues was to transfer the message of Christ to other people, not to simply babble in church with like people. Then I quoted verse 33 (NASB), *"for God is not a God of confusion but of peace"*.

In 2004, I was reading multiple chapters on the same day. On this day I read 1 Corinthians 12-14 (NASB), so I only wrote one or two lines about chapter 14, "Tongues may be more appropriate as a prayer language than for public consumption," referring to verse 14. *"God is not a God of confusion but of peace"* (v. 33). Then, *"all things must be done properly and in an orderly manner"* (v. 40).

That year, I wrote a prayer about a lot of this, "What gifts have You given me for the church? Faith and prophecy (teaching). Am I using them to build up, edify, the body? Am I loving? Help me grow in love, faith, and hope. What about tongues for me? Use the gift in my prayer life as led by the Spirit. God help me mature in faith and Christianity. I have a long way to go, but I have come a long way. Thank You."

In 2015, I wrote, "Pursue love. Love is action. It does not just come or come out." I continued, "Conduct in church. Prophesy, tongues." Then I quoted verse 26, *"Let all things be done for building up."* And verse 33,

> **For God is not a God of confusion but of peace.**
>
> **1 Cor. 14:33**

"For God is not a God of confusion but of peace." Lastly, verse 40, *"But all things should be done decently and in order."*

DIGGING DEEPER

Rather than get into the controversy of tongues and prophesy, let's focus on the bigger message Paul was giving to the Corinthian church. He was saying some of the spiritual gifts were causing confusion in the worship time in the church. That is not what God intended with spiritual gifts. In fact, again, verse 33 says, *"For God is not a God of confusion but of peace."* And again, he says, *"But all things should be done decently and in order"* (v. 40).

If there is something causing confusion or dissention in your church worship service, maybe it is time to take a look at it. Today, one of the biggest issues of contention in churches is the volume (sound) of the worship service. Maybe that is an issue that is dividing your church or causing confusion or dissention. What does Paul say about it? He says, *"that the church may be built up"* (v. 5). And he says, *"strive to excel in building up the church"* (v. 12). Again, he says, *"Let all things be done for building up"* (v. 26).

Prayer

Lord, let us not divide over spiritual gifts. Let us build the church up through spiritual gifts. May our churches be places where people are comfortable, both the believer and the non-believer. May they be places where You are lifted up and the church is built up. And may they be places where all things are done decently and in order, places where You are lifted up, not spiritual gifts and not the gifts of men. In our houses of worship, may You increase and we decrease. Bless Your church, Almighty God. In Jesus' name, we pray. Amen.

MY THOUGHTS

1 CORINTHIANS 15

Immovable

In 1 Corinthians 15, Paul announces the resurrection not only of Jesus, but ours! Do you believe you will be physically resurrected? Please read or listen to 1 Corinthians 15.

COMMENTS

Sometimes, when you read a passage of scripture, you just need to shout the amen, so amen, hallelujah!

At the beginning of the introduction of 1 Corinthians, I stated there were two firsts in 1 Corinthians. One was the recording of the first celebration of the Lord's Supper in chapter 11. Here in this chapter, is the second first. This is the first announcement of the resurrection, and we are going to cover that. But before we do, let's go back to my three journals from 1994, 2004, and 2015 on 1 Corinthians 15.

> Be steadfast, immovable, always abounding in the work of the Lord, knowing that your toil is not in vain in the Lord.
>
> 1 Cor. 15:58

In 1994, I wrote mostly about the end of chapter 15 (NASB), "Baptism for the dead? I'd like to hear a sermon on this verse." Referring to verse 33, I wrote, "Wow, what a verse! *'Bad company corrupts good morals.'"* Then I moved on to verses 56 and 57, *"The sting of death is sin . . . but thanks be to God, who gives us the victory through our Lord Jesus Christ."* And then that great last verse, verse 58, *"be steadfast, immovable, always abounding in the work of the Lord, knowing that your toil is not in vain in the Lord."*

In 2004, I wrote, "Reader's Digest version of the gospel, 1 Corinthians 15:3-4. 1 Corinthians 15:14 and 17 lay it out. If Christ had not been raised from the dead, our faith is worthless and we are still in our sins. But because Jesus was resurrected, we too will be." I moved on to verse 26, "Jesus conquered the last enemy, death."

In 2015, I repeated some of those same themes. I was referring to verses 3-8 when I wrote, "Resurrection proof." I continued, "I work hard for Jesus, Ezra, Gideons, life, though it is not I, but the grace of God that is within me, referring to verse 10." Moving on, I wrote, "Without a resurrection, your faith is futile and we are still in our sins." Then, once again, verse 33, *"'Bad company ruins good morals.'* We see this over and over." I continued, "The last enemy to be destroyed is death. And Jesus will raise us from death, thereby defeating it. So, with the hope of resurrection and eternal life, *'be steadfast, immovable, always abounding in the work of the Lord, knowing that in the Lord your labor is not in vain'"* (v. 58).

DIGGING DEEPER

There are so many important points in this chapter. Let's go back to verses 3 and 4, that summary of the gospel, *"that Christ died for our sins in accordance with the Scriptures, that he was buried, that he was raised on the third day in accordance with the Scriptures."* Yes, that is a summary of the gospel, but it also says twice, *"in accordance with the Scriptures."* God is not a God of surprises. He already told us what would happen. This is a fulfillment of what was already written in the scriptures.

We also have to cover this issue about the resurrection. Paul writes:

And if Christ has not been raised, then our preaching is in vain and your faith is in vain. We are even found to be misrepresenting God, because we testified about God that he raised Christ, whom he did not raise if it is true that the dead are not raised. For if the dead are not raised, not even Christ has been raised. And if Christ has not been raised, your faith is futile and you are still in your sins (vv. 14-17).

Verse 20 says, *"But in fact Christ has been raised from the dead"*. I love the "buts" in scripture! Without the resurrection, we have no Christianity, we have no faith. Paul goes on to say as much, *"If the dead are not raised, 'Let us eat and drink, for tomorrow we die'"* (v. 32). Without a resurrection, without Jesus' resurrection, there is no building block for Christian faith.

Let's go to verses 51 and 52, *"Behold! I tell you a mystery. We shall not all sleep, but we shall all be changed, in a moment, in the twinkling of an eye, at the last trumpet. For the trumpet will sound, and the dead will be raised imperishable, and we shall be changed."* There is a resurrection, not only Jesus' resurrection but our own future resurrections. For those of us who believe in the resurrection, *"Death is swallowed up in victory. O death, where is your victory? O death, where is your sting?"* (vv. 54-55).

Because we believe in the resurrection, we believe in the resurrection of Jesus, we believe in our future resurrections, we can say verse 58 together, *"Therefore, my beloved brothers, be steadfast, immovable, always abounding in the work of the Lord, knowing that in the Lord your labor is not in vain."* Hallelujah! Praise God!

Prayer

Thank You for the resurrection. Thank You for Your own resurrection and thank You for our resurrections. Thank You that You have defeated death and we have eternal life, all of us who believe in Your resurrection. Hallelujah, Lord! We give You the praise, glory, and honor. In Jesus' name, amen!

MY THOUGHTS

Collections

Today, we conclude our devotions in 1 Corinthians with the last chapter, chapter 16. Paul encourages the Corinthians to support the church and missions. Do you agree with Paul and support your local church and various missions? Please read or listen to the last chapter of 1 Corinthians.

COMMENTS

In 1994, on 1 Corinthians 16 (NASB), I wrote in my journal, "Paul's travel plans were in the Lord. Thank you for a wide door for effective service. He is doing the Lord's work. *'Be on the alert, stand firm in the faith, act like men, be strong. Let all that you do be done in love'* (vv. 13-14). *'If anyone does not love the Lord, he is to be accursed'''* (v. 22).

As we close out 1 Corinthians, remember in 2004, I was reading multiple chapters at a time. I read 1 Corinthians 15 and 16 and wrote a lot more about 1 Corinthians 15 and only this on chapter 16, "Help us do all things in love."

In 2015, I finished 1 Corinthians 16 with these words, "Paul ends 1 Corinthians with an appeal for an offering to take to Jerusalem. He also expects the Corinthian church to *'help me on my journey, wherever I go'* (v. 6), a personal appeal for funds, as well, and an appeal to help Timothy on his way. Giving was a part of the early church. Just about everywhere Paul went, he took up a collection, or an offering, for the Jewish Christians in Jerusalem. That is what he refers to in the first few verses of this chapter."

DIGGING DEEPER

Let's look at a couple of things.

He says in verse 2, *"On the first day of every week, each of you is to put something aside and store it up".* What does that say to you? If the early church attended worship services on the first day of the week to celebrate the resurrection of Jesus, then Paul is saying each time you go to church, you are to put something aside, or give an offering.

Is that your practice? Are you a giver to your church body? I believe tithing is still a principle we ought to be following today. Are you tithing ten percent of your income to your local church, congregation, or assembly?

If you do not believe in tithing, I hope, at least, you are giving offerings to the church that educates you, teaches you, and disciples you. That is the first offering Paul is talking about, an offering to help someone else, an offering to help the Jewish Christians in Jerusalem.

But he also infers people ought to help him and Timothy in their ministries. He says in verse 6, *"so that you may help me on my journey, wherever I go."* In verse 11, when he refers to Timothy coming their way, he says, *"Help him on his way".* As I wrote in my journal, giving was a part of the early church. Is it part of your faith, part of your Christianity, today?

> Be watchful, stand firm in the faith, act like men, be strong. Let all that you do be done in love.
>
> 1 Cor. 16:13-14

Finally, let's refer to verses 13 and 14, *"Be watchful, stand firm in the faith, act like men, be strong. Let all that you do be done in love."*

Paul wrote 1 Corinthians so they would work together to advance the gospel. What prevented them from doing so, was arrogance and one-upmanship. Rather than coming together, they were becoming a divided church.

We have gone through the arguments Paul has made back to the Corinthian church in his letter. As he closes his arguments he says, again, *"Be watchful, stand firm in the faith, act like men, be strong. Let all that you do be done in love"* (vv. 13-14).

Prayer

Paul signs off with this prayer, *"The grace of the Lord Jesus be with you. My love be with you all in Christ Jesus. Amen"* (vv. 23-24). I echo the prayer of Paul to each one of you as well, *"The grace of the Lord Jesus be with you. My love be with you all in Christ Jesus"* (vv. 23-24). Until next time, God bless you. Amen.

MY THOUGHTS

THIRTEEN DAYS IN 2 CORINTHIANS

2 CORINTHIANS 1

Comfort

Today, we begin our study in 2 Corinthians. About a year after writing 1 Corinthians, Paul writes again to the church at Corinth in Southern Greece. The Corinthian church got up-ended by visits from some of Paul's opponents. Several openly rebelled against Paul. He sent Titus there to calm things down, which, for the most part, succeeded.

But there was still a rebellious minority who continued to reject Paul and his gospel. They argued Paul suffered too much to really be a Spirit-filled apostle of Jesus. So the central theme of 2 Corinthians is the relationship between suffering and the power of the Holy Spirit in Paul's life, his ministry, and his message.

2 Corinthians is the most personal of all of Paul's letters, filled with deep emotion. He writes to do a few things: strengthen the faithful majority and purify the church. Secondly, to offer the rebellious minority one more chance to repent before he returns to judge them.

What is its relevance today? Have you ever had to defend yourself? In his most autobiographical letter, Paul provides a model of how to keep our composure while defending ourselves and reaching for reconciliation. Let's jump into Paul's emotionally charged letter, 2 Corinthians. Please read or listen to 2 Corinthians 1.

COMMENTS

I will be using three of my personal Bible reading journals for 2 Corinthians. The first journal is from 1994 when I was thirty-nine years old. The second journal is from 2004 when I read the Bible chronologically at forty-nine years old. The third journal is from 2015 when I was sixty years old; so, perspectives from three different decades.

Let's start with my journal from 2015. I wrote, "God comforts us in our afflictions so we can comfort others in theirs. As in most cases, we have nothing to give without Jesus giving to us first." I continued, "Paul became a Christian. That didn't mean an easy life afterward. Difficulty and Christianity help us to rely, not only on ourselves, but on God." Next, I wrote, "We pray for one another in our afflictions. We are to behave *in the world with simplicity and godly sincerity, not by earthly wisdom, but by the grace of God*" (v. 12).

In 2004, I was reading the Bible chronologically. I was in the Book of Acts, and the passage of 2 Corinthians 1-4 took place during the portion I was reading in Acts. So I read 2 Corinthians 1-4 on this day, but only made comments on what I read in Acts, not on 2 Corinthians.

In 1994, I was reading a chapter a day. On this day, I read 2 Corinthians 1 and wrote, "The word 'comfort' appears ten times. God comforts us in all our affliction so we can comfort others in their affliction with the comfort we received from God. Comfort is abundant through Christ. If we are not comfortable, we are not receiving God's abundant comfort when we are afflicted. Help me be comfortable in You, O Lord." I finished with, "Conduct in the world should be based on holiness, godly sincerity, and grace."

DIGGING DEEPER

Referring back to my journal in 2015, I wrote, when Paul became a Christian, it did not mean his life became easy. Let's look at verses 8 and 9, *"For we do not want you to be ignorant, brothers, of the affliction we experienced in Asia. For we were so utterly burdened beyond our strength that we despaired of life itself. Indeed, we felt that we had received the sentence of death. But that was to make us rely not on ourselves but on God."*

As we read the writings of Paul, we surely understand that he understands suffering and affliction on behalf of Christ. You may be suffering today. You may be afflicted. You may be in a part of your life where you are questioning even God Himself. So let's get some comfort out of 2 Corinthians 1. Verses 3 and 4 say, *"Blessed be the God and Father of*

> **Blessed be the God and Father of our Lord Jesus Christ, the Father of mercies and God of all comfort, who comforts us in all our affliction.**
>
> **2 Cor. 1:3-4**

our Lord Jesus Christ, the Father of mercies and God of all comfort, who comforts us in all our affliction, so that we may be able to comfort those who are in any affliction, with the comfort with which we ourselves are comforted by God."

Jesus suffered. Paul suffered. You may be suffering. Verses 5 and 6 say, *"For as we share abundantly in Christ's sufferings, so through Christ we share abundantly in comfort too. If we are afflicted, it is for your comfort and salvation; and if we are comforted, it is for your comfort, which you experience when you patiently endure the same sufferings that we suffer."* Though it may be difficult, we need to endure the suffering so we eventually can gain the comfort of Jesus. We learn as Paul learned, when we are suffering, we rely not on ourselves, but on God.

Paul wrote in verse 10, *"He delivered us from such a deadly peril, and he will deliver us. On him we have set our hope that he will deliver us again."* If you are suffering, I hope you say as Paul, "On Him, I have set my hope and he will deliver me."

Let's look at one last thought in this chapter, verse 12. Paul says, *"For our boast is this, the testimony of our conscience that we behaved in the world with simplicity and godly sincerity, not by earthly wisdom but by the grace of God".* Regardless of what you are going through, I hope you can proclaim that you behave in the world with simplicity, godly sincerity, not earthly wisdom, but by grace, even as you suffer.

Prayer

Father, I pray for any today who may be in pain, who may be suffering, who may be under any kind of affliction. I pray, Lord, that through suffering, through discomfort, we all learn to rely on You and not on ourselves.

And Lord, I pray any who are suffering, who are in difficult circumstances, could say they continue to behave in the world with simplicity and godly sincerity, not on earthly wisdom, but under Your grace. As they do, Lord, that will be a testimony to those around them.

You remind us in this chapter, Lord, You will comfort us in our affliction. Please do so to those who need Your touch even this day. Lord, may we comfort those around us who are also suffering under affliction as You comfort us. As we comfort them, Lord, may it be a testimony to them of Your grace, Your mercy, and Your love to us and to those we try to comfort. We reach out to You today and we ask You to reach back and comfort us. We ask it, in Your precious name. Amen.

MY THOUGHTS

2 CORINTHIANS 2

Do Christians Smell?

In 2 Corinthians 2, Paul discusses pain and suffering. Do you have strained relationships? Are you willing to initiate reconciliation? Please read or listen to 2 Corinthians 2.

COMMENTS

In 1994, I wrote in my personal Bible reading journal, "Criticism comes from love, not to make people sorrowful. We want to make people happy, but sometimes we need to say the tough things. We then need to be forgiving. Am I an aroma, a sweet fragrance?" I finished with, *"who is adequate for these things?"* (v. 16 NASB).

Ten years later, in 2004, I read 2 Corinthians 1-4, all on the same day, and did not write any notes on this chapter.

In 2015, I wrote in my journal, "Over the Pacific." I was flying that day and probably crossed the date line, so I did not know which day it was. I read on the plane on my way to Australia for a Gideon assignment. I read 2 Corinthians 2 and 3 together on that day. Related to chapter 2, I wrote, "Express abundant love. We must be careful not to be outwitted by Satan. We are not ignorant of his ways. We face him in ministry, but we must not succumb to his ways." Then I wrote, "We smell. Christians smell. An aroma to those interested in being saved. A stench of death to those who won't listen."

DIGGING DEEPER

Have you ever caused someone pain? Have you been the cause of their pain? In chapter 2, Paul takes the blame for causing the Corinthian church the pain he heard about. An important point here is whether Paul is guilty or not of actually causing the pain, he takes the blame. That may be the case in a relationship you are facing right now. Whether it is your fault or not, do you need to take the blame for causing the pain?

I remember a few instances in my life when this was certainly the case. Relationships sometimes get strained between parents and children. Sometimes between bosses and employees. And sometimes between, again, children and parents.

The first instance was when I was a child and had a strained relationship with my mother. The second instance is when I worked for a Christian company and ended up having a strained relationship with the boss. The third is my own relationship as a parent with one of my children. In each instance, there was plenty of blame to go around. In each instance, the Lord eventually led me to seek forgiveness from each of them.

In one instance, it took a drive from Denver to Colorado Springs to go and face the person and ask for forgiveness. In the other two instances, I wrote letters seeking their forgiveness, and in each case, I was forgiven. In such cases, you hope they would also ask for forgiveness, but that does not always happen. It did happen in one instance, and it was very, very refreshing.

Paul says it this way in verse 4, *"For I wrote to you out of much affliction and anguish of heart and with many tears, not to cause you pain but to let you know the abundant love that I have for you."*

Maybe this devotion has brought to mind a strained relationship you may be in right now. I cannot tell you what to do, I can only share how the Word of God touches my life, and how I try to respond from time to time, and then try to obey what I believe I am hearing from the Word and from the Lord. That is why we read the scriptures. It is not just for knowledge sake. It is to impact how we live our lives.

Again, maybe this devotion has caused you to think about a strained relationship. I do not know what God will lead you to do, but He led me in one instance to take a sixty-mile drive and sit with that person and ask for forgiveness. And, in the other two instances, to write a note. Maybe He will lead you to do something similar.

As He does, though it may be difficult, I encourage you to follow His lead. Because, remember, I wrote in my journal, in one of those passages, as Christians, we smell. Verses 15 and 16 say, *"For we are the aroma of Christ to God among those who are being saved and among those who are perishing, to one a fragrance from death to death, to the other a fragrance from life to life."* Will you be a sweet aroma to

> **For we are the aroma of Christ to God among those who are being saved and among those who are perishing, to one a fragrance from death to death, to the other a fragrance from life to life.**
>
> **2 Cor. 2:15-16**

the one you are in a strained relationship with? Will you go the extra Christian mile? Will you turn the other cheek to be able to remedy that strained relationship?

Can we do it in our own strength? Probably not. Let's continue with how Paul finishes this chapter. He wrote, *"Who is sufficient for these things? For we are not, like so many, peddlers of God's word, but as men of sincerity, as commissioned by God, in the sight of God we speak in Christ"* (vv. 16-17). You may feel insufficient to remedy the situation. We all do. But as Christians of sincerity, commissioned by God, we speak in Christ. As Paul did, and as I did, may you go and do likewise.

Prayer

Father, we come before You. We pray, Lord, if we have caused pain in someone else's life, You would remind us of that today. You would bring to mind any strained relationship we may have. And Lord, regardless of whose fault it is, may we be the ones to go and try to remedy the situation.

First, Lord, would You put the desire in our heart to do so? Secondly, would You put the words in our mouth or in our pens or in our keyboards to type or write exactly what You want us to say? May we be sincere Christians who desire to speak as You would speak to those we have caused pain or have some affliction with.

Thirdly, Lord, would You go before us to those people and as we go to them, would You have us well received? May they hear the sincerity of our hearts and receive our request for forgiveness.

And lastly, Lord, though we may expect a, "Please forgive me too," we may not get it. Please, Lord, help us get through that in a patient, enduring way so we do not get more hurt because we went and asked forgiveness and they did not.

As Christians, as representatives of You, help us as we go try to remedy strained relationships. Go with us; go before us. In Jesus' name, amen.

MY THOUGHTS

2 CORINTHIANS 3

Unveiled

2 Corinthians 3 is a hard chapter to understand. Sometimes our faces, minds, and hearts are still under a veil of confusion. But, where the Spirit of the Lord is, there is freedom. Are you veiled or free? Please read or listen to 2 Corinthians 3.

COMMENTS

As we get into 2 Corinthians 3, I want to remind you what I do is share my personal Bible reading journals. I am not a pastor. I am not seminary-educated. I am just a guy who reads his Bible every day and tries to figure out what the Lord is saying through the passage and to me. In this passage, there is a lot of difficulty; that is why I go to church and get taught the Word of God. Teaching the Word of God is not my intent in *Day by Day Through the Bible*. My intent is to relate to common folks, like you and me, who should be reading our Bibles and seeing what the Lord is saying to us on a daily basis.

As I look at my English Standard Version Study Bible on this chapter, there are more footnotes than words in the passage itself. In my Bible, three-quarters of the page is footnotes instead of the Word of God. When I read a passage like this, if I have a hard time with the passage, I do read all the footnotes so I can get an understanding of what other people think the passage says. But *Day by Day* is not a Bible study, so I do not intend to read you all the footnotes on 2 Corinthians 3.

I do encourage you to get a good study Bible and do your own Bible study, not just read daily devotions, but feed yourself in the scriptures daily. I also encourage you to be part of a Bible-believing church where you can get an understanding of what these kinds of passages mean.

With that backdrop, let's go to my journal in 1994, when I read 2 Corinthians 3 (NASB), and wrote, "We are letters being read by those around us." I continued, "Comparison of Moses and the law came

> **Where the Spirit of the Lord is, there is liberty.**
>
> **2 Cor. 2:17**

with such glory Moses wore a veil. How much more glory comes with the Holy Spirit? The law is dead, but the Holy Spirit remains forever." Then I wrote, "The veil is removed in Christ," and finished with, *"where the Spirit of the Lord is, there is liberty"* (v. 17).

The summary of the chapter might be a little chopped up in my journal. Remember, that was back in 1994. Secondly, I just wrote a summary of what I was getting out of the scriptures. Truly, I never intended to be sharing any of this publicly. Those were my journal entries as I read this passage many years ago.

I also selected to share my journal in 2004, when I read the Bible chronologically. There again, I read 2 Corinthians 1-4 on the same day and did not have an entry on this chapter.

In 2015, you might remember from yesterday, I was flying over the Pacific on a flight from Denver to Australia. I went across the date line as I was reading my Bible on the airplane reading 2 Corinthians 2 and 3 that day. I wrote about chapter 3, "After my 'Christian work,' do I leave letters of changed lives? My effectiveness is not authored in me. It comes from God, always. Having the Spirit of God results in freedom. Transform me, Lord, into your image. May people see the Spirit of God in me."

DIGGING DEEPER

I only have one verse underlined in this chapter in my Bible, verse 17. I want to close with that verse and some thoughts about it. However, we will start with the verse before it and finish with the verse after it, *"But when one turns to the Lord, the veil is removed. Now the Lord is the Spirit, and where the Spirit of the Lord is, there is freedom. And we all, with unveiled face, beholding the glory of the Lord, are being transformed into the same image from one degree of glory to another. For this comes from the Lord who is the Spirit"* (vv. 16-18).

That is what happens when we come to faith in Jesus. The veil gets lifted from our faces, our minds, and our hearts. The things of the Spirit begin to make sense to us. The scriptures, the Word of God, begin to enlighten us because the veil of misunderstanding, or hardness of heart, is lifted. I praise God for that in my life. I hope you do too. It is almost worth shouting a hallelujah for! When the veil is lifted, we have freedom in Christ! Not a freedom to be misused or abused, but a freedom to lead us closer to Him.

As the last verse in this chapter says, *"being transformed into the same image"*. That is what we are trying to do. We are trying to become Christ-like as we live our lives here on this earth. Doing so only comes from the Lord, it only comes from the Spirit. We will not do it in our flesh. We will do it when led of the Spirit, when the veil is lifted from us, and we behold the glory of the Lord.

Prayer

Lord, we thank You. Those of us whose veil has been lifted and have life in the Spirit and in You, thank You that You are transforming us into Christ-likeness.

For some, the veil is still over your eyes. Maybe the veil is still over your heart. May you be willing to have God lift it right now. May the Spirit of the living God infiltrate your heart and your mind so you can also be transformed. May you, for the very first time, behold the glory of the Lord. Holy Spirit, lift the veil from anyone praying this prayer right now. Thank You and we give You all the glory. In Jesus' name, amen.

MY THOUGHTS

2 CORINTHIANS 4

Light in Darkness

2 Corinthians 4 is one of my favorite chapters of scripture. I will share why. Do you share light in the darkness? Please read or listen to 2 Corinthians 4.

COMMENTS

In 1994, after reading 2 Corinthians 4 (NASB), I wrote, *"Therefore, since we have this ministry, as we have received mercy, we do not lose heart"* (v. 1). Then I wrote, *"the god of this world has blinded the minds of the unbelieving"* (v. 4). Then I quoted verse 7, *"we have this treasure in earthen vessels"*. Next, I referred to verse 16, *"'Therefore we do not lose heart'*. My inner man is renewed day by day by spending time in the Word and prayer. I believe the Bible ministers to the inner man as this verse indicates. Look at things that cannot be seen, rather than things, though seen, that are temporal."* That was my journal entry in 1994.

This passage took on a whole new light in 1998. In 1998, I was asked to go on my first International Scripture Blitz overseas for The Gideons International; I went to Thailand. I spent two weeks in Thailand, one week in Bangkok, and one week in Chiang Mai. The first seven verses of this chapter were our theme during that International Scripture Blitz. That is why this passage has become so important to me, so valuable to me. Not only was it the theme of my first International Scripture

Blitz as a Gideon, but it has been a theme for me ever since. So many times, when I share about the Gideon ministry, I use this text to share about the Gideons.

Let's go through the first seven verses of 2 Corinthians 4. *"Therefore, having this ministry by the mercy of God, we do not lose heart"* (v. 1). I absolutely believe I have this ministry from the Lord, the ministry of The Gideons International of which I have been a volunteer for over forty years. Obviously, if I have done this for over forty years, I have not lost heart.

The next verse in my English Standard Version Study Bible says, *"But we have renounced disgraceful, underhanded ways. We refuse to practice cunning or to tamper with God's word"* (v. 2). In the New King James Version, it says something more like, "we do not handle the Word of God deceitfully."

As members of The Gideons International, we have the privilege to handle the Word of God. I remember very specifically one time placing Bibles in a large Marriott Hotel in Denver. We were checking room after room after room, hundreds of rooms, looking at the Bibles making sure they were okay and putting them back in drawers. I was going room to room, and God stopped me as I was holding a Bible in my hand. He said to me, "You are handling My Word." What a privilege to be able to place the Word of God in a hotel room or in the hands of someone here or around the world.

Verses 3 and 4 say, *"And if our gospel is veiled, it is veiled to those who are perishing. In their case the god of this world has blinded the minds of the unbelievers, to keep them from seeing the light of the gospel of the glory of Christ".* It is so true. I have been all over the world and have seen the god of this world blind the eyes of those who are perishing. They cannot, or will not, see the light of the gospel. But verse 5 goes on to say, *"For what we proclaim is not ourselves, but Jesus Christ as Lord, with ourselves as your servants for Jesus' sake."* Although we go as members of The Gideons International, we do not proclaim ourselves. We hand out the Word of God that teaches people and leads people to Jesus.

> **And if our gospel is veiled, it is veiled to those who are perishing.**
>
> **2 Cor. 4:3**

Verse 6 says, *"For God, who said, 'Let light shine out of darkness,' has shone in our hearts to give the light of the knowledge of the glory of God in the face of Jesus Christ."* The god of this age has blinded those around the world so they cannot see the light of the gospel. But, the Lord has given us the privilege to take the gospel around the world and let light shine in the darkness, just as it shown in my dark heart at one point in my life. So many times, when I used this passage as a message in a church, I called it "Shining Light in the Darkness."

Verse 7 says, *"But we have this treasure in jars of clay (or earthen vessels) to show that the surpassing power belongs to God and not to us."* We have this treasure, we have the gospel within us and we get to take it around the world. What a privilege, what an honor to be able to serve this way in my life.

I remember sharing this very passage in the People's Republic of China a few years ago, imagine that. Those people, by the billions, have been led by the god of this world into blindness. But there we were, shining the light in the darkness in the People's Republic of China. Praise the Lord!

Now you have a pretty good understanding of why this particular chapter in scripture, this particular set of verses, means so much to me.

DIGGING DEEPER

Before we leave 2 Corinthians 4, let's highlight a couple more thoughts. Verse 14 says, *"knowing that he who raised the Lord Jesus will raise us also with Jesus"*. We thank the Lord for a guaranteed resurrection from the dead.

In verse 16, Paul says, *"So we do not lose heart. Though our outer self is wasting away, our inner self is being renewed day by day."* Can you say the same thing? Can you say your inner self is being renewed day by day? We can be sure that will happen day by day as we spend time in God's presence, time in His Word, and time with Him in prayer.

I need to be renewed day by day. That is why I do not skip a day in God's Word. Each and every day I spend a little bit of time with the scriptures and with the Lord in prayer. I hope you do, too. I hope you make it a habit to renew your inner self day by day.

Prayer

Lord, I thank You for the hope I find in this chapter of scripture. Though the gospel is veiled by the god of this world to so many, we have the chance to shine the light into the darkness of their hearts and their lives.

You have given us this treasure, this message, in earthen vessels, ourselves, so we can share it with someone else. Thank You that You shined the light in our dark heart so we can now share it with someone else.

Because we have that light shining in our own hearts, Lord, we do not lose heart, but we renew our inner self day by day with You in Your Word and in prayer. O, God, thank You that You are never too busy for us, though we seem to be sometimes too busy for You. Forgive us, Lord. When we do carve out time to be with You, renew our inner spirit each and every day. We give You the praise and thanks when You do. In Jesus' name, we pray. Amen.

MY THOUGHTS

2 CORINTHIANS 5

Life in a Tent

In 2 Corinthians 5, Paul, a tentmaker, describes life in a tent. But he says we get to exchange our tents for heavenly bodies as new creations in Christ. Is your tent wearing out? Do you long for a heavenly body? Please read or listen to 2 Corinthians 5.

COMMENTS

I actually have a journal entry in all three journals on this chapter. Let's start with 1994 (NASB), *"we walk by faith, not by sight'* (v. 7). That's hard to do. Hebrews 11:1 says, *'faith is the assurance of things hoped for, the conviction of things not seen.'* It's tough to be blind and walk. It's hard to look beyond what we see in the physical and in our mind's eye. Faith takes depending on God, not us." Then I wrote about verse 14, *"the love of Christ controls us"*. Then verse 15, "All that *'live should no longer live for themselves, but for Him who died and rose again on their behalf.'*"

In 2004, reading the Bible chronologically, I read 2 Corinthians 5-9 (NASB) on the same day. I wrote, "You speak through Your Word, *'for we walk by faith, not by sight'* (v. 7). *'For the love of Christ controls us . . . He died for all, so that they who live might no longer live for themselves, but for Him who died and rose on their behalf'"* (vv. 14-15). Then I wrote, *"we are ambassadors for Christ"* (v. 20).

In 2015, I was reading a couple of chapters a day. I read 2 Corinthians 4 and 5 on the day I finally arrived in Australia. If you would like to learn a little about international travel, I wrote in my journal, "I lost a day traveling. Twenty-four hours from home to here." That was from Denver, Colorado to the Gold Coast in Australia.

In my journal, I wrote, "Life is more than physical," looking at verses 1-7. Then, *"Yes, we are of good courage . . . we make it our aim to please him"* (vv. 8-9). *"For the love of Christ controls us"* (v. 14).

Next, I referred to verse 15 and wrote, "Galatians 2:20, restated. Verse 15 says, *'and he died for all, that those who live might no longer live for themselves but for him who for their sake died and was raised.'"* I was saying that was a restatement of Galatians 2:20, which says, *"I have been crucified with Christ. It is no longer I who live, but Christ who lives in me. And the life I now live in the flesh I live by faith in the Son of God, who loved me and gave himself for me."*

I continued in my journal, "My life doesn't matter. Only Christ living through me matters." Then I quoted, *"Therefore, if anyone is in Christ, he is a new creation. The old has passed away; behold, the new has come"* (v. 17). Then I wrote, "Yes! Yes! Thank You!" I finished chapter 5 with, "We are ambassadors for Christ proclaiming the reconciliation, referring to verse 20."

> Therefore, if anyone is in Christ, he is a new creation. The old has passed away; behold, the new has come.
>
> 2 Cor. 5:17

DIGGING DEEPER

Let's go back to some of the key points of this chapter. Interestingly, Paul, the tentmaker, begins chapter 5 with the illustration of the body being a tent. He says in verse 1, *"For we know that if the tent that is our earthly home is destroyed, we have a building from God, a house not made with (human) hands, eternal in the heavens."* Then he says in verse 2, *"For in this tent we groan, longing to put on our heavenly dwelling."*

I am not sure I would have said that in my twenties or my thirties, but now in my sixties, yeah, my tent is groaning! In verse 6, Paul says, *"We know that while we are at home in the body we are away from the Lord."* One of these days, we are going to give up this tent, this body, and have our heavenly bodies. Hallelujah!

Then Paul encourages us to walk by faith, not by sight and make it our aim to please Him, referring to verses 7 and 9. Why should we do this? Why should we walk by faith and not by sight? Why should we make it our aim to please Him? Paul tells us in verse 10, *"For we must all appear before the judgment seat of Christ, so that each one may receive what is due for what he has done in the body, whether good or evil."* Though we are not saved by our works, we are going to be judged by what we have done on earth, in this body. Let's read it again, *"For we must all appear before the judgment seat of Christ, so that each one may receive what is due for what he has done in the body, whether good or evil"* (v. 10).

I love verse 17, *"Therefore, if anyone is in Christ, he is a new creation. The old has passed away; behold, the new has come."* I have been a Christian since I was fifteen years old. I started reading the Bible the day I became a Christian. I have always believed in this verse. I am so thankful I am a new creation in Christ, old things have passed away, all things became new for me. I hope that is true for you; in Christ, you are a new creation. You no longer hold onto the things of the past but allow God to mold you and shape you each and every day.

Prayer

Lord, we may be stuck in this tent, this human body, as we live here on earth. We know the tent, this human body, ages, it groans, it will be destroyed. But we are so thankful You are preparing for us a new body, a heavenly body, to live eternity in.

We are also so thankful, Lord, old things have passed away, all things become new when we believe in You. We are so thankful, Lord, we do not have to carry our baggage from the past into our future. Father, I give You permission to continue to set aside the old things in my life and make me new in You. Thank You for making me a new creation. In Jesus' name, I pray. Amen.

MY THOUGHTS

2 CORINTHIANS 6

Unequally Yoked

In 2 Corinthians 6, Paul warns us not to get yoked with unbelievers. In marriage, or in life, are you partners with light or darkness? Please read or listen to 2 Corinthians 6.

COMMENTS

As I looked in my journal in 1994 concerning this chapter, I noticed there were two days between 2 Corinthians 5 and 2 Corinthians 6. Those two days were a Saturday and a Sunday, indicating I skipped the weekend in my daily quiet time. This is 1994, I am thirty-nine years old, so let me explain.

On Saturdays, I usually go to a Gideon prayer breakfast where we always read about a chapter of scripture. So I did get my daily time in the Word there on Saturday. And Sunday I went to church, and there we heard, probably read, a passage of scripture. I picked up my Bible reading on Monday. I am not making excuses, but some of us, as Christians, do.

I will explain the way somebody told it to me a few years ago. They said, "If you skip two days a week in your Bible reading, you miss a hundred days a year spending time in God's Word." This friend of mine shared when he got that revelation, it was startling to him. He decided to stop taking the weekends off. I, too, decided that a long time ago, and very rarely do I substitute a Gideon prayer meeting or church for my own time in God's Word on the weekends.

My daily Bible reading is not a ritual. It is not a check-off on a to-do list. It is not a "have-to"; it is a "want-to". I get something from the Lord each and every day I am in the Word. Why wouldn't I want to do that? So if you have been taking weekends off, I hope you reconsider after today's devotion.

Now, on to my journal entry in 1994 on 2 Corinthians 6, "Lord allow me to be a credit to the ministry, giving no cause for offense in anything, in order that the ministry may not be discredited." I also wrote, "Be careful about serious association with unbelievers, which means associate with believers."

In 2004, ten years later, I was reading chronologically, so I read 2 Corinthians 5-9. I made some notes about chapter 5 and some notes about chapter 8, but no notes on chapter 6.

In 2015, remember I was in Australia on a Gideon assignment. I was reading a couple of chapters a day, so I read 2 Corinthians 6 and 7 on this day and wrote, "Paul is all-in, referring to verses 4 and 5, and 8-10." Let's step aside from the journal and read verses 4 and 5, *"but as servants of God we commend ourselves in every way: by great endurance, in afflictions, hardships, calamities, beatings, imprisonments, riots, labors, sleepless nights, hunger"*. Yes, I would say Paul is all-in.

I continued in my journal, "Nowhere does the Word of God say, following God is easy or without persecution or suffering. Yet, God also provides purity, knowledge, patience, kindness, the Holy Spirit, genuine love, truthful speech, the power of God, and weapons of righteousness. He says to us in verse 14, separate from lawlessness, darkness, unbelievers, idols, unclean things."

> **Do not be unequally yoked with unbelievers. For what partnership has righteousness with lawlessness? Or what fellowship has light with darkness?**
>
> **2 Cor. 6:14**

Let's focus on verses 14 and 15, about being unequally yoked. The Word of God says, *"Do not be unequally yoked with unbelievers. For what partnership has righteousness with lawlessness? Or what fellowship has light with darkness? . . . Or what portion does a believer share with an unbeliever?"* If you have been a Christian for any length of time, you have probably heard this principle that Christians should not be yoked with unbelievers. Most often it is referred to regarding marriage.

The illustration Paul uses is a yoke; something that connects two animals together. In his context, remember, he is writing to a Corinthian church that is divided. He is saying to the believers, do not link up with the unbelievers, the ones criticizing Paul.

We seem to have broadened the application to not only marriage, but to business relationships. Most Christians, most pastors, say it is not a good idea to get married to someone who is not a believer. So often, love blinds, and we think we are strong enough we can convert the unbeliever in the marital relationship. Yes, that can happen. Yes, it has happened. But so has the alternative where the unbeliever takes the believer away from his/her beliefs, out of the church, and neutralizes his/her faith.

It is the same in business relationships. Oftentimes Christians say they should not partner with someone who is an unbeliever. Surely, partnerships between unbelievers and believers have worked. But, also, so many of them have run into significant problems, differences in philosophy, as to how to run the business.

So both in marriage and in business, I agree with, *"Do not be unequally yoked with unbelievers"* (v. 14). Though the illustration is agricultural, we realize it is the same when we become yoked together with somebody, one person's conduct and direction of life can strongly influence or control the other's.

DIGGING DEEPER

The application from 2 Corinthians 6, may be, if you are a young person, be careful. Be careful who you hang with, who you are yoking with. Be careful who you are allowing to influence your character, your direction in life. Pray God brings you a believing spouse, someone who shares your Christian values and hopefully can grow with you in your lives together.

For young businesspeople, be careful who you go to work for, or who you work with. Be careful about the influence of the unbeliever on your life. Though some of us are older, and maybe had bad experiences when yoked together with unbelievers, might we heed the same warning. Whatever stage we are at in our lives, be careful who we let influence our lives. I believe there is godly wisdom in the scriptures, and this is one of those places. It may not be culturally popular, but I believe in the long run, it will pay off.

Prayer

Father, help us not become unequally yoked. Help us be careful who we associate with in this life. Protect us, Lord. Bring good people into our lives, people who can influence us to the good in our Christian walk. Lord, help me resist any temptation to become unequally yoked. Guide and direct my steps, Almighty God. In Jesus' name, we pray. Amen.

MY THOUGHTS

2 CORINTHIANS 7

Godly Grief

Today, we cross the halfway point in 2 Corinthians. 2 Corinthians has thirteen chapters, and we are now in chapter seven. Please read or listen to 2 Corinthians 7.

COMMENTS

As we look at the first verse of chapter 7, it says, *"Since we have these promises"*. We need to go back to chapter 6 to see what those promises were, so let's do that. Chapter 6 ended with the concept of being unequally yoked, *"Do not be unequally yoked with unbelievers"* (v. 14). Chapter 7:1 basically concludes that discussion. So we need to look at the verses between 6:14 and 7:1.

Paul was arguing there is no reason to be yoked with unbelievers because we have so many promises, so many blessings, in the Lord. He quotes the Old Testament when he shares these promises we have as believers. He writes:

For we are the temple of the living God; as God said,
I will make my dwelling among them and walk among them,
and I will be their God,
and they shall be my people.

Therefore go out from their midst,

and be separate from them, says the Lord,

and touch no unclean thing;

then I will welcome you,

and I will be a father to you,

and you shall be sons and daughters to me,

says the Lord Almighty (2 Cor. 6:16-18).

Those are the promises Paul opens chapter 7 with. He says, *"Since we have these promises, beloved, let us cleanse ourselves from every defilement of body and spirit, bringing holiness to completion in the fear of God"* (v. 1). So 7:1 really concludes the argument at the end of chapter 6. Now, let's go to my journals on chapter 7.

In 1994, reading the NASB version, I wrote, "Perfect holiness, referring to verse 1," which we just discussed. Then I wrote, *"Great is my confidence in you"* (v. 4). Then I put, "Comfort," and I put down the number of times I saw the word "comfort" in this chapter. I came up with at least six times. Then I wrote, "Sorrow should lead to repentance," and I quoted verse 16, *"I rejoice that in everything I have confidence in you."*

In 2004, I was reading chronologically, and I read chapters 5 through 9 in one day. I referred to some of the chapters in my journal, but nothing on this chapter that year.

In 2015, I was still in Australia, still reading two chapters a day, when I read chapters 6 and 7 together. I wrote about chapter 7, "Try as best as we can to be holy." Then, "Be sorry for any wrongdoing. Godly grief produces repentance that leads to salvation." Then lastly, "Comfort one another."

In our book introduction, we learned Paul had sent a letter to the Corinthians that caused them some problems. Then he sent Titus there to get some information and try to smooth things over. In verse 8, he said, *"For even if I made you grieve with my letter, I do not regret it—though I did regret it".* So he understands his letter caused some problems with the Corinthians. But after he sent Titus there and Titus came back, Titus gave him a positive report about things that were going on with the Corinthian church. So Paul is comforted.

> For godly grief produces a repentance that leads to salvation without regret, whereas worldly grief produces death.
>
> 2 Cor. 7:10

Verse 10 says, *"For godly grief produces a repentance that leads to salvation without regret, whereas worldly grief produces death."* What do you think the difference is between godly grief and worldly grief? This is a good time to look at a footnote in my English Standard Version Study Bible:

godly grief. Grief that comes from God is characterized by **repentance**, i.e., remorse caused by having lost God's approval and the consequent resolve to reverse one's conduct and live for God. **worldly grief**. Grief that comes from the world, i.e., a remorse brought about by losing the world's approval, leads to a resolve to regain that approval, and this **produces death**, or divine judgment (p. 2232).

DIGGING DEEPER

Are you sorry for something you have done? Do you have godly grief or worldly grief? Is your sorrow leading you to repent and therefore leading you to salvation? Or is your sorrow or your grief causing guilt feelings you cannot seem to get out from under?

Those guilty feelings—I am not good enough, I should not have done it, I will never be forgiven—might be worldly grief which leads to death. If this devotion has brought worldly grief to your mind, hopefully, you will change it into godly grief, leading to repentance, leading to forgiveness, leading to cleansing, maybe even leading to salvation. Paul thought that was happening with the Corinthian church. I hope that is what is happening to you.

Paul closes this chapter with a thought for the Corinthian church, the same thought I have for you. *"I rejoice, because I have perfect confidence in you"* (v. 16). That confidence is that you will turn your worldly grief into godly grief.

Prayer

Father, we pray for anyone hurting today. If You have brought something to their mind they are sorrowful over, can You turn that worldly grief into godly grief? May we have the courage to repent without regret, accept Your forgiveness, and turn our hearts toward You. *"(L)et us cleanse ourselves from every defilement of body and spirit, bringing holiness to completion in the fear of God"* (v. 1). In Your name, we pray. Amen.

CLUB 365

Thank you for using *Day by Day Through the Word* devotions. If *Day by Day* is touching your life, please visit ezraproject.net to see how you can add listening to your visual daily devotions through Club 365. By joining Club 365, you can hear each passage of the *Day by Day* devotion while you are reading it. Check out Club 365 at ezraproject.net. See how you can add to your blessings of *Day by Day* with ADDBIBLE, audio daily devotions. God bless you!

MY THOUGHTS

2 CORINTHIANS 8

Give Generously

In 2 Corinthians 8, Paul covers giving. What are your thoughts about giving to your church and other Christian nonprofit organizations? Please read or listen to 2 Corinthians 8.

COMMENTS

In 1994, on 2 Corinthians 8 (NASB), I wrote, "Give financially to support the work of the ministry." Then I referred to verse 11, *"finish doing it also'.* Complete what I start." And related to verse 15, "God's supply line. Not too much. No lack." Then referring to verse 21, "Be honorable in the sight of God and men."

In 2004, I read 2 Corinthians 5-9 (NASB) on the same day and had a couple entries related to this chapter. Quoting verse 7, *"But just as you abound in everything, in faith and utterance and knowledge and in all earnestness and in the love we inspired in you, see that you abound in this gracious work also."* Then I quoted verse 11, *"But now finish doing it also, so that just as there was the readiness to desire it, so there may be also the completion of it by your ability."*

In 2015, I read 2 Corinthians 8 and 9 on the same day. Remember, I was in Australia at the time on a Gideon assignment. I referred to chapter 8, "Give according to our means and beyond to the Lord. God blesses accordingly and for what is honorable to God."

DIGGING DEEPER

2 Corinthians 8 is a great chapter about our attitude toward giving. Let's go over some of the key verses. Verse 3, *"For they gave according to their means, as I can testify, and beyond their means, of their own accord"*. Principle one is, we can only give according to our means. If God has blessed you, you may have more to give. If you have limited means, you give according to your means. But the tail end of this verse says, but they also gave beyond their means of their own accord. In other words, they were not arm-twisted to give more. They wanted to give more, a little bit beyond what they thought they could give initially.

Verse 7 says, you do well in many things, Corinthian church. So you can also do well in the act of giving. Actually, the verse says, *"But as you excel in everything—in faith, in speech, in knowledge, in all earnestness, and in our love for you—see that you excel in this act of grace also."* This act of grace is the act of giving. So principle two in giving is to excel in giving.

Principle three comes in verse 10. It says, complete what you pledged, or complete what you started. The middle of the verse says, *"this benefits you, who a year ago started not only to do this work but also to desire to do it."* Verse 11 then says, *"So now finish doing it as well"*. Maybe you have given a faith pledge to your church, or to a building program, or to a missions organization. This verse tells us, complete the task. Do what you said and finish. In any kind of church giving campaign, we should not only start eagerly, but we should finish eagerly.

> **Whoever gathered much had nothing left over, and whoever gathered little had no lack.**
>
> **2 Cor. 8:15**

Principle four is, God meets the need. It is found in verse 15. Paul writing, *"As it is written, 'Whoever gathered much had nothing left over, and whoever gathered little had no lack.'"* Whether you have much or whether you have little, God can meet the need.

Those are four wonderful principles about our attitude toward giving. How do you measure up on those four principles?

Do you give according to your means, and sometimes beyond your means? Do you excel in the act of giving? Do you honor your pledges? Do you start strong and finish strong in your giving? And lastly, do you praise God because He meets the need, whether you have much or whether you have little?

Finally, verse 21 says, *"for we aim at what is honorable not only in the Lord's sight but also in the sight of man."* I hope how you give, what you give, and your attitude toward giving, is honorable in the sight of God and also in the sight of man.

Prayer

Lord, we thank You that You give us means, You equip us, You bless us with a standard of living, whatever it is. And You tell us to give according to our means. Let each of us be a part of meeting the needs of Your kingdom-building here on earth.

You set a principle of the tithe. It is my understanding that if all Christians gave ten percent, there would be no needs in the church today. We thank You for the challenge in this chapter about our heart, about our attitude, about giving.

Help us, Lord, to give according to our means. Help us to excel in giving. Help us to not only start well, but to finish well in our giving. Help us realize whether we have much or little, You provide exactly what we need. May our attitude and our actual giving be honorable in Your sight. We pray it, in Jesus' name. Amen.

MY THOUGHTS

2 CORINTHIANS 9

Cheerful Givers

2 Corinthians 9 is a continuation of chapter 8, with more biblical principles on giving. Do you give? Cheerfully? Please read or listen to 2 Corinthians 9.

COMMENTS

Chapter 8 had some principles of giving; we outlined four yesterday. Chapter 9 continues with more thoughts about giving.

In 1994, at thirty-nine years old, I read 2 Corinthians 9 (NASB) and wrote, "Be prepared to give." Then I wrote, related to verse 6, "The law of the harvest. How we sow is a measure of what we reap." Then, "Give with joy to help others." Then, referring to verse 8, "*God is able to make all grace abound to you, so that always having all sufficiency in everything, you may have an abundance for every good deed'.* God is very complete."

Ten years later, in 2004, at forty-nine years old, I was reading the Bible chronologically, so I read 2 Corinthians chapters 5-9 (NASB) on the same day. I had a couple of references to this chapter starting with verse 10, "*Now He who supplies seed to the sower and bread for food will supply and multiply your seed for sowing and increase the harvest of your righteousness.'* Stay the course. More seed is coming. Plant. Your harvest is coming."

Eleven years later, in 2015, at sixty years old, I was still in Australia reading 2 Corinthians chapters 8 and 9 on the same day. I wrote about chapter 9, "Guidelines on giving." I was referring to verses 6 and 7. "And God's multiplication, referring to verse 10."

2 Corinthians 9 continues the discussion Paul had in chapter 8 about giving. This is a subject most of us do not like to hear about. We certainly do not like to be preached at about it. But there are scriptural principles, as Christians, we should understand concerning our heart toward giving.

> Each one must give as he has decided in his heart, not reluctantly or under compulsion.
>
> 2 Cor. 9:7

Here is one of the more famous passages we hear when discussing giving, *"The point is this: whoever sows sparingly will also reap sparingly, and whoever sows bountifully will also reap bountifully. Each one must give as he has decided in his heart, not reluctantly or under compulsion, for God loves a cheerful giver. And God is able to make all grace abound to you, so that having all sufficiency in all things at all times, you may abound in every good work"* (vv. 6-8).

Verse 10 goes on to say, *"He who supplies seed to the sower and bread for food will supply and multiply your seed for sowing and increase the harvest of your righteousness."* In chapter 8, we learned that each one gives according to their means. That is all we can do. We cannot give more than what God has blessed us with, but we are to give according to our means.

DIGGING DEEPER

In chapter 9, Paul enhances that when he says, *"whoever sows sparingly will also reap sparingly"* (v. 6). In other words, if you are not giving according to your means, if you are withholding, or if you become selfish about what God has given you, you may also reap sparingly. The same principle applies with the continuation of the verse, those who *"sows bountifully will also reap bountifully"* (v. 6). That may also relate back to 8:3, *"they gave according to their means"* but some, *"beyond their means"*. That may be bountifully.

Each one of us need to give as we have decided in our hearts. Not reluctantly, nor under compulsion. In other words, we do not give because we have to, and we do not give because we are pressured to give. We give after prayerful consideration, time with the Lord, according to what He has put in our hearts.

In both The Gideons International work I do, and in the Ezra Project, I have had plenty of opportunities to appeal for money. Many, many times when I get to that point, I stop, and if there are couples in the room, say, "Please pray with your spouse. Allow the Lord to tell you what amount to give. Sometimes He will give it one way to our spouse and one way to you. After you pray, then talk to each other and see what the Lord has laid on your hearts to give."

For example, once in a missions pledge in our church, after Terry and I prayed, we talked about what the Lord laid on our hearts. On her heart, He laid $50 a month. On my heart, it was $600. Amazing, it was equal, exactly the same amount! So pray before you give, then do what God lays on your heart, *"not reluctantly or under compulsion, for God loves a cheerful giver"* (v. 7). And why wouldn't you give cheerfully after He has laid on your heart what to give?

Usually in my appeals, after that prayer I say, "And Lord give us the courage to give what You laid on our hearts." Sometimes the amount might surprise us, so I pray for courage to be obedient to what one hears from the Lord.

Verse 8 gives us a promise about our giving, *"And God is able to make all grace abound to you, so that having all sufficiency in all things at all times, you may abound in every good work."* What that says to me is God is able. He is the one that gives us everything anyway. He gives us the sufficiency so we can give generously what He has laid in our hearts.

The promise continues in verse 10, *"He who supplies seed to the sower and bread for food will supply and multiply your seed for sowing and increase the harvest of your righteousness."* In one way, this tells me He supplies seed for me. He is the one that gives me everything I have so I can even give at all. And when I give, He gives me more seed. In other words, He gives me more so I can give again. Another way I read this is, He supplies me. When I sow seed, when I provide bread for food, He will give me more seed. And He will increase my harvest. I hope you want that. I hope you want God to increase your harvest.

Prayer

Lord, we thank You for more principles on giving. Help us understand. Help us hear from You. Help us be cheerful givers. Help us sow our seed bountifully so You will give us more seed so we can sow more and we can increase our harvest for You. What a blessing that You have entrusted us with seed anyway. So with a smile on my face, may I bountifully sow the seeds You give me.

And, Lord, we look forward to the harvest. We look forward to a harvest of meeting people's needs, meeting our churches' needs, meeting the needs of expanding the kingdom here on earth. We look forward to a harvest when it is all over, and you say, *"Well done, good and faithful servant"* (Matt. 25:21). Water the seeds we sow, Lord, and then give us more seed. In Jesus' name, amen.

MY THOUGHTS

2 CORINTHIANS 10

Influence

In 2 Corinthians 10, Paul defends himself. Have you ever had the need, or desire, to defend yourself? Do you use your god-given gifts to influence those around you? Please read or listen to 2 Corinthians 10.

COMMENTS

In 1994, in my journal, I wrote concerning this chapter, "Need to be commended by the Lord, not by self." Sometimes I write my prayers too, and I wrote that day, "For attitude." So needing to be commended by the Lord and not myself, I prayed for my own attitude.

In 2004, when I was reading the Bible chronologically, I read chapters 10-13 on one day and closed out 2 Corinthians. I summarized some of the verses in chapter 10, "I am so weak. Lord, strengthen me. Continue to grow me up in the faith. Help my thoughts become obedient. Help me boast only in You."

In 2015, I am still in Australia. I read 2 Corinthians 10 and 11. My entries in my journal concerning chapter 10 were, "Lord, give me weapons of divine power to destroy strongholds. There seem to be more and more strongholds and we are not winning. Take my thoughts captive for You. Paul may not have been gifted physically or verbally, referring to verse 10."

I continued, "We don't compare ourselves with others. Only in service to the calling God has placed on my life. I have a certain area of influence God assigned and no more. Like Paul, my prayer is *'our area of influence among you may be greatly enlarged'* (v. 15). May I not boast but be commended by You."

> For the weapons
> of our warfare are
> not of the flesh but
> have divine power to
> destroy strongholds.
>
> 2 Cor. 10:4

After handling many of the issues facing the Corinthian church in the first nine chapters of this book, Paul now turns in the next few chapters to defending himself. Paul first reminds the Corinthian church the battle between them and him is not in the flesh, it is in the Spirit. *"For the weapons of our warfare are not of the flesh but have divine power to destroy strongholds. We destroy arguments and every lofty opinion raised against the knowledge of God, and take every thought captive to obey Christ"* (vv. 4-5).

That is such an important principle. If you are in a battle, whether it is in a relationship, your job, within a church, within a ministry, the battle is not flesh to flesh. It is a spiritual battle. In such battles, we need divine power. We need to be sure our thoughts are captive in Christ. Certainly, it is hard to put aside our own agendas, to put aside what we think about in the flesh, but we must because it is a spiritual battle. Paul says it clearly, *"For though we walk in the flesh, we are not waging war according to the flesh"* (v. 3).

Have you ever wondered what Paul was really like? We might get a glimpse into him here in verse 10. He writes, *"For they say, 'His letters are weighty and strong, but his bodily presence is weak, and his speech of no account.'"* From that verse, I do not think Paul was an imposing figure. Maybe he came with that thorn in his side, weakening him physically. It also says, his speech was of no account, which is amazing. You would think Paul was a great orator, but from that verse, it does not sound like he was a spellbinding speaker.

But what he needed he had. He had the power of the Holy Spirit within him, and the ability to profess truth wherever he went. Look what he says in verse 13, *"But we will not boast beyond limits, but will boast only with regard to the area of influence*

God assigned to us, to reach even to you." I love that. I love what the verse implies. It says to me in ministry, I am only to deal with the area of influence God has assigned to me, and I do believe God has assigned me a few areas of influence for Him.

DIGGING DEEPER

What about you? What area of influence has God assigned to you? Do you have an area of ministry in your life? It does not have to be full time. You do not have to be a pastor. I believe God has assigned all of us an area of ministry, an area of influence.

What has God called you to do? What does God want you to do? What is the area of influence God wants you to minister in? If you know it, minister in it. If you do not know it, after this devotion, take some time to think about it.

Let's go back to verse 13, *"But we will not boast beyond limits, but will boast only with regard to the area of influence God assigned to us".* What is your area of assignment? Ask the Lord. Pray about it. Seek it out and then be bold enough to do it.

Paul concludes the chapter with this thought, *"Let the one who boasts, boast in the Lord. For it is not the one who commends himself who is approved, but the one whom the Lord commends"* (vv. 17-18).

Yes, we all have an area of influence, something God has given us to do. But we do not boast in ourselves. We understand as we started this chapter, it is not a battle between our flesh. Whatever we are asked to do is a spiritual assignment. So how could we boast?

We can be thankful God has given us some area of influence in His kingdom. We can hope we will do all we can to be obedient and He will be well pleased. He is the one that will commend us.

Prayer

Lord, help me find my area of influence. Help me find what You have placed me on this earth to do. Help me find the place where You want me to serve in Your kingdom. And Lord, help me understand it is not from my flesh, but it is a spiritual battle, therefore, I need Your help.

Lord, help me realize I might be like Paul. I might not have much bodily stature. I might not even be able to speak eloquently. But like You used Paul, You can use me because You assigned me an area of influence.

Lord, I pray You find me faithful. I pray when it is all over, You will have commended me for that which You have assigned me to do. And we will give You the glory. In Jesus' name, amen.

MY THOUGHTS

2 CORINTHIANS 11

Sincere and Pure Devotion to Christ

We are coming down the home stretch of 2 Corinthians, only chapters 11, 12, and 13 to go. In chapter 11, Paul warns against being led astray to a different gospel. Do you know the one true gospel? Please read or listen to 2 Corinthians 11.

COMMENTS

The danger Paul faced in the Corinthian church is the same danger we face today in our churches. Let's look at the initial verses of this chapter, *"But I am afraid that as the serpent deceived Eve by his cunning, your thoughts will be led astray from a sincere and pure devotion to Christ. For if someone comes and proclaims another Jesus than the one we proclaimed, or if you receive a different spirit from the one you received, or if you accept a different gospel from the one you accepted, you put up with it readily enough"* (vv. 3-4).

Powerful words for the Corinthian church and for us as believers today. I have challenged some pastors to do a little survey, to stand in front of their church and ask five to ten people what the gospel is, or what it takes to be saved. Could they get five to ten consistent answers?

Then go outside the church; go to people who say they are Christians and ask them what it means to be a Christian. The answers are all over the map. That is exactly what Paul is warning in these verses. Let's look at them again, *"But I am afraid that as the serpent deceived Eve by his cunning, your thoughts will be led astray from a sincere and pure devotion to Christ. For if someone comes and proclaims another Jesus than the one we proclaimed, or if you receive a different spirit from the one you received, or if you accept a different gospel from the one you accepted, you put up with it readily enough"* (vv. 3-4).

> But I am afraid that as the serpent deceived Eve by his cunning, your thoughts will be led astray from a sincere and pure devotion to Christ.
>
> 2 Cor. 11:3

Where are we going to find the one true gospel? We are going to find it in the Word of God. But we have many who are deceiving the people in the churches today. Paul explains it this way, *"For such men are false apostles, deceitful workmen, disguising themselves as apostles of Christ. And no wonder, for even Satan disguises himself as an angel of light. So it is no surprise if his servants, also, disguise themselves as servants of righteousness. Their end will correspond to their deeds"* (vv. 13-15).

Those are some tough words from the Apostle Paul. Tough words that our churches need to hear today. As Christians, we need to be careful not to be *"led astray from a sincere and pure devotion to Christ"* (v. 3). We must be careful not to follow another Jesus, not to follow a different spirit, not to follow a different gospel.

DIGGING DEEPER

How do you know what your preacher is preaching if you do not measure it against the yardstick of the Word of God? As Paul said, *"So it is no surprise if his servants, also, disguise themselves as servants of righteousness"* (v. 15). Servants of whom? Servants of Satan himself.

I heard it said recently, today we have "notional Christianity"; whatever we want it to be, it is. That cannot be according to God's Word. It reminds me of a flight I was on recently. I sat down next to a thirty-something year-old woman. She said, as she began to share her spiritual journey, that her spirit was mixed with Judaism, Islam, Catholicism, and a variety of other things. I got out a New Testament and pointed out John 14:6. I had her read, *"I am the way, and the truth, and the life. No man comes to the Father except through me."* After reading it, she closed the Testament. I asked her, "What do you think?" She said, "I pick and choose what I believe out of the books I read."

That is exactly what Paul is warning here in chapter 11 of 2 Corinthians. Our very practical application from this chapter today is to guard ourselves from another Jesus, a different spirit, a different gospel from the one you accepted. Guard your *"sincere and pure devotion to Christ"* (v. 3). How are you going to know the one true gospel? Stay in God's Word. Stay in *Day by Day Through the Bible*. We cover the gospel many, many times in the various books we go through.

Prayer

Father, please guard our hearts against another Jesus, against a different spirit, against a different gospel. Do not let Satan come as an angel of light to us. Please, Lord, guard Your church against Satan using his servants in pulpits to disguise truth and righteousness. You said the gates of hell will not prevail against the church. We pray it so. And we pray it so in our own lives as well. In Jesus' name, we ask it. Amen.

MY THOUGHTS

2 CORINTHIANS 12

A Thorn in Our Flesh

Today we are in the second-to-last chapter of 2 Corinthians, chapter 12. Do you get spiritually arrogant at times? Or, has God provided a thorn in your flesh to keep you humble? Please read or listen to 2 Corinthians 12.

COMMENTS

In 1994, when I read 2 Corinthians 12, I wrote, "Paul's thorn in the flesh, to keep me from exalting myself. Maybe that's why things go wrong, don't always happen just the way we want, is to help keep us from exalting ourselves. And that God works through our weaknesses."

In 2004, ten years later, I was reading the Bible chronologically, finishing with chapters 10-13 together. I referred to one verse out of chapter 12, verse 9, "Let your grace be sufficient for me."

In 2015, eleven years after 2004, remember I spent most of what we were reading in 2 Corinthians in Australia. I am on the plane, once again, finally on my way home, reading 2 Corinthians 12 and 13. I wrote, "Paul caught up in the third heaven. Heard things he cannot share. Wow." I continued, "To keep him humble, he had the thorn of flesh, which he wanted removed. God said, 'No.'"

In these last few chapters of 2 Corinthians, remember Paul is defending himself. The Corinthians had visitors who shared their spiritual credentials and their spiritual experiences. Maybe they were more articulate than Paul. The Corinthians were divided between Paul and these other messengers. Here, Paul, in a strange way, shares one of his spiritual credentials, *"I know a man in Christ who fourteen years ago was caught up to the third heaven"* (v. 2). Paul's hesitancy to boast of his vision is reflected in his use of the third person. But he is definitely referring to himself in the illustration. Think about what he says in verse 4, *"and he heard things that cannot be told, which man may not utter."*

After his Damascus Road experience, where Jesus confronted Paul, Paul did not go to Jerusalem to learn the gospel. Paul had direct, personal experiences with Jesus. That may be what he is referring to here.

> **So to keep me from becoming conceited because of the surpassing greatness of the revelations, a thorn was given me in the flesh, a messenger of Satan to harass me, to keep me from becoming conceited.**
>
> **2 Cor. 12:7**

He goes on to say in verse 7, *"So to keep me from becoming conceited because of the surpassing greatness of the revelations, a thorn was given me in the flesh, a messenger of Satan to harass me, to keep me from becoming conceited."* Can you imagine what Paul saw? The *"surpassing greatness of the revelations"* (v. 7), hearing things, seeing things, that cannot be told. And just to be sure Paul keeps from getting too arrogant, too cocky, too conceited, he gets a messenger from Satan to harass him. This story from Paul is enough to keep me as humble as I can be so none of this ever happens to me.

Three times Paul pleads to the Lord that it would leave him, this thorn of flesh, this messenger of Satan. But Jesus says to him, *"My grace is sufficient for you, for my power is made perfect in weakness"* (v. 9). So Paul prayed three times that this thorn would be removed. Did Jesus answer his prayer? Yes, but not the way Paul wanted it answered; but He did answer his prayer.

DIGGING DEEPER

Has that happened to you? Do you pray for something, but it does not turn out the way you want? Just remember, God may have answered your prayer, just not the way you wanted it. Paul gets it. He says, *"Therefore I will boast all the more gladly of my weaknesses, so that the power of Christ may rest upon me. For the sake of Christ, then, I am content with weaknesses, insults, hardships, persecutions, and calamities. For when I am weak, then I am strong"* (vv. 9-10).

Do we get it when God decides not to answer our prayer the way we want? Do we understand He may be keeping us weak so we can be made strong through Him? Can we say, like Paul, *"For the sake of Christ, then, I am content with weaknesses, insults, hardships, persecutions, and calamities"* (v. 10)? I do not think I can say that. I get bad news and my countenance changes. I get bad news and I get knocked off my spiritual rocker. So often, after I experience insults, hardships, persecutions, and calamities, I need to filter it through my quiet time to get myself spiritually back on track.

But I also believe what scripture tells me; I need You, every hour I need You. In my flesh, I can do nothing, but hallelujah, Christ in me, the hope of glory. I think I can say with Paul, when I am weak, He makes me strong.

Do you have a thorn in your flesh? Do you have something that bothers you, that keeps you from being conceited spiritually? Have you asked God to remove it, and has He said, "No"? Can you see it like Paul, *"My grace is sufficient for you, for my power is made perfect in weakness"* (v. 9). Friends, we might have a strange prayer today.

Prayer

Lord, thank You for the thorn in our flesh. Thank You for whatever it takes for us not to become spiritually conceited. Thank You for the thorn in our flesh that keeps us weak so You can be made strong through us. In a strange way, Lord, might we praise Your name for that thorn in our flesh. For that which keeps us weak so You can be seen strong through us. Thank You. In Jesus' name, amen.

MY THOUGHTS

Test Yourself

Today brings us to the last chapter of the great book of 2 Corinthians, chapter 13. Paul covered the one true gospel throughout 2 Corinthians. The Corinthians were challenged to stand firm after hearing false teachings. Have you been exposed to false teachings? Test yourself, are you standing firm? Please read or listen to 2 Corinthians 13.

COMMENTS

As we finish 2 Corinthians, let's look at these last entries of journals from 1994, 2004, and 2015. Starting out with 1994 (NASB), "He was crucified for our weaknesses, referring to verse 4." Then, *"Test yourself to see if you are in the faith; examine yourselves'* (v. 5). Or do you not know that Jesus Christ is in you? Do what is right even though I should appear unapproved. Do nothing against the truth."

From 2004 (NASB), "Test me. Examine me. Be Jesus in me. Help me stand for truth. *'Finally, brethren, rejoice, be made complete, be comforted, be like-minded, live in peace; and the God of love and peace will be with you'* (v. 11). Praise God, I can come to You and You forgive my weaknesses and use me anyway. Thank You."

From 2015, on that plane ride all the way home from Australia, I wrote, "Our weaknesses can strengthen us. In our weaknesses, God offers power. Examine me.

Test me. Is Christ in me? *'Aim for restoration, comfort one another, agree with one another, live in peace'"* (v. 11).

That ends the journal entries from those various decades: 1994, 2004, and 2015. I hope you enjoyed the use of those journals walking us through 2 Corinthians. Let's look at a couple of concepts out of this last chapter before we close 2 Corinthians.

Paul says to the Corinthians, and to us, in verse 5, *"Examine yourselves, to see whether you are in the faith. Test yourselves. Or do you not realize this about yourselves, that Jesus Christ is in you?—unless indeed you fail to meet the test!"* What is the test Paul is referring to? I refer to my English Standard Version Study Bible footnote on verse 5, "The **test** to **see** if **Christ is in** the Corinthians will be their response to Paul and his call to repent since God's message and the messenger are one."

> **Examine yourselves, to see whether you are in the faith. Test yourselves. Or do you not realize this about yourselves, that Jesus Christ is in you?**
>
> **2 Cor. 13:5**

The test is the same for us today. *"Examine yourselves, to see whether you are in the faith. Test yourselves. Or do you not realize this about yourselves, that Jesus Christ is in you ?"* (v. 5). Is Jesus Christ in you? Remember in chapter 11 Paul said, *"But I am afraid that as the serpent deceived Eve by his cunning, your thoughts will be led astray from a sincere and pure devotion to Christ. For if someone comes and proclaims another Jesus than the one we proclaimed, or if you receive a different spirit from the one you received, or if you accept a different gospel from the one you accepted, you put up with it readily enough"* (vv. 3-4).

That is the test. Is Christ in you? Or have you been led astray by another Jesus, a different spirit, or a different gospel? The same test Paul is giving to the Corinthians he gives to us. Paul proclaims in verse 8, *"For we cannot do anything against the truth, but only for the truth."* I hope you can shout that as loud as Paul could shout it. You too can do nothing against the truth, but only for the truth. After this devotion today, do what Paul is asking us to do, examine yourself to see whether you are in the faith.

Paul finishes the book by saying, *"Finally, brothers, rejoice. Aim for restoration, comfort one another, agree with one another, live in peace; and the God of love and peace will be with you"* (v. 11). Paul wrote this letter to the church of Corinth because they had been up-ended by visits from Paul's opponents. Several openly rebelled against Paul. They argued Paul suffered too much to really be a Spirit-filled apostle of Jesus. In the church of Corinth, there was a rebellious minority who continued to reject Paul and his gospel.

The central theme of 2 Corinthians was the relationship between suffering and the power of the Holy Spirit in Paul's life, ministry, and message. He wrote to strengthen the faithful majority and purify the church and to offer those in rebellion one more chance to repent before he returned to judge them. Verse 11 closes out Paul's desire for the Corinthian church. *"Aim for restoration, comfort one another, agree with one another, live in peace; and the God of love and peace will be with you."*

DIGGING DEEPER

Let's wrap up 2 Corinthians with an application to our lives today. Did you once hear the gospel? Did you once hear the truth of the gospel? Did you accept the truth of the gospel at one time in your life? If so, have you stood firm? Have you stayed strong, have you stayed true to the one true gospel of Jesus Christ?

Or since you heard the truth of the gospel, have you heard a different gospel? A different spirit? Maybe, even, a different Jesus? Has it turned your head away from the one true gospel? If so, Paul is saying repent, come back to the one true gospel of Jesus Christ. I hope you heed his invitation today.

There may be some of you who have never heard the true gospel of Jesus Christ. I share it like Paul shared it in chapter 5, *"For the love of Christ controls us, because we have concluded this: that one (Jesus) has died for all (us), therefore all have died; and he (Jesus) died for all, that those who live might no longer live for themselves, but for him who for their sake died and was raised"* (vv. 14-15).

That is the gospel in a nutshell. *"Therefore, if anyone is in Christ, he is a new creation. The old has passed away; behold, the new has come"* (2 Cor. 5:17).

Please accept the love of Christ. Please accept the forgiveness of Jesus and the fact that He died on the cross for your sins so you can be forgiven. Please set aside your life in the flesh and allow the Holy Spirit to enter your life and live by the Spirit from now on. Please accept the offer to become a new creature in Christ. Let your old self pass away and become new in Jesus.

Prayer

Please say this prayer to Jesus. Confessing to God that I am a sinner and believing that the Lord Jesus Christ died for my sins on the cross and was raised for my justification, I do now receive and confess Him as my personal Savior. Amen.

CONCLUSION

That would be a great ending to the study of 2 Corinthians. If you made a decision for Christ, please let us know. Please go to ezraproject.net, to our contact page, where you can let us know you received Jesus as your Lord and Savior. We would love to know so we can pray for you as you grow in Christ.

We look forward to being together again on another book of the Bible. In Jesus' name. Thank you. Amen.

MY THOUGHTS

SIX DAYS IN GALATIANS

GALATIANS 1

One True Gospel

Today, we begin the Book of Galatians. It is one of the earliest writings of Paul, dated around 48 A.D., which is only about fifteen years after the death, burial, and resurrection of Jesus. The theme of Galatians is believers do not have to become Jews or follow the outward ceremonies of the Law of Moses. New Christians are to live in the guidance and the power of the Spirit. Galatians is about freedom in Christ, but not a license to sin. It also contains one of my favorite verses, which we will get to tomorrow.

What does freedom in Christ mean to you? Does it mean what many people think, that even if I continue in sin, Jesus has to forgive me? Please read or listen to Galatians 1.

COMMENTS

Throughout Galatians, I will refer to three of my personal Bible reading journals, one written in 1999, another in 2008, and one from 2012. I have journaled my daily Bible reading for over thirty-five years and have read the Book of Galatians nearly twenty times in those thirty-five years. Let's get started with the Book of Galatians.

In 1999, I wrote, "Paul defends his credentials in the opening sentence, *'not sent from men nor through man, but through Jesus Christ'* (v. 1 NASB). He also gives God glory in his greeting. He then gets right to the point, why are you Galatians turning away from the gospel so soon? There is one gospel, it is simple, but not easy. Man wants to complicate it with religion; Paul is trying to keep it pure."

I continued writing, "Paul clarifies the gospel he preached came directly through Jesus Christ, not man. That is why he knew it to be absolute truth. After Paul was converted, he went to the desert for three years, not to seminary or to Peter. Jesus formulated Paul's message. He then went to Jerusalem to meet Peter and James. Then he headed back out into the field."

As I look into these journals, which I do not do very often, I find some very interesting personal anecdotes that were going on in my life. I will share some from 1999. My oldest son, Jason, was a pretty good baseball player. He got a scholarship to Texas Tech University, and he was in his senior year, the final days of his college career.

His college career ended just a few days before and the Major League Baseball draft was going on. In my journal, I wrote, "Major League Baseball draft yesterday. Twenty-two rounds. The catcher from the Texas Tech Red Raiders was drafted by the Rockies in the third round. Another player from Tech was drafted, fifteenth round to Arizona. Three other Tech players were taken. Jason Huth waits out today. I pray for good news." We will pick up that story with chapter 2.

In 2008, when reading Galatians 1, I personalized it a little more, "Paul, not sent from men, but through Jesus Christ and God the Father. Do I believe that about myself in the Ezra Project and in the Gideons? If so, I better take it way more seriously." I wrote on, "If anyone preaches a gospel contrary to the true gospel, he is to be accursed, according to verses 8 and 9. There is a lot of false gospel being preached and believed today. It should be accursed. God set apart Paul *from my mothers' womb*' (v. 15 NASB). Do I feel that way about my calling? Again, if so, I need to take it way more seriously."

> Much of Christianity today is deserting a biblical gospel for a different gospel.

In 2012, I wrote, "Probably the earliest New Testament writing, Galatians, before 50 A.D. within 15-20 years of the death and resurrection of Jesus. Paul identifies himself as an apostle, which means one who was sent, not from man, but through Jesus Christ and God the Father. Those are his credentials. Jesus Christ *'gave himself for our sins to deliver us from the present evil age'* (v. 4). Paul is *'astonished'* (v. 4) the Galatians are so quickly deserting the one true gospel, not that there is another one. Much of Christianity today is deserting a biblical gospel for a different gospel. Go back to Paul, he says, *'let them be accursed'* (v. 9). The true gospel may not please men, but it is still the unchanging true gospel. We need to please God, rather than men, and stand for the one true gospel of Jesus Christ."

DIGGING DEEPER

As we kick off Galatians 1, it is pretty clear Paul is saying, *"I am astonished that you are so quickly deserting him who called you in the grace of Christ and are turning to a different gospel"* (v. 6). That is the general theme of this book. And, as Paul states, *"For I would have you know, brothers, that the gospel that was preached by me is not man's gospel. For I did not receive it from any man, nor was I taught it, but I received it through a revelation of Jesus Christ"* (vv. 11-12).

Those are two good themes to think about today. Where did you receive the news about Jesus Christ? Where did you receive your gospel? Is it man's view or is it a biblical view? We look forward to having Paul clarify the gospel of Jesus Christ in the Book of Galatians.

Prayer

Lord Jesus, teach us Your one true gospel as we go through the Book of Galatians. Help us not turn aside to any other gospel but the one true gospel of Jesus Christ. Teach us, Lord, through the Book of Galatians. In Your name, we pray. Amen.

MY THOUGHTS

GALATIANS 2

Crucified with Christ

Galatians 2 contains one of my favorite verses, see if you can find it. Paul claims to be crucified with Christ. What does that mean, and can you claim the same? Please read or listen to Galatians 2.

COMMENTS

That is a powerful chapter of scripture. Let's dissect it by looking at journal entries from 1999 (NASB), 2008 (NASB), and 2012.

In 1999, I wrote, "Paul visits Jerusalem and compares his gospel with the pillars, Peter, James, and John. *'(K)nowing that a man is not justified by the works of the Law but through faith in Christ Jesus'*" (v. 16). Then, referring to verse 20, I wrote for myself, *"'crucified with Christ; . . . it is no longer I who live, but Christ lives in me'* and *'I live by faith.'"*

Yes, there is that favorite verse of mine, Galatians 2:20, *"I have been crucified with Christ. It is no longer I who live, but Christ who lives in me. And the life I now live in the flesh I live by faith in the Son of God, who loved me and gave himself for me."*

Going back to that personal anecdote I referred to yesterday about the baseball draft, my entry today says, "I am the proud father of a professional baseball player! Jason Huth drafted yesterday by the Cincinnati Reds in the 26th round. Twenty-six, the number he wore on his uniform. He gets a chance to play. That's what he wanted. We're all so excited and happy for Jason. It was his highest draft of his three. He got drafted by San Francisco out of high school in the forty-second round. After junior college by Montreal, I think it was in the forties. He's headed for Florida Instructional League, then rookie ball in Billings, Montana."

Yeah, that was a pretty exciting day in the Huth family. You may wonder if you ever saw Jason Huth's name in a Major League box score. Well, no. He did play two years of Minor League ball before giving up his baseball career, getting married, and starting a family.

Back to the more spiritual aspects of today's devotion. In 2008, I wrote, "Paul got the gospel from Jesus, not from men. But he submitted his message to the apostles for confirmation that he was on the right course. We need to be careful our message, our gospel, is in line with true Christianity too. That is why I am under the authority of my pastor in the Ezra Project. Submit, yes; but back down on what Jesus has entrusted to us, no. Paul confronted Peter publicly for the sake of the gospel. That took assurance he had the gospel right."

I continued, "The question of that day was whether Christians had to become Jews first. Paul said no; Peter was not sure if salvation was only in Christ or also in keeping the law. We have such issues today and they need to be addressed and solved. For example, is Jesus the only way, or do many paths lead to salvation?

> Is Jesus the only way, or do many paths lead to salvation?

'(N)evertheless knowing that a man is not justified by the works of the law but through faith in Christ Jesus' (v. 16). And the verse I try to live by, Galatians 2:20." That was my entry in 2008.

DIGGING DEEPER

The question in chapter 2 is, what is the true gospel? I wish preachers today were concerned about the gospel they preach. Oh, how we need a true, consistent gospel message from our churches today.

What is the true gospel? According to Paul in Galatians 2, it is pretty clear. I close with two verses. Verse 16, *"yet we know that a person is not justified by works of the law but through faith in Jesus Christ"*. And once again, that great verse, verse 20, *"I have been crucified with Christ. It is no longer I who live, but Christ who lives in me. And the life I now live in the flesh I live by faith in the Son of God, who loved me and gave himself for me."*

Prayer

Father, thank You for the one, true gospel. We are not justified by works we do in this life. We are justified through faith in Jesus Christ and Christ alone. Thank You as we read Your Word, the gospel becomes very clear. Father, we thank You for Jesus, the author and finisher of our faith, in whose name we pray. Amen.

MY THOUGHTS

GALATIANS 3

Is Being Good, Good Enough?

Galatians 3 clarifies the gospel message. Paul makes the way to heaven clear. Do you think being a good person is what it takes to get into heaven? How good is good enough? Please read or listen to Galatians 3.

COMMENTS

The best way to go back through Galatians 3 is to look at the journal entries I used for those three years I selected. Beginning with 1999, I wrote, "Salvation comes by faith, not by works or obedience to the law. Judaizers were trying to make Gentiles Jews first, as a condition of salvation. Paul opposed it. Today it may be like becoming a religion, Baptist, Methodist, Catholic, before becoming a Christian. Paul argues against it. Faith, belief, is what it takes. The promise of faith and belief was to Abraham, not through the law. Paul is trying to point the Jews back to the promise God gave Abraham of Jesus, which was before the law. The law was to point us to Jesus. It did not need to enslave Gentile believers."

My notes in 2008 (NASB) clarify this more, "Salvation by works or by faith? *'Even so Abraham believed God and it was reckoned to him as righteousness'* (v. 6). He was before the law even existed." Quoting verse 14, *"in Christ Jesus the blessing of Abraham might come to the Gentiles, so that we would receive the promise of the Spirit through faith."* Continuing, "The law defines sin for us. It is neutral. It may condemn us by defining our behavior, but it cannot save us." Verse 22, *"But the Scripture* (the law) *has shut up everyone under sin, so that the promise by faith in Jesus Christ might be given to those who believe."*

In 2012, bringing even more clarity to this chapter, I wrote, "Paul challenges the Galatians in verse 2, *'Did you receive the Spirit by the works of the law, or by hearing with faith?'* Obviously by hearing, not by works. Then he jumps back past the Law of Moses, all the way back to Father Abraham. Abraham was justified by faith, not by works of the law. In Abraham, not Moses, all the nations will be blessed. If we choose to live under the Law of Moses, we have to keep the whole law or be cursed, according to verse 10. Christ became the curse for us through crucifixion so we can skip the law and be justified by faith. Freedom in Jesus."

I continued, "Salvation comes by faith, not by keeping the law. So why the law? It was a step between Abraham and Christ. It defines sin and provided a sacrificial system of temporary forgiveness. If the law could give life, there was no need for Jesus. Once Christ came, the intermediary step was no longer necessary. We don't have to go through Judaism to faith. We go directly through Jesus now."

Paul was making the argument in his day, they only needed Jesus for eternal life. These new-found Christians did not have to go back through the law, which no one in the past could keep anyway, and try to come up with some way to salvation.

DIGGING DEEPER

How does this apply to us today? For some in Christianity, we still combine salvation and works. What Paul was arguing here is salvation is in Christ alone, not in our works. When you ask people if they are going

> **For some in Christianity, we still combine salvation and works.**

to heaven, some say, "Yes" or "Maybe". When you ask them, "Why?" they say they are a good person, or they have never killed anybody, or they have "done good" in their life. If Paul was here, he would argue against that and say, "Being good is not good enough. Doing good works is not good enough. What we need is faith in Jesus Christ." That was the ticket then, that is the ticket to heaven today.

Prayer

Father, we thank You for the Word that clarifies our theology. We thank You for Your Word that clarifies how we gain eternal life, and it is through Jesus Christ and His sacrificial gift on the cross at Calvary. It is not by being good or good enough.

We thank You Lord, because none of us could live up to the letter of the law. Thank You for salvation in Christ and Christ alone, in whose name we pray. Amen.

MY THOUGHTS

GALATIANS 4

Adopted

Galatians 4 is about adoption, being grafted in, becoming joint heirs. Are you in the family of God? How does one get in, or is it automatic? Please read or listen to Galatians 4.

COMMENTS

Sometimes, it is hard to put ourselves into the context of what Paul writes. Let's see if we can simplify this passage by looking at some journal entries.

In 1999, I wrote, "We were slaves to sin. We couldn't free ourselves, then God acted. He sent a Redeemer, someone to buy us out of slavery and free us. He not only did that, He made us kin to the one who redeemed us. He made us family members, joint heirs with the Redeemer so we could inherit the Father's kingdom. Wow! What a story! From slaves to joint heirs. It's better than winning the lottery!"

Sometimes I get a little excited about what I read in the scriptures, but I continue in my journal, "Before you learn the gospel, you served false gods and worshiped in vain. Then I tell you the truth of the gospel, you get excited, you follow gladly. I leave, others come in, tickle your ears with the new message that takes you back to the false gods and vain worship, but you follow. Are you interested in truth or trendy philosophy? Fight for the truth."

I continued, "Paul validates the Old Testament by quoting from it. He cites Genesis and Isaiah, the law and the prophets. He argues we can be free or under bondage, our choice. I choose freedom in Jesus Christ." I hope that journal entry simplified chapter 4 a little bit.

But let's go on to 2012 and get a little bit different perspective. "An underage heir cannot receive his inheritance until he comes of age. Jews and Gentiles were 'underage', enslaved to elementary principles of the Mosaic Law or paganism until the fullness of time had come, and that's Jesus. Now we can inherit it all. Once we accept Jesus, why would we want to go back to the former religious principles?" That is referring to verse 9.

I went on to another thought as I continued to write. "Paul longs to be with the Galatians. He loves the church he planted and does not want them to stray away from the truth. Paul continues dismissing the need for the law by again, going back before the law to Abraham and his two sons. He uses Ishmael as an example of one born into slavery and Isaac as a miracle birth into freedom because Sarah was barren yet bore Isaac in her old age. The Gentiles have a miracle chance to be grafted into the family of God through Jesus. They do not need to be slaves first and go back under the law to be free in Jesus."

DIGGING DEEPER

Let's summarize the principles of chapter 4 by quoting a couple of verses. We start with verses 4-7, *"But when the fullness of time had come, God sent forth his Son, born of woman, born under the law, to redeem those who were under the law, so that we might receive adoption as sons. And because you are sons, God has sent the Spirit of his Son into our hearts, crying, 'Abba! Father!' So you are no longer a slave, but a son, and if a son, then an heir through God."* What a promise from the Word of God today.

The Galatians heard that good news. We have heard that good news. But then Paul follows up with a question in verse 9, *"But now that you have come to know God, or rather to be known by God, how can you turn back again to the weak and worthless elementary principles of the world?"* What a question for us today. Once we know God, why would we turn back to the elementary principles of the world?

We have been offered the greatest gift, to be adopted in the family of God as sons, as joint heirs. If you have never received that, receive it today. Receive that gift from Jesus. And for those of us who have, let's not turn back to the elementary principles of the

> Once we know God, why would we turn back to the elementary principles of the world?

world when we have the greatest gift of all, an inheritance with Jesus, our Savior, and Redeemer.

Prayer

God, keep us focused. Keep us focused on the right things. Keep us focused on the wonderful gift of salvation, an inheritance in Christ we have in Jesus. Help us forget the elementary principles, the things of this world, that so easily ensnare us. Keep us focused on You. In Jesus' name, we pray. Amen.

MY THOUGHTS

GALATIANS 5

Walk by the Spirit, Not by the Flesh

Galatians 5 ends with the fruit of the Spirit. Can you name the fruit of the Spirit? How do people see you walking in the fruit of the Spirit in your life? Please read or listen to Galatians 5.

COMMENTS

In 1999, when reading Galatians 5 (NASB), I wrote in my Bible reading journal, "Faith, not religious systems, saves the soul. The law, though perfect, cannot save because we cannot keep it. If we fail at any part of it, we are lost and need a Savior. Jesus made entry into heaven easier. Forgiveness is easier than perfection."

Referring to verse 7, I wrote, "'*You ran well; who hindered you from obeying the truth?*' That's what Paul is asking. Many start out their Christian lives well, but they fade quickly. It's easier to believe in a lie than the truth. Verse 17 says, '*For the flesh sets its desire against the Spirit, and the Spirit against the flesh; for these are in opposition to one another.*' Yet Paul says, live and walk in the Spirit. I suppose it's a choice. Obey the flesh or the Spirit every day." That was my journal entry in 1999.

In 2012, I wrote, "Once one has accepted the free gift of forgiveness through Jesus Christ, there is no need, no advantage, to try to gain salvation through good works. Good works should be a result of salvation in Christ, but it is not a means to salvation. Paul twice says, *'faith working through love'* (v. 6) and *'through love serve one another'* (v. 13). Love is the reason for good works, not justification."

I continued, "Walk by the Spirit, not by the law. Walking by the Spirit of God, the Holy Spirit helps prevent fulfilling the desires of the flesh. The desires of the flesh and the desires of the Spirit are opposites. We cannot go both ways, but it's a constant battle. We are to set aside the desires of the flesh and express the fruit of the Spirit." Like in Galatians 2:20

> Once one has accepted the free gift of forgiveness through Jesus Christ, there is no need, no advantage, to try to gain salvation through good works.

we read earlier, we are to crucify *"the flesh with its passions and desires"* (v. 24) and according to verse 25, walk by the Spirit and *"live by the Spirit"*.

That is easier said than done, isn't it?

DIGGING DEEPER

How is your walk? Are you walking according to verse 1, in the freedom of Christ because Christ has set us free? Or are you still walking with the yoke of slavery to sin and to the flesh? We all experience the battle going on in us between the flesh and the Spirit, as summarized in verse 17, *"For the desires of the flesh are against the Spirit, and the desires of the Spirit are against the flesh, for these are opposed to each other"*. It is a wrestling match between our flesh and between our Spirit. Yet we see the fruit of the flesh, and it is not very good, while we desire the fruit of the Spirit which would make our lives so much easier and so much more gratifying.

What do we do? We take Paul's advice. In verse 16, he says, *"But I say, walk by the Spirit, and you will not gratify the desires of the flesh."* Again, Paul says in verse 25 (NASB), *"If we live by the Spirit, let us also walk by the Spirit."* Go back to verse 1 where he says, *"stand firm therefore, and do not submit again to a yoke of slavery."* Paul continues his advice to us in verse 13, *"For you were called to freedom, brothers. Only do not use your freedom as an opportunity for the flesh, but through love serve one another."*

What Paul is saying is, fight off the desires of the flesh and walk in the Spirit of God. Can we do it? It is not easy, but Paul reminds us in verse 24, *"And those who belong to Christ Jesus have crucified the flesh with its passions and desires."* As Christians, let's live by the Spirit, let's walk by the Spirit, let's enjoy the fruit of the Spirit which is *"love, joy, peace, patience, kindness, goodness, faithfulness, gentleness, self-control; against such things there is no law"* (vv. 22-23).

Prayer

Jesus, thank You for crucifying my flesh. Thanks for crucifying the passions and the desires of my flesh and filling me with the Holy Spirit when I came to saving faith in You. Now Lord, help me continue to walk by the Spirit, to live by the Spirit, so I can ward off the desires of the flesh and enjoy the fruit of the Spirit.

Lord, I know it is not easy, but with Your help, I can be victorious, and I will give You the praise and the glory. In Jesus' name, amen.

MY THOUGHTS

GALATIANS 6

Restoration

Today, we wrap-up Galatians with chapter 6. Throughout Galatians, Paul raised and addressed concerns about the church in Galatia. His goal was to keep them on the right track and restore their faith in the one true gospel. Have you wandered off the path? How can the Book of Galatians bring you back? Please read or listen to Galatians 6.

COMMENTS

This concludes the Book of Galatians. Let's finish up with a couple journal entries, starting in 1999, "Help one another in the walk of faith. Also, worry about myself, my own work. Don't compare myself with others. Do what God has asked me to do. What I sow, I will reap. Don't grow weary, don't lose heart, keep helping. Do good to all, especially those of faith." I think what this means is what this verse says, *"Bear one another's burdens"* (v. 2). Help each other out.

We need to understand what this chapter begins with. Verse 1 says, *"Brothers if anyone is caught in any transgression, you who are spiritual should restore him in a spirit of gentleness."* Why? Because we also are tempted from time to time and we may need to be restored by somebody else.

We hear of people who fall in sexual sin, sexual temptation, and it is easy to point the finger at them. In my early Christian days, I was pretty good at pointing the finger at those who failed spiritually. But as I grew in my faith, I began to understand I am so close to falling myself. I am far less critical today when I hear of Christians who fail or who fall to some moral sin.

> **We owe it to each other to be less critical, less judgmental, and more willing to restore someone with a spirit of gentleness.**

Let's look at the encouragement from Paul here in these first few verses. *"Brothers, if anyone is caught in any transgression, you who are spiritual should restore him in a spirit of gentleness. Keep watch on yourself, lest you too be tempted"* (vv. 2-3). We owe it to each other to be less critical, less judgmental, and more willing to restore someone with a spirit of gentleness. We are to bear one another's burdens.

That means we pray for one another. We help one another in times of need. Aren't you glad you are in the body of Christ when you have a great need? When I got prostate cancer several years ago, I had some brothers saddle up to me, pray for me, stay in touch with me, and it meant so much to me as they helped me bear my burden.

On to verses 7 and 8, key verses in the scripture, *"Do not be deceived: God is not mocked, for whatever one sows, that will he also reap. For the one who sows to his own flesh will from the flesh reap corruption, but the one who sows to the Spirit will from the Spirit reap eternal life."*

In the last chapter, we read about the fruit of the flesh and the fruit of the Spirit. It is true, whatever we sow is what we are going to reap. Sow to the Spirit and not to the flesh. Sometimes when we sow, we do not see the harvest immediately. But the next verse encourages us. *"And let us not grow weary of doing good, for in due season we will reap, if we do not give up"* (v. 9).

There are times in my own life when I have prayed and prayed and prayed for certain things; but I have not yet seen the fruit. I have not seen or reaped the harvest yet. But I am not going to give up, because this verse tells me in due season, if I don't give up, I will reap.

DIGGING DEEPER

What have we learned from the Book of Galatians? Paul made a strong argument that Christians, the new Christians of that day, and even we, are saved by faith and faith alone in Jesus Christ. It is not by works, it is not by being circumcised, or becoming a Jew before we become a Christian. It is not by following the Law. It is by faith in Christ alone.

In Galatians, we find the true gospel of Jesus Christ. Paul concludes, *"For neither circumcision counts for anything, nor uncircumcision, but a new creation"* (v. 15). It is not that we are Jewish or Gentile, it is that we are a new creature, thanks to Jesus.

Galatians is a book about freedom in Christ, as we go back to chapter 5 verse 1, *"For freedom Christ has set us free; stand firm therefore, and do not submit again to a yoke of slavery."* Because of Jesus, we can be free. Let's not be yoked by the slavery of sin in our lives anymore.

Prayer

Thank you, Jesus, for the Book of Galatians that reminds us there is one true gospel and it is You, Jesus Christ. Because of that, we can be free from the yoke of slavery of sin. We have the power to fight off the desires of the flesh and live and walk by the Spirit. Thank You for the lessons learned. Help me walk by the Spirit and not by my flesh. In Jesus' name, we pray. Amen.

MY THOUGHTS

SIX DAYS IN EPHESIANS

EPHESIANS 1

In Him

Today, we begin the Book of Ephesians. Ephesians is one of the epistles in the New Testament. We will look at my English Standard Version Study Bible book introduction to help us understand more about Ephesians.

The Apostle Paul visited the Asian port city of Ephesus and pastored the church there for about three years. Ephesus boasted of the temple of Artemis, one of the Seven Wonders of the ancient world and a grandiose theater where over 20,000 Ephesians chanted, "Great is Artemis of the Ephesians." That is the environment Paul was in.

About five years after his visit, Paul was imprisoned in Rome, around 62 A.D. From there, he wrote back to the Ephesians. There was no specific occasion or problem that inspired the letter.

The two main themes of the Book of Ephesians are: 1) Christ has reconciled all creation to Himself and to God; 2) Christ has united people from all nations to Himself and to one another in His church. These two things happen by faith alone through His grace.

Paul also encourages the Ephesians, and us, to attribute gratitude to our Lord Jesus Christ. We will find some of the greatest doctrines of our faith in Ephesians: grace, eternal election, and redemption by the blood of Christ.

The Book of Ephesians is also about God's gifts to the church: apostles, prophets, evangelists, pastors, and teachers, all gifts to mature the body of Christ. We will also hear the most complete explanation that salvation is by grace alone, through faith alone, through Christ alone. Also, we see a complete description of the armor of

God needed by every believer to do battle against Satan. We will learn about Jesus as the head of the church. We will hear the term "in Christ" ten times in this letter, a favorite expression of the Apostle Paul. Ephesians is six chapters; we will take them one per day. Please read or listen to Ephesians 1.

COMMENTS

To help us through the Book of Ephesians, I selected three of my personal Bible reading journals. One from 1992, when I read the New Testament, one from 2002, when I was reading a book a month, and one from 2012, when I read twenty books that year, including Ephesians. So, twenty years apart, three different decades.

From the journal in 1992, after reading Ephesians 1 (NASB), I wrote, *"be holy and blameless before him"* (v. 4). I went on to write, "He lavishes His grace upon us, according to verse 8, *'that the God of our Lord Jesus Christ, the Father of glory, may give to you a spirit of wisdom and of revelation in the knowledge of Him'"* (v. 17). I finished with, "Your heart may be enlightened, referring to v. 18."

Before I look into my journal in 2002, 2002 was a very special year in my life. It was the year we started the Ezra Project. When I looked for journals concerning Ephesians, I found this one in 2002, and my reading of Ephesians happened to coincide exactly with the first week I started the Ezra Project, after leaving a position in the consulting world.

In 2002, I read Ephesians three times in the month of April. Yes, friends, sometimes it is good to stay in a book for a long time and let that book go through you as you go through the book over and over. That is what it was like for me in 2002, as I was reading Ephesians.

Here is how I started my journal entry on April 1, 2002, "The first day of the rest of my life! Today I begin a dream, a passion, to work on the Ezra Project full-time. What a way to begin, the day after Easter. Praise God for this marvelous opportunity."

On the first day of the Ezra Project, I read the whole Book of Ephesians, and wrote as a summary, "In Him, you were far off but brought near. A book about the church. Very appropriate after Ezra and Nehemiah laid the foundation for the Ezra Project, now I read about the audience. Thank You, Lord, for guiding my schedule of reading in 2002."

In February, I read the Book of Ezra. In March, I read the Book of Nehemiah. That is what I was referring to as I was leading up to April 1st, now in Ephesians. I look forward to sharing more stories about the beginning of the Ezra Project as we go through the Book of Ephesians, but let's look at 2012.

In 2012, I read Ephesians 1 on two different days, so I split it up. I read fourteen verses on the first day and verses 15-23 on the second day. Sometimes it is good to slow down the pace of your Bible reading and take it a bit slower. I wrote about the first fourteen verses, "What or who am I by the will of God?", referring to verse 1. "We have access to *every spiritual blessing in the heavenly places*' (v. 3). We are to *'be holy and blameless before him'*" (v. 4).

Next, I referred to verse 7, *"In Him',* Jesus alone, we have redemption through His blood or through His death on the cross. We also have forgiveness through that very same act." I went on to write, "When one hears the word of truth and believes, he is sealed by the Holy Spirit who guarantees our inheritance, eternal life, until we acquire it upon death."

> **Jesus is above every rule and authority, above every name that is named. He is head of over all things, including His church.**

On the second day, I finished chapter 1 starting with verse 15, "What does Paul pray for those in Ephesus? The spirit of wisdom and knowledge of the Father, enlightened hearts, to know the hope He has for each one of us, an inheritance and the greatness of His power." I continued, "Jesus was raised from the dead, is seated at the right hand of the Father, according to verse 20. Jesus is above every rule and authority, above every name that is named. He is head of over all things, including His church."

DIGGING DEEPER

What do we have in Christ? Verse 3, *"every spiritual blessing in the heavenly places"*. Secondly, He has chosen us *"in him before the foundation of the world, that we should be holy and blameless before him"* (v. 4). In Him, we have been predestined for adoption as sons through Jesus Christ, *"according to the purpose of his will"* (v. 5). And, *"In him we have redemption through his blood, the forgiveness of our trespasses, according to the riches of his grace"* (v. 7). In Him, we have *"all wisdom and insight making known to us the mystery of his will"* (vv. 8-9), and *"In him we have obtained an inheritance"* (v. 11). And, in Him, after we heard the word of truth and accepted it, we are sealed with the promise of the Holy Spirit who guarantees our inheritance, eternal life, referring to verses 13 and 14.

We praise the Lord according to verses 18-20:

> *having the eyes of your hearts enlightened, that you may know what is the hope to which he has called you, what are the riches of his glorious inheritance in the saints, and what is the immeasurable greatness of his power toward us who believe, according to the working of his great might that he worked in Christ when he raised him from the dead and seated him at his right hand in the heavenly places.*

In Him, we have it all. In Him, we have everything we need. In Him, we can live a spiritual life on earth.

Prayer

Hallelujah, Lord Jesus! Thank You for every blessing we just read about in Ephesians 1. Thank You that in You, we have been saved from an eternal death and given an inheritance of eternal life. Our prayer is one of thankfulness, a grateful heart, for Your powerful redemptive work on the cross. To God be the glory. Great things You have done. Amen.

MY THOUGHTS

EPHESIANS 2

Not by Works

In Ephesians 2, there is a great passage in scripture, one of the most famous passages in all the Bible. Look for it in Ephesians 2. Are we saved by what we do or by what we believe? Please read or listen to Ephesians 2.

COMMENTS

Did you catch the power verse in Ephesians 2? Let's see if the journals reveal it to us. In 1992, I wrote, "We are dead in our trespasses and sins, all of us, according to verse 1. But God gives us life in Christ, according to verses 4 and 5. So it is by His actions (grace), not our own works, we attain salvation. It is a gift from God we receive, not earn," referring to verses 8 and 9.

I went on to write, "Having no hope without God, referring to verse 12", and *"have been brought near by the blood of Christ'* (v. 13 NASB). He also eliminated the division between Jews and Gentiles with salvation for all men."

In 2002, remember, I was transitioning from a consulting practice into full time in the Ezra Project. It does not always go easy. There is a reference to that in my journal entry. "My former boss and owner is still under my skin over ownership share payoff. He decided to pay me over five years! Unbelievable! And it is contingent upon me abiding by my 1997 employee nine-page contract. Unbelievable. Thankfully, we can take these things to the Lord." I made a note about my prayer that day, "A better attitude. To put the consulting business behind me. You deal with him as David prayed against his enemies. To move on to success in the Ezra Project."

Then I read Ephesians 2 (NKJV) and wrote in that journal, "We *'were dead in (the) trespasses and sins'* (v. 1). We all once conducted ourselves in the lusts of our flesh, *'by nature children of wrath',* referring to verses 1-3. I continued, *"'But God'* (v. 4). Hallelujah! *'(M)ade us alive together with Christ'* (v. 5). Raised us up together and made us sit together in the heavenly places in Christ Jesus. *'For by grace you have been saved through faith'* (v. 8). *'But now in Christ Jesus you who once were far off have been brought near by the blood of Christ'* (v. 13). Praise God!"

Yes, that power verse has been referred to in both my journal entries in 1992 and 2002. Let's see if we find it again in 2012.

In 2012, I split chapter 2 into the first ten verses on the first day, and verses 11-22 on the second day. Concerning the first ten verses, "We are all dead in sin, following Satan, carrying out the desire of our body, passion of our flesh, and we are *'by nature children of wrath'* referring to vv. 1-3. This is human nature. Born in sin. We are not good and learn evil. We are evil, sinful, and must be taught good. Raising children illustrates this. I never had to teach my kids to be mean, selfish, or to lie. It all came naturally. *'But God', 'But God, being rich in mercy'* (v. 4) and love offers grace to make *'us alive together with Christ—by grace you have been saved—'* (v. 5). Saved from what? From being dead in our sin. From God's wrath. Grace is a gift from God to sinners. We cannot work out our salvation. It is not a result of works. We are dead in sin. God offers us mercy, love, and grace. We accept it by faith and gain eternal salvation through Jesus Christ. Praise God!"

> **This is human nature. Born in sin. We are not good and learn evil. We are evil, sinful, and must be taught good.**

Thus ends my journal entries, so let's find that power verse. We are going to lead up to it as we look at chapter 2.

Oftentimes we hear the question, "Is man basically good or basically evil?" The first few verses of Ephesians 2 answer that question very clearly. *"And you were dead in the trespasses and sins in which you once walked, following the course of this world, following the prince of the power of the air, the spirit that is now at work in the sons of disobedience— among whom we all once lived in the passions of our flesh, carrying out the desires of the body and the mind, and were by nature children of wrath, like the rest of mankind"* (v. 1-3).

Are we basically good or basically evil? We are *"by nature children of wrath"* (v. 3), *"sons of disobedience"* (v. 2), *"following the prince of the power of the air"* (v. 2), the devil himself. We are born with a sin nature. But that is not the end of the story. Praise God for the "buts" in scripture. Verses 4-6, *"But God,"* *"But God, being rich in mercy, because of the great love with which he loved us, even when we were dead in our trespasses, made us alive together with Christ—by grace you have been saved—and raised us up with him and seated us with him in the heavenly places in Christ Jesus".* Shout the Hallelujah! Because of God's rich mercy, His great love, His saving grace, we can be snatched out of our trespasses and our sins and seated in the heavenly places.

How does this happen? Here are the power verses of Ephesians. Verses 8 and 9, *"For by grace you have been saved through faith. And this is not your own doing; it is the gift of God, not a result of works, so that no one may boast."* We can only be saved by the grace of God. No other way. There is no way for us to be good enough.

DIGGING DEEPER

If you are asked why God should let you into heaven, would you say, "I have been a good person"? That is not what Ephesians chapters 1-3 say. We are hopeless, destined for an eternity in hell, as sons of disobedience and children of wrath. But God, but God, by His grace, not your own doing, opens heaven to us as a gift.

Have you ever received that gift, that gift of grace? If so, verse 13 gives us our assurance, *"But now in Christ Jesus you who once were far off have been brought near by the blood of Christ."* But it is conditional, *"in Christ Jesus".* It is for those of us who have accepted the gift of God, the forgiveness of sins by His grace.

If you have never done it, do it today. Find a Bible. Reread Ephesians 2:8-9, and receive the gift of God's grace, the forgiveness of your sins. Let's pray.

Prayer

Father, we thank You for Paul who makes it very clear we are sons of disobedience, we are children of wrath, we are hopeless without You. But we also thank You he articulates the plan of salvation very clearly in Ephesians 2. It is by Your mercy, Your great love, Your saving grace we can join You in the heavenly places. It is by grace we have been saved through faith in our Lord Jesus Christ. Thank You for the assurance of eternal life from verses like these.

And for those who have never received that gift, Lord Jesus, open their hearts today. Let them repent of their sins. Let them call on that great love, that great mercy, and Your saving grace. And assure them, Lord, it is not about their goodness or their badness. It is about You and Your gift to us, eternal salvation through the blood of Jesus Christ. To that, we can shout the hallelujah and the amen.

MY THOUGHTS

EPHESIANS 3

Revealing the Mystery of the Ages

Today brings us to Ephesians 3. Do you know the mystery of the ages? Please read or listen to Ephesians 3.

COMMENTS

Let's take a look at my journals on Ephesians 3. In 1992, I was thirty-seven years old. I read Ephesians 3 and wrote, "Strengthen my inner man. Ground me in Your love. Fill me with the fullness of God."

In 2002, at forty-seven years old, the year I started the Ezra Project—in fact, the very month I started the Ezra Project—I read Ephesians 3 (NKJV), and wrote, "Mystery, that Gentiles, non-Jews, would become fellow heirs, partakers of the promise of Christ through the gospel." Next, I quoted verse 12, *"in whom we have boldness and access with confidence through faith in Him."* Then referring to verse 20, "He *'is able to do exceedingly abundantly above all that we (can) ask or think'"*.

And I wrote a prayer concerning the Ezra Project, "Bless the Lord. Guide and direct me this day in the Ezra Project: Secretary of State filing, office furniture, funding, and help with the PowerPoint presentation." You can see I am bathing this ministry in prayer and seeking God's help in every way.

I mentioned earlier, I read Ephesians more than once in the month of April. Let's flip to another day when I read Ephesians 3, so we can relate more to growing the Ezra Project from its very beginning. On April 14, fourteen days after the start of the Ezra Project on April 1st, I read Ephesians 3 and wrote, "For what reason? To reveal the mystery that Gentiles should be fellow heirs with Jews. Paul understood his purpose and he fulfilled it. Acts 9:15 defines Paul's purpose, *'Go, for he is a chosen vessel of Mine to bear My name before Gentiles, and kings, and the children of Israel.'* He spent the remainder of his life doing so. I hope now, I am a chosen vessel of His to go and proclaim the power of His Word to His children."

Referring to my prayer, "You have given people assignments in life. I believe You have given me mine: to be a man of Your Word. Being a Gideon for twenty-two years has been a fulfilling part of my assignment. Now the second part, the Ezra Project: Reconnecting God's people to God's Word. I accept my assignment. I am very excited about it and look forward to watching You work in it, like You have in my life in The Gideons." Continuing my prayer, "Funding is confusing now. I thought 'so-and-so' was going to be there for me in a significant way. This week he said funds would come through the church and they are struggling to pay their bills. It will be interesting to watch You work in this, Lord."

Now let's look at 2012, when I was fifty-seven years old. I look at my journal date, and it is actually our thirty-seventh wedding anniversary. On that day, I was reading Ephesians 3 and wrote, "God called Paul *'to preach to the Gentiles'* (v. 8). He is part of revealing the mystery of Christ which was not revealed to previous generations and that is, *'Gentiles are fellow heirs . . . partakers of the promise in Christ Jesus through the Gospel'* (v. 6). Paul gets *'to preach to the Gentiles the unsearchable riches of Christ'* (v. 8). Paul's prayer, *'be strengthened with power through his Spirit in your inner being, so that Christ may dwell in your hearts through faith— (be) rooted and grounded in love, . . . to comprehend . . . the fullness of God'* (vv. 16-19). Reminder, God *'is able to do far more abundantly than all that we ask or think'"* (v. 20).

Let's take a look at Ephesians 3. In verse 3, Paul reminds the Ephesians he did not receive the revelation of the mystery of Christ from the other apostles; he got it directly from Christ in a revelation. In verse 6, He describes that mystery, *"This mystery is that the Gentiles are fellow heirs, members of the same body, and partakers of the promise in Christ Jesus through the gospel."*

I am not Jewish. You probably aren't, either. So aren't you glad this mystery was revealed and we were grafted in with the Jews to have a chance at eternal life? In verses 7-9, Paul declares his role in revealing this mystery, *"Of this gospel I was made a minister according to the gift of God's grace, which was given me by the working of his power. To me, though I am the very least of all the saints, this grace was given, to preach to the Gentiles the unsearchable riches of Christ, and to bring to light for everyone what is the plan of the mystery hidden for ages".*

Paul reminds himself and those in Ephesus, he once persecuted the church, so he is the least of those who should be bringing the good news to the Gentiles. In the later verses of chapter 3, Paul prays for the Ephesians:

For this reason I bow my knees before the Father, from whom every family in heaven and on earth is named, that according to the riches of his glory he may grant you to be strengthened with power through his Spirit in your inner being, so that Christ may dwell in your hearts through faith—that you, being rooted and grounded in love, may have strength to comprehend with all the saints what is the breadth and length and height and depth, and to know the love of Christ that surpasses knowledge, that you may be filled with all the fullness of God (vv. 14-19).

What a prayer! Are you *"strengthened with power through his Spirit"* (v. 16)? Does Christ dwell in your heart? Are you *"rooted and grounded in love"* (v. 17)? Do you *"know the love of Christ"* (v. 19)? Are you *"filled with all the fullness of God"* (v. 19)?

DIGGING DEEPER

Chapter 3 closes with a couple of great, great verses; one I quote often, verse 20, *"Now to him who is able to do far more abundantly than we think or imagine,"* is the way I learned it, *"according to the power at work within us, to him be glory in the church and in Christ Jesus through all generations, forever and ever. Amen."* Yes, Jesus can do far more abundantly than we can think or imagine. Do you believe it? I quote that often because I have seen it in my own life. God has blessed me so often beyond what I can think or imagine. I hope you have had similar experiences. Let's pray in thanks.

> Jesus can do far more abundantly than we can think or imagine.

Prayer

Father, we thank You that You revealed the mystery of the ages to Paul. That mystery is we, as Gentiles, are included in the plan of salvation. Paul's revelation said it was from the very beginning. It was never for just the Jews. It was always for every person from every tongue and every tribe and every nation.

We thank You as participants in the gospel, we can be strengthened with power through Your Spirit, You can dwell in our hearts, we can be rooted and grounded in love, and we can be filled with the fullness of You. Thank You, thank You, thank You. And, as partakers in the gospel, we can be assured You can do far more abundantly than we can ask or think. Your power is at work in us. To God be the glory. Thank You, thank You, thank You. Amen.

MY THOUGHTS

EPHESIANS 4

Walk Worthy

In Ephesians 4, we are instructed to walk in a manner worthy of the calling to which we have been called. There are some pretty high standards in this chapter, like be angry and sin not, let no corrupt talk come out of your mouth, and be kind to one another. How is your walk? Please read or listen to Ephesians 4.

COMMENTS

Looking back in my journal in 1992, I wrote a few phrases related to this chapter. "1) Walk worthy of His calling; 2) One, one, one, one in Christ; 3) Growing up in Him; 4) Truth is in Jesus."

Ten years later, in 2002, this was the very week I started the Ezra Project. We started on April 1st. On the fifth day of the month, I wrote this in my journal, "Had a great day yesterday. Opened the bank account for the Ezra Project, then went to the Secretary of State and registered the name. Wrote the first check from the account to 'Secretary of State.' I have never done those things before, and it's putting flesh on an idea I've had for years. It's happening!"

Five days into the Ezra Project, I was pretty excited. Then I read Ephesians 4 (NKJV), and wrote, *"walk worthy of the calling with which you were called"* (v. 1). Then, "Grace was given to each one of us, referring to verse 7." And then, "I hope He has given to me to be a teacher *'for the equipping of the saints for the work of ministry'"* (v. 12).

I continued to write, "Causing *'growth of the body'* (v. 16)," and then *"put off. . . the old man"* (v. 22). Then, "Live verses 29 and 32." What are verses 29 and 32? *"Let no corrupting talk come out of your mouths, but only such as is good for building up, as fits the occasion, that it may give grace to those who hear."* Yes, I think I ought to live by that verse. And what is verse 32? *"Be kind to one another, tenderhearted, forgiving one another, as God in Christ forgave you."* And, yes, I think I ought to be kind to one another and be tenderhearted, forgiving, as God has forgiven me."

In 2002, I was reading a book a month, so I was reading Ephesians more than once in the month of April when I started the Ezra Project. Turning to the second record of when I read Ephesians in April 2002, which was on the 16th, I wrote, "Disappointed, but not dismayed. The guy I was depending on is putting in $1,500 a month for six months, a far cry from the tone of his earlier discussions. The Lord is teaching me not to depend on man, but solely on Him. A good place to be."

Concerning the first six verses of Ephesians 4 (NKJV), I wrote, "I have been beseeched. The Word of God often has the answers to specific life challenges, *'walk worthy of the calling with which you were called'* (v. 1), *'just as you were called in one hope of your calling'* (v. 4). I know I am called to do this. Thanks for the confirmation and assurance to move on because You are with me. Hallelujah!"

The next day, I finished Ephesians 4, and wrote in my journal, "Lifted up. God raised my spirits yesterday. I bought office furniture and visited a ministry that is support based. They are going to loan me training material to learn to do the same. Over and over in my mind and heart I said, 'I can do this!' Thank You, Jesus, for your peace and comfort yesterday, the day after I got word I was getting far less than I anticipated from what I thought would be a major funding source."

> **Jesus gifted people to equip saints for the work of ministry and building up the body of Christ. We are to grow up in Christianity.**

Next, I read Ephesians 4:4-16, "Grace was 'given' to each one of us. Thank You. I believe He has given me as a teacher *'for the equipping of the saints for the work of ministry'* (v. 12), to edify the body of Christ, speaking the truth in love, causing growth of the body." Of course, I am relating these readings to the beginning of the Ezra Project ministry.

The next day, I finished Ephesians 4 and wrote, "The truth is in Jesus." I continued, "Put off former conduct, deceitful lusts. Put on true righteousness, holiness. Renew spirit of your mind. Work so we can give to those in need. Be kind to one another, tenderhearted."

As I share my journal entries from that first month of the Ezra Project in 2002, you get a little inside information about how it is to start a ministry.

Ten years later in 2012, my journal entry indicates we were on a cruise, my favorite kind of vacation. It was the first day of the cruise and I was reading Ephesians 4, "Walk in a manner worthy of my calling, referring to verse 1. I have been called to be a man of His Word: Gideons and Ezra Project and my own personal life. Walk and act accordingly."

Then, "Unity. One body, one spirit, one hope, one Lord, one faith, one baptism in God the Father. No 'coexist' bumper sticker stuff here." Then I wrote, "Jesus gifted people to equip saints for the work of ministry and building up the body of Christ. We are to grow up in Christianity." I continued, "We are to put off the old self and put on a new self. Give no opportunity to the devil." I finished by writing, "I need to work on my mouth at all times and be kind and tenderhearted to one another." The prayer notes were, "To be tenderhearted, to be a blessing to others on this cruise."

DIGGING DEEPER

Let's summarize the key points of Ephesians 4. Starting with verse 1, *"walk in a manner worthy of the calling to which you have been called"*. I believe I have been called by God to do certain things. Do you? Do you know your calling?

Verse 22, *"put off your old self"*. Verses 23 and 24, *"be renewed in the spirit of your minds, and to put on the new self"*. Have you done it? Have you set your old self aside, renewed your mind in the things of God, and put on a new self?

How about the challenge of verse 26, *"Be angry and do not sin; do not let the sun go down on your anger".* And another challenge in verse 29, *"Let no corrupting talk come out of your mouths, but only such as is good for building up, as fits the occasion, that it may give grace to those who hear."* I wish I could say my life has been 100% true to that verse. You know different and I know different, but it is still something we can strive for.

And that last verse, *"Be kind to one another, tenderhearted, forgiving one another, as God in Christ forgave you."* Same thing. I wish I could say my whole life I was always kind to someone and tenderhearted. I know it is not true in my life, probably not true in yours, either. But these are standards in scripture we can strive for. And when we fail, we can forgive one another, as this verse says, because Christ has forgiven us when we fail. Chapter 4 has a lot of standards to live by. Let's pray it so, in our lives.

Prayer

Father, we thank You for the challenges of scripture. The challenges of how we are to live our lives on a regular basis. Lord, Your standards are high because You are holy and You ask us to be holy. These are aspects of a holy life.

Lord, help us walk in a manner worthy of Your calling. Help us put off our old selves, renew our minds, and put on a new self, more pleasing to You. Guard our mouths, Holy Spirit, so we can be uplifting instead of tearing down other people. And, Lord, even when it is uncomfortable, help us be kind to one another, tenderhearted to those around us. When we fail, Lord, thank You for Your forgiveness which reminds us to forgive others when they fail around us. Thank You for principles to live by. In Jesus' name, amen.

MY THOUGHTS

EPHESIANS 5

Marriage According to God

Ephesians 5 is about walking in love, and husbands and wives. Wives are to submit to their husbands, and husbands are to love their wives. If you are married, is this what you see in each other? Please read or listen to Ephesians 5.

COMMENTS

In 1992, at thirty-seven years old, after reading Ephesians 5, I had a lot to write about, *"be imitators of God'* (v. 1). *'(W)alk in love'* (v. 2). Be careful how we talk, referring to verses 4-6. Let our actions be done in the light, referring to verses 8-15. Because *'Christ will shine on you'* (v. 14). Make *'the most of your time'* (v. 16). Give thanks, referring verse 20."

Then I wrote, *"'husband is the head of the wife'* (v. 23). Husbands must act accordingly, and so must wives. Husbands need to lead, but wives need to learn to follow, not lead, referring to verse 23. Wives need to be subject to their husbands. Husbands need to love their wives as Christ loved the church. He sacrificed it all for them, men, referring to verses 24 and 25. Husbands love wives as if she was a part of your own body. Nourish and cherish her, referring to verses 28 and 29. Wives respect your husbands, referring to verse 33. With the list of how to treat a husband and wife, no wonder there are so many divorces and broken homes. Men are not willing to be men, and women aren't willing to be wives. But this formula would work. It's God's formula for marital success."

In 2002, in the first entry on Ephesians 5 (NKJV) in that first week of starting the Ezra Project, I wrote, *"'be imitators of God'* (v. 1). *'(W)alk in love'* (v. 2), *'have no fellowship with the unfruitful works of darkness, but rather expose them'* (v. 11), *'walk circumspectly, not as fools but as wise'* (v. 15), *'understand what the will of the Lord is'* (v. 17). Nourish and cherish Terry."

My second entry on Ephesians 5 was about twenty days after the beginning of the Ezra Project. I have another interesting note in my journal, "Terry went to a luncheon with two girlfriends yesterday. In her prayer time, one felt led of the Lord to have a fundraising dinner for the Ezra Project. She mentioned it at the luncheon, and another woman said her husband was a gourmet chef, a confirmation to her. The other then offered to host it. Another confirmation. The first friend also talked to her husband about it, and he said the Lord was telling him the same thing. Praise the Lord! And this is all going on and I had nothing to do with it. The Lord is expanding the Ezra Project without me."

Stepping aside from the journal for a moment, that was the first fundraiser the Ezra Project ever had. These ladies put that fundraiser together a couple months later, and that launched the Ezra Project.

Back to the day I was reading Ephesians 5 (NASB) in 2002, I split the chapter up in a couple of days, so the first day was the first fourteen verses. *"'(B)e imitators of God'* (v. 1). *'(W)alk in love'* (v. 2). No *'foolish talking'* (v. 4). *'Walk as children of light'* (v. 8), *'no fellowship with the . . . darkness'"* (v. 11).

The next day, I had another interesting journal entry concerning the Ezra Project. It was on a Saturday, "Moving into the Blair Foundation office today. Went to Fort Morgan and visited a couple of guys that I used to work with when I was a consultant. They said they would help with the Ezra Project. Praise the Lord! And Terry got a $75 check from another girlfriend. Every little bit helps right now."

On that day, I read Ephesians 5:15-21 (NASB) and wrote, "If I could live these verses, my trouble would be over! I redeem the time pretty well. I am a good organizer and time manager. Heck, I teach it. I try hard to understand what the will of the Lord is. I don't drink, and I hope I am filled with the Holy Spirit. Verse 19 is the challenge, *'speaking to one another in psalms and hymns and spiritual songs, singing and making melody in your heart to the Lord.'* This attitude would be great; to live life with a song in my heart, making melody throughout the day. Being joyful, happy, and contagious. Wow, wouldn't that be nice!"

Then I wrote, *"giving thanks always for all things to God the Father in the name of our Lord Jesus Christ'* (v. 20). I am pretty thankful, but *'all things'* (v. 20)? I can be more thankful." Then I wrote, *"'submitting to one another in the fear of the Lord'* (v. 21)? I can do a lot better at this too. Submitting to people. I'm not much on submission. So, in summary, I need to make melody and submit more."

The next day, I read Ephesians 5:22 through the end of the chapter and wrote, "Submission is difficult for many women partly because men have abrogated their role as spiritual leader in the home. Women would have a hard time submitting to a man who is not a father or a husband, but primarily

> This is a biblical model for marriage, not a cultural model in today's world. But I will take a biblical model over culture any day.

a breadwinner, consumed with his occupation, not his wife or his family." Then I referred to a part of my prayer that day, "To love my wife. Thank You for her." And, "Let no corrupt words come out of my mouth, but words of edification."

In 2012, at fifty-seven years old, I read Ephesians 5 on that cruise on the coast of Bermuda. I wrote, *"'walk in love'* (v. 2), and thanksgiving. *'Walk as children of light'* (v. 8), *'and try to discern what is pleasing to the Lord'* (v. 10). Expose the darkness, *'understand what the will of the Lord is'* (v. 17). Give thanks always. Submit to one another. Wives submit to their husbands. Husbands love your wives. Wives respect your husbands."

My prayer note that day was, "Thank You for a biblical marriage of thirty-seven years. For Terry, bless her. Bless me. Bless us together in You."

My journal entries summarized the important points of this chapter. I wrote in one of those journals, if the formula for marriage would follow Ephesians

5, there would be a lot less divorce. I realize this is a biblical model for marriage, not a cultural model in today's world. But I will take a biblical model over culture any day.

The balancing act of a marriage is clear in scripture. Wives submit to your own husbands. You notice, the scripture never tells a wife to love her husband. scripture tells a wife to submit to her husband, to respect her husband. I do not know why that is the case, but I think maybe it is because love comes naturally for a woman. Women love their husbands. They do not have to be told to do so. But, for us men, husbands are to love our wives. And the dimension of that love is defined in the scriptures, *"as Christ loved the church and gave himself up for her"* (v. 25). So, our love for our wives must be all-in.

If that dimension of love was not enough, Paul goes on to say, *"husbands should love their wives as their own bodies"* (v. 28). How many of us are in love with our own bodies? We are to love our wives as much as we love ourselves. Scripture goes on to say we are to nourish and cherish it, so we are to nourish and cherish our wives. Men, we are instructed to leave our fathers and mothers and hold fast to our wives and become one flesh.

The formula for a successful biblical marriage is right here in Ephesians 5. The question to all of us who are married is not do we know it, but can we do it? I spend time in God's Word to change how I live my life, not to just gain knowledge.

DIGGING DEEPER

How is your marriage? Is it based on these principles? If not, maybe you and your spouse can look these verses over and consider how you can change your marriage based on a biblical model.

I wrote in my journal, I was thankful Terry and I have a biblical model of marriage. At the time, we had been married for thirty-seven years. Today, as I write this, we celebrated our forty-third wedding anniversary yesterday. I think both of us would praise God for a biblical marriage. How about you?

If you are not married, or not married yet, when the time comes, consider building your marriage on a biblical base. Ephesians 5 is a great place to start.

Prayer

Father, thank You for reminding us how You constructed marriage. You modeled it after Your love for Your own church, Your bride. You remind us, as husbands, to love our wives, nourish our wives, cherish our wives. And You remind wives to submit to and respect their husbands. In the opening verses of this chapter, You remind us to *"be imitators of God"* (v. 1) and to *"walk in love"* (v. 2). If we do those two things, we will have great marriages.

Thanks for the reminders of how to live life according to biblical principles. In the name of Jesus, we pray. Amen.

MY THOUGHTS

EPHESIANS 6

The Whole Armor of God

We conclude the Book of Ephesians with chapter 6. Paul covers raising children and the armor of God. Are you dressed for battle? Please read or listen to Ephesians 6.

COMMENTS

In 1992, when reading Ephesians 6, I wrote in my personal Bible journal, "'*Children, obey your parents*' (v. 1). '*Fathers, do not provoke your children to anger*' (v. 4). But what if bringing them up in the discipline and instruction of the Lord, provokes them to anger? Like one of my sons saying, 'Quit jamming your religion down our throat.' Or, 'That's okay if you believe the Bible is right.' What's a father to do then?"

Then concerning verse 13, "*stand firm.*" And, "Spiritual armor: truth, righteousness, peace, faith, salvation, the Word of God, and pray at all times." My prayer after reading Ephesians 6 was fairly simple, "God help me work with You at home. I need Your peace and intelligence."

Ten years later in 2002, I was reading Ephesians (NKJV) more than once in the same month. The first entry I made on Ephesians 6 was, "*whatever good anyone does, he will receive the same from the Lord*' (v. 8). Be strong and stand."

A few days later, I read Ephesians 6 again, and I had one of the journal entries about the beginning of the Ezra Project, "Going to the Blair Foundation Ezra Project office for the first time today. Another exciting step." Earlier, I shared I bought office furniture I put in the office over the weekend. This was a Monday; the first time I went to the Ezra Project office.

As we close out Ephesians 6 today, and the Book of Ephesians altogether, I will leave the beginning of the Ezra Project, as well. I hope you enjoyed some of the insights of the very beginning of this ministry, the first week and the first month of the Ezra Project many years ago. We thank God for His blessing on the Ezra Project and sustaining this ministry since 2002.

In 2002, related to Ephesians 6, I wrote concerning the first nine verses, "Be obedient. Also, honor others. Please God by doing so and we will be pleasing to men and each other."

The next day, I finished Ephesians 6 with these words, "Christianity is proactive: be strong, put on, wrestle, take up, withstand, stand, girded, shod, taking, being watchful. If we do not actively participate, we are weak and subject to the attacks of the devil. No wonder Christianity is soft. We are not proactive." I wrote a prayer note after reading these verses, "For my weakness, strengthen me. For the armor to be real to me and to be used by me."

Ten years later, in 2012, after reading chapter 6 on a cruise, I wrote, "'*Children, obey your parents*' (v. 1). Honor your parents. Fathers, don't make your children mad, but bring them up in Christian faith." I continued, "We fight spiritual battles; therefore, we need to be strong in the Lord. Do all to withstand evil, then stand firm. Faith extinguishes all the flaming attacks of the evil one. The only offensive weapon is the Word of God." We were on a cruise in the Caribbean. I share those journal entries to remind us, even on vacation, spend time in the Word each and every day.

Thus ends my journal entries on Ephesians 6, so let's look at the chapter. I mentioned in one of the journals, the struggle as a father to bring up my children in the ways of the Lord. Sometimes I got resistance. Maybe you did too as a parent.

Verse 4 says, *"Fathers, do not provoke your children to anger, but bring them up in the discipline and instruction of the Lord."* As I brought them up in the discipline and instruction of the Lord, sometimes I think it made them angry. If you are a struggling parent today, I encourage you to follow the scriptural principles of raising your children, *"do not provoke your children to anger, but bring them up in the discipline and instruction of the Lord"* (v. 4) and let the Holy Spirit work it out in their hearts.

The next section in Ephesians 6 is about work. Verses 7 and 8 say, *"rendering service with a good will as to the Lord and not to man, knowing that whatever good anyone does, this he will receive back from the Lord".* I hope if you have a job, that is how you work. Render service to the Lord throughout the day, it is your testimony as a Christian. Let your light shine before men. I realize it is not always comfortable, but it is right to be a testimony of your Christianity before those you work with.

Lastly, we are encouraged as Christians to be strong, stand for the Lord. Ephesians 6 reminds us we are in a spiritual battle and therefore, we need spiritual armor. Verse 12, *"For we do not wrestle against flesh and blood, but against the rulers, against the authorities, against the cosmic powers over this present darkness, against the spiritual forces of evil in the heavenly places."* As Christians, we do not like to realize this, but Satan has dominion over the earth right now. This verse reminds us that is the battle we are in.

DIGGING DEEPER

In one of my journals, I said we need to be proactive Christians. One action item is to take up the whole armor of God. "Take up" means it is something we need to do. If we do not, we are not protected against the onslaught of the enemy. But if we take up the whole armor of God, *"you may be able to withstand in the evil day, and having done all, to stand firm"* (v. 13). That is the protection God offers us in the battleground of life.

With the armor God provides, we can stand firm. We *"can extinguish all the flaming darts of the evil one"* (v. 16). In the armor of God, we are to pray at all times in the spirit. The armor of God gives us: truth, righteousness, peace, faith, salvation, the Word of God, and prayer. By being proactive, by taking on our armor, we can withstand the fiery darts of the enemy. I encourage you to proactively put on the full armor of God. It is a gift, but one that will do us no good unless we receive it and use it. Praise God for the armor He gives us to live this life victoriously in Him.

Let's close our time in the Book of Ephesians by going back to my journal in 2002, the year I started the Ezra Project. After reading Ephesians a couple of times in the month of April, I wrote a summary, "What does Paul say? He tells us who we are in Christ, where we are without Him, where we are because of Him, and how to act as believers. What I get most is, I was dead, subject to the lusts of the flesh and wooings of the devil. But because of the redemptive work of Jesus, I am alive and can choose to follow the Holy Spirit and alter my conduct accordingly. What freedom! I can live with a song in my heart now, thanks to Jesus Christ."

> **He tells us who we are in Christ, where we are without Him, where we are because of Him, and how to act as believers.**

That was my summary of the Book of Ephesians in 2002. I pray you have been blessed by our time in the Book of Ephesians. Let's pray.

Prayer

Father, we thank You for this great book of scripture. We thank You for some of the great doctrines of faith we were reminded of in this book:

- We are saved by grace and grace alone and not by works.

- We have been redeemed by the blood of Jesus Christ and that alone.

- You have gifted the church to grow the saints with apostles, prophets, evangelists, pastors, and teachers.

We thank You for the reminder You are the head of the church. We thank You for this great description of the armor of God, Your gift to help us live life.

Finally, Lord, we thank You for reminding us over ten times we are *"in Christ"*, the best place to be to live this thing called life. We thank You for lessons learned in the Book of Ephesians. Holy Spirit, remind us to be doers of the Word and not hearers only. In Jesus' name, we pray. Amen.

MY THOUGHTS

FOUR DAYS IN PHILIPPIANS

Walking Worthy of the Gospel

Today, we begin one of my favorite New Testament books, the Book of Philippians. Let's look at my English Standard Version Study Bible book introduction to help us get familiar with this wonderful book.

Paul wrote this letter to the Roman colony of Philippi—most likely from prison in Rome—around 62 A.D. The church in Philippi was the first church he founded in Europe. The first convert there was Lydia. Paul and Silas were imprisoned for exorcising a demon from a fortune-telling slave girl, but God miraculously delivered them. Paul probably visited Philippi numerous times.

The theme of his letter is encouragement. He wanted the Philippians to live as citizens of a heavenly colony with a growing commitment to serve God and each other. He thanked them for their latest gift of support for his ministry. With Paul being in jail, they could have abandoned him, but they remained faithful.

Though the Philippians appeared to be a pretty healthy congregation, Paul encouraged them to keep growing in their faith, to press on. Spiritual progress takes effort, and he encourages them to work out their salvation with fear and trembling, knowing it is God who works in them, *"both to will and to work for his good pleasure"* (2:13).

Philippians is a joyful, almost exuberant, book. The words "joy" and "rejoice" appear over a dozen times in just four chapters. There are several familiar verses in this wonderful book of encouragement. We will discover them as we read a chapter a day.

Chapter 1 focuses on our manner of life. Are you growing in the Lord? Do you walk worthy of the gospel? Please read or listen to Philippians 1.

COMMENTS

To help us through the Book of Philippians, I selected three of my personal Bible daily reading journals. One from 1986, one of the very first journals I wrote when I was thirty-one years old; one from 1994, when I was thirty-nine; and one from 2012, when I was fifty-seven.

Let's begin with 1986 when I was using a New American Standard Bible (NASB) in my daily devotions. That year, I read Philippians 1 and cited various verses that touched my heart:

- Pray with joy, referring to verse 4.
- *For I am confident of this very thing, that He who began a good work in you will perfect it until the day of Christ Jesus* (v. 6).
- *I know that I will remain and continue with you all for your progress and joy of faith* (v. 25), answer to tempting thoughts that this isn't going to work out.

Eight years later, in 1994, still reading from the NASB, I read Philippians 1, and wrote, "A great chapter":

- *For I am confident of this very thing, that He who began a good work in you will perfect it until the day of Christ Jesus* (v. 6).
- *I long for you all with the affection of Christ Jesus* (v. 8).
- *My circumstances have turned out for the greater progress of the gospel* (v. 12).
- *In every way . . . Christ is proclaimed* (v. 18).
- Exalt Christ in that which I do, referring to v. 20.

In 2012, I actually split Philippians 1 into two days, so I read verses 1-11 on the first day, and wrote, "If Paul wrote this letter from prison in Rome, Timothy must have been there with him. Thank those who partner with me in ministry. Bring Your good work in me to completion. Grow love in me. Grow knowledge and understanding in me. Guide me to be pure and blameless. Let my light be filled with the fruit of righteousness."

The next day, I finished the chapter, verses 12-30, and wrote, "Regardless of Paul's circumstances, his testimony for Christ stood tall. People were talking about Jesus, good and bad, but either way, they were discussing Christ and Christianity and Paul rejoices. When we need help, we need the prayers of others and the Holy Spirit for our deliverance. referring to verse 19."

"(T)o live is Christ, and to die is gain" (v. 21). "Is that true for me? Through my cancer episode, I had to consider it and believe. I believed it."

I referred to verse 22, "As we live in the flesh, it needs to mean fruitful labor for the kingdom.

"'Let your manner of life be worthy of the gospel of Christ' (v. 27). O, let it be so for me, Lord."

I ended by summarizing verse 29, "Believe in God = suffering for God."

Those were my personal Bible reading journal entries from various times in my life reading Philippians 1. Let's take a brief look at this wonderful chapter.

DIGGING DEEPER

We will begin with one of these most quoted, familiar verses, *"And I am sure of this, that he who began a good work in you will bring it to completion at the day of Jesus Christ"* (v. 6). I referred to that verse in several of my journals. It reminds us that our faith walk is a work in progress. We must continue to grow in our faith. We must continue to allow the Lord to work in us and through us. Christianity is not a destination; it is a journey.

Paul gives us some examples of maturity and growth:

And it is my prayer that your love may abound more and more, with knowledge and all discernment, so that you may approve what is excellent, and so be pure and blameless for the day of Christ, filled with the fruit of righteousness that comes through Jesus Christ, to the glory and praise of God (vv. 9-11).

What steps are you taking to ensure your love for God and others is maturing? How do you develop your spiritual knowledge, discernment, and understanding? Make a list of how you believe you are more pure, more blameless, as you grow in Christ. Think of an example of the demonstration of the fruit of righteousness in you. The answers to these questions are concrete demonstrations of maturity as our faith grows in Jesus.

Paul encourages the Philippians and us to continue to grow in our walk with Jesus. Paul wrote:

Some indeed preach Christ from envy and rivalry, but others from good will. The latter do it out of love, knowing that I am put here for the defense of the gospel. The former proclaim Christ out of selfish ambition, not sincerely but thinking to afflict me in my imprisonment. What then? Only that in every way, whether in pretense or in truth, Christ is proclaimed, and in that I rejoice (vv. 15-18).

From prison, Paul keeps an encouraging, uplifting spirit. Even in tough circumstances, he rejoices that Christ is being proclaimed. How does your life proclaim Jesus to people? Some who see you may accept your Christian faith. Some may reject it. But as Paul says: *"What then? Only that in every way, whether in pretense or in truth, Christ is proclaimed"* (v. 18).

If you do not feel your life proclaims Jesus in the way you know would please Him, what steps can you take? I hope the list begins with prayer and Bible study.

Let's look at another famously quoted verse, *"For to me to live is Christ, and to die is gain"* (v. 21). Do you feel that way or do you cling to this life? Paul had an eternal perspective. Do you? Is your life Christ, as Paul proclaims, *"For to me to live is Christ"* (v. 2)? If you were arrested for being a Christian, would there be enough evidence to convict you?

> **If you were arrested for being a Christian, would there be enough evidence to convict you?**

Paul continues, *"Only let your manner of life be worthy of the gospel of Christ, so that whether I come and see you or am absent, I may hear of you that you are standing firm in one spirit, with one mind striving side by side for the faith of the gospel"* (v. 27). How would others describe your life? As a light shining for Christ? Or as a dim candle flickering in the wind? If asked to describe how your manner of life is worthy of the gospel of Christ, how would you describe it?

And what would be that manner of life? It is how you live, publicly, and privately. Are you *"standing firm in one spirit, with one mind"* (v. 27)? What does that mean? How are you standing firm in your faith? How are you standing firm as a testimony for Christ? How are you striving through the faith of the gospel? How does your life proclaim the gospel?

These are challenging concepts in Philippians 1 but remember the theme of this book is encouragement. I hope as we read these verses, you are encouraged to continue to grow in your walk in Jesus, so your light may shine before men. Let's pray.

Prayer

Father, thank You for the opening chapter of the Book of Philippians. We are reminded it is You who works in us and You will complete that good work in us.

We are also reminded to live in a manner worthy of the gospel so our lives reflect Your gospel. Some people seeing our lives will accept the gospel, and some will reject it. But either way, in pretense or in truth, Christ is proclaimed through our lives.

We pray You would see our manner of life worthy of the gospel. Thanks for Your words of encouragement in Philippians 1. We are all a work in progress. Continue to complete what You have started in each one of us. To God be the glory. In Jesus' name, we ask it. Amen.

MY THOUGHTS

PHILIPPIANS 2

God is at Work in You

In the second chapter of the Book of Philippians, Paul reminds us God is at work in each of us for His good pleasure. We are reminded to give up self and serve others as Jesus did. Are you still selfish, or are you serving others? Please read or listen to Philippians 2.

COMMENTS

In 1986, I read Philippians 2 (NASB), and wrote in my personal Bible reading journal:

- Terry and me: *"make my joy complete by being of the same, maintaining the same love, united in spirit, intent on one purpose"* (v. 2).
- *Do not merely look out for your own personal interests, but also for the interests of others* (v. 4).
- *For it is God who is at work in you, both to will and to work for His good pleasure* (v. 13).

And I wrote in big capital letters: "PTL!" (Praise the Lord.)

In 1994, I followed a similar pattern while reading Philippians 2 (NASB):

- I want us to be of the same mind, maintain the same love, be united in spirit, intent on one purpose, referring to verse 2, which has been a theme verse for my relationship with Terry since 1983.

- Excellent way to live. Look to others, not self, referring to verses 3 and 4.
- Have this attitude. Empty self. Humble self, referring to verses 5-11.
- Work out your salvation for God is at work in you, referring to verses 12 and 13.
- Don't grumble, referring to verse 14.
- Hold fast the word of life, referring to verse 16.
- Hold men like him in high regard, contrasting verses 2:21-3:11.

In 2012, I read Philippians 2 over two different days. On the first day I wrote:

- There is encouragement in Christ. Comfort from love, participation in the spirit, and affection and sympathy in one another referring to verses 1-11.
- Be humble. Count others as more significant than self. This is hard to do. Look after your own interests and then the interest of others. That's easier.
- Jesus was the form of God, deity. He is not a man or just a prophet. He is unique; equal with God, referring to verse 6.
- He took on the likeness of men. He didn't become human. He took on the likeness of men, but He was still the form of God, referring to verse 7.
- Jesus humbled Himself to the point of death. Judas nor Jews nor Pilate had any control or authority over Him, referring to verse 8.

Then I wrote, "What is the name above every name? Lord, Old Testament for Yahweh. Jesus Christ is Lord or Yahweh."

The next day, I finished Philippians 2:12-30, and wrote:

- Salvation is not an end, it's the beginning. Once saved, we are to continue to mature by working out our salvation with fear and trembling. And we are not alone or on our own. It is God who works in you. God, continue Your work in me, referring to verses 12 and 13.

- Be blameless, innocent, without blemish. Share as light, holding fast to the word of life. That is what working out salvation looks like, referring to verses 15 and 16.
- Paul wants fruit for his labor, his calling, as we all do, referring to verse 16.
- Timothy put Christ above his own interests, referring to verses 20-22.
- We should receive fellow workers for Christ with all joy, and honor such men, referring to verse 29.

DIGGING DEEPER

Philippians 2 is full of wonderful instructions as to how to live this Christian life:

So if there is any encouragement in Christ, any comfort from love, any participation in the Spirit, any affection and sympathy, complete my joy by being of the same mind, having the same love, being in full accord and of one mind. Do nothing from rivalry or conceit, but in humility count others more significant than yourselves (vv. 1-3).

As Christians, we should be comforted in the love of Christ, in the Spirit of God. And we should demonstrate that same love to others. As best we can, we should count others as more significant than ourselves. *"Let each of you look not only to his own interests, but also to the interests of others"* (v. 4). Certainly, we are all selfish. We care about our own interests. But we are also to set that aside and look to the interests of others, remembering the Word of God says, *"love your neighbor as yourself"* (Mark 12:31).

The next few verses give the example of how Jesus did this Himself. He, who was of God, came down from heaven and became like a human being, giving up His godliness to become like us, because He cared for our interests. Because He humbled

Himself, even to the point of death, God has highly exalted Him. And then we see one of these famous verses in the Book of Philippians, *"The name that is above every name, so that at the name of Jesus every knee should bow, in heaven and on earth and under the earth, and every tongue confess that Jesus Christ is Lord, to the glory of God the Father"* (vv. 10-11).

Yes, that means every knee will bow, every tongue confess. I have this crazy picture in my mind, when Jesus comes it is not going to be a 5'8" guy riding on a horse. He will encompass the whole sky. It will be as if you and I looked down on an anthill. That is how God will look at the earth. He could hold it in His hand. And when people see that, they will know they were wrong. They will know Jesus is Lord, and truly every knee will bow and every tongue will confess at that moment Jesus is Lord.

> **We are to do things without grumbling, without questioning. We are to be blameless, innocent children of God.**

In the meantime, we are to mature in our Christian faith. We are to work out *"our own salvation with fear and trembling, for it is God who works in you, both to will and to work for his good pleasure"* (v. 12). Praise the Lord He is at work in each one of us. And as He is, we are to work out our salvation. In other words, we are to continue to grow in our faith walk. We are to do things without grumbling, without questioning. We are to be blameless, innocent children of God. We are to shine as lights in the world, and we are to hold fast to the word of life. Holding fast to the word of life or staying connected to God's Word will help us work out our salvation and mature in our faith in Jesus.

All these principles are worth applying to our daily lives. I am not saying I am good at all of them. I am saying, we should strive to work on them and get better at each one. Let's pray.

Prayer

Father, thank You for Your love, thank You for Your Holy Spirit, thank You for completing my joy. Thank You for humbling Yourself, coming in human form, and dying on the cross so I might have salvation in You.

I look forward to the day when my knee will bow, my tongue will confess that You have been my Lord. Continue to do a work in me, Lord, to mature me to faith in You. Allow me the privilege to shine before men in a crooked and twisted generation.

And, Holy Spirit, help me hold fast to Your Word. Draw me into Your Word each and every day of my life. Continue to work out Your salvation in me. Continue to work in me, both to will and to work for Your good pleasure. For it is in Jesus' name we ask all these things. Amen.

MY THOUGHTS

PHILIPPIANS 3

Press On

I n Philippians 3, Paul enumerates his resume; he explains to the believers at Philippi why he is uniquely qualified to write them this letter. What is your spiritual resume? Paul counts it all loss to serve Jesus. Can you? He reminds us to press on in our growth as Christians. Are you still growing, or are you spiritually relaxing? Please read or listen to Philippians 3.

COMMENTS

In 1986, I read Philippians 3 (NASB), and wrote:
- I count all things to be loss in view of the surpassing value of knowing Christ Jesus my Lord, for whom I have suffered the loss of all things and count them but rubbish so that I may gain Christ, referring to verse 8.
- *Forgetting what lies behind and reaching forward to what lies ahead, I press on toward the goal for the prize of the upward call of God in Christ Jesus* (vv. 13-14).

In 1994, it appears I missed two days of Bible reading. Looks like I read Philippians 2 on a Friday and missed Saturday and Sunday and picked up Philippians 3 on Monday. I do go to a Gideon International prayer breakfast on Saturdays, so

I get Bible reading when I go there. And certainly, I get Bible reading in Sunday at church. However, if you are in the habit of skipping your Bible reading on weekends, a friend of mine once told me if you miss two days a week, you miss a hundred days a year in the Word of God. When he figured that out, he stopped skipping weekends.

On that Monday, I read Philippians 3, and wrote, "Put my confidence in Jesus, not in my flesh, not in who I am. I want to know Christ Jesus, my Lord, better. Help me forget what lies behind and reach forward to what lies ahead."

In 2012, I was far more mature in my Bible reading. I was on a cruise and still read the Word of God each day. I split this chapter into two different days, reading verses 1-11 on the first day and writing:

- We must be watchful for any who preach a different gospel, referring to verse 2.
- Christians worship by the Spirit of God, glory in Christ Jesus, and put no confidence in the flesh or works for their salvation, referring to verse 13.
- Our goal should be to know Christ Jesus, referring to verse 8.
- Our righteousness comes through faith in Christ, referring to verse 9.

The next day, I finished Philippians 3, reading verses 12-21:

- Christianity is active, a journey. We reach for our future in Christ, *"straining forward"*, referring to verse 13.
- *I press on toward the goal* (v. 14).
- Can I say to anyone, *"Join in imitating me"?* (v. 17).
- Follow good examples. Be careful. There are others who are enemies of the cross. Their *"minds set on earthly things"* (v. 19).
- *Our citizenship is in heaven . . . we await a Savior, the Lord Jesus Christ* (v. 20).

Let's take a look at Philippians 3. Let's begin with that first word, *"Finally"*. Interesting Paul uses the word 'finally,' but there are two more chapters to go! And then Paul gives us his resume. He was, *"circumcised on the eighth day, of the people of*

Israel, of the tribe of Benjamin, a Hebrew of Hebrews; as to the law, a Pharisee; as to zeal, a persecutor of the church; as to righteousness under the law, blameless" (vv. 5-6). In other words, He is very Jewish.

That is quite a stout resume. What is your spiritual resume? When did you accept the Lord? When did the Lord become the Lord of your life? Were you baptized? Did you grow up in a Christian family? Are you the first generation in a Christian family? Do you study God's Word? Are you part of a home group? Are you zealous for your Christian faith? Are you striving for righteousness? Would anyone call you blameless?

But then Paul shifts gears and he says, *"Indeed, I count everything as loss because of the surpassing worth of knowing Christ Jesus my Lord"* (vv. 7-8). Would you count

> **What is your spiritual resume?**

your career as loss? Would you count your friends as loss? Would you count your spirituality, your relationship with Jesus, as the most important thing in your life?

"(T)he righteousness of God depends on faith" (v. 9). We should know the power of His resurrection, that we should share in His sufferings. We should become like Him, referring to verses 9 and 10. Then Paul tells us he has not attained that level yet, and nor have we. *"(B)ut I press on to make it my own, because Christ Jesus has made me his own"* (v. 12). *"Forgetting what lies behind and straining forward to what lies ahead, I press on toward the goal for the prize of the upward call of God in Christ Jesus"* (v. 13). Are you pressing on? Are you straining forward? Or are you relaxing in your Christianity?

Paul says in verse 17, *"join in imitating me"*. None of us would probably ever say that, but what if somebody decided to imitate your Christianity? What kind of a Christian would they be?

Finally, in verses 20 and 21, he reminds us, *"But our citizenship is in heaven, and from it we await a Savior, the Lord Jesus Christ, who will transform our lowly body to be like his glorious body, by the power that enables him even to subject all things to himself."* Do you live like your citizenship is in heaven or here on earth?

DIGGING DEEPER

Write down your spiritual resume. When and where did the spiritual significant events happen in your life? You might think of those milestones as you share your testimony with others.

Secondly, count them all as loss. Strive toward the surpassing worth of knowing Christ Jesus as your Lord. And how do you know Christ Jesus? By spending time in His Word, and in prayer, and in a church.

Lastly, take time to think about what it would be like for you to press on in your faith, to strain forward to what lies ahead. What is God calling you to do with your life? Do you know? If not, you may want to spend time with the Lord and ask Him, "What is the call on my life?"

And finally, strive to live as citizens of heaven and not sojourners on the earth. Let's pray.

Prayer

God, I give You all the glory for working in me and through me. Thank You for the principles to live by in Philippians 3. Amen.

MY THOUGHTS

PHILIPPIANS 4

Think on These Things

In this last chapter of the Book of Philippians, we are to be anxious for nothing, guarding our hearts and minds in Jesus, thinking on godly things, and leaning on God who strengthens us. Do you fret or do you have the peace of Christ? Where is your mind? On the things of the world or the things above? Please read or listen to Philippians 4.

COMMENTS

Let's look at my journals from 1986, 1994, and 2012 one last time.

In 1986, after reading Philippians 4 (NASB), I wrote:

- *Therefore, my beloved family whom I long to see, my joy and crown, so stand firm in the Lord, my beloved* (v. 1).

- *Be anxious for nothing, but in everything by prayer and supplication with thanksgiving let your requests be made known to God. And the peace of God, which passes all understanding, shall guard your hearts and your minds in Christ Jesus* (vv. 6-7).

- *For I have learned to be content in whatever circumstances I am* (v. 11).

In 1994, I was very brief concerning Philippians 4. I wrote one line, *"Let your gentle spirit be known to all men"* (v. 5).

In 2012, I was splitting the chapters in Philippians into two readings. I read Philippians 4:1-9 at the conclusion of that cruise and wrote in my personal Bible reading journal:

- Paul was a man of love, referring to verse 1.
- Euodia and Syntyche were believers. They needed to resolve their dispute in the Lord. They may have needed intervention of another Christian to help do so, referring to verse 3.
- The Philippians did a lot of things right. They should rejoice, not be anxious. How? Be reasonable. Pray. Be thankful. Exchange anxiety for the peace of God. Also, focus our minds on the good stuff. We get easily distracted by thinking about the wrong things causing anxiety, yet we can have the peace of God, referring to verses 3-9.

> **We get easily distracted by thinking about the wrong things causing anxiety, yet we can have the peace of God.**

The next day, I finished Philippians 4:10-23 and wrote:

- 'Joy' or 'rejoice' occur twelve times in these four short chapters. This is a joyful book compared to other letters Paul writes to churches. Paul doesn't speak from need, *"for I have learned in whatever situation I am to be content"* (v. 11). It may be easier for Paul, single, no one depending on him but himself, easier to adapt to economic circumstances than me, but I still need to learn to be content in God's provision, whatever level that may be.
- Paul faced it all. I have not, referring to verses 12 and 13.
- The Philippian church was always a giving church, referring to verses 15 and 16.
- Paul does not seek the gift. I do through Ezra Project appeals, but I, like Paul, seek the fruit that increases to your credit, referring to verse 17.
- God supplies the giver's needs according to His riches in glory. I pray it so for all Ezra donors, referring to verse 19.

DIGGING DEEPER

Philippians 4 has several power verses. Let's go over them.

"Rejoice in the Lord always; again I will say, rejoice" (v. 4). How are you doing with that one? I cannot say I rejoice always. When I was diagnosed with cancer seven years ago, my first response was not rejoicing.

"Do not be anxious about anything, but in everything by prayer and supplication with thanksgiving let your requests be made known to God. And the peace of God, which surpasses all understanding, will guard your hearts and your minds in Christ Jesus" (vv. 6-7). I can say it has been my joy to experience the benefits of this verse. Rather than getting anxious about a lot of things, I take my stuff, the good, the bad, and the ugly, to the Lord by *"prayer and supplication with thanksgiving"* (v. 6), I make my request known to God. And experiencing the peace of God is a great benefit. And yes, friends, the peace of God surpasses all understanding. It will guard your hearts and your minds in Christ Jesus. What a blessing.

One way of preventing anxiety is to think on the right things, *"Finally, brothers, whatever is true, whatever is honorable, whatever is just, whatever is pure, whatever is lovely, whatever is commendable, if there is any excellence, if there is anything worthy of praise, think about these things"* (v. 8). We can reroute our minds on what we think about. Rather than dwell on all those "what-ifs" that most likely will never occur, think on the things listed here in Philippians 4.

"I can do all things through him who strengthens me" (v. 13). Are you content in your circumstances? Paul says he has learned to be content in every circumstance, whether he has been brought low or whether he's abounding. He says, *"I have learned the secret"* (v. 12), and the secret is *"I can do all things through him who strengthens me"* (v. 13). Keep that in mind when you are facing difficult circumstances. You can make it through as you depend on Jesus.

And the last power verse: *"And my God will supply every need of yours according to His riches in glory in Christ Jesus"* (v. 19). This verse is often misquoted, so look at it again. Many people say, "And my God shall supply all <u>my</u> needs according to His riches in glory." That is not what it says. It says, *"And my God will supply every need of <u>yours</u>"* (v. 19). This is not a selfish prayer. This is a prayer of thanks for those who give. I pray this verse every week for those who give to the Ezra Project. I sincerely pray God meets the needs of those who give. I believe God is able to meet all of your needs according to His riches in glory.

As we close out Philippians, let's go back to our introduction. The church at Philippi was the first church Paul founded in Europe. This letter was a letter of encouragement to that church. He wanted the Philippians—and us—to live as citizens of a heavenly colony with growing contentment to serve God and each other.

He also encouraged them to press on and continue to grow in their faith and spiritual maturity. He encourages us to do the same today. He reminded them, and us, that spiritual progress takes effort, and he encouraged them to work out their salvation, reminding them it was God who was at work in them.

That encouragement is for us today, our spiritual growth takes effort, but God is at work in us. He reminded the Philippian church to rejoice and be joyful. He reminds us the same today. I hope you are encouraged by our time in the Book of Philippians. Let's thank the Lord.

Prayer

Father, we thank You for this wonderful, short book packed with power verses reminding us that You began a good work in us and You are continuing it. You remind us You will come again and every knee shall bow and every tongue confess that You are Lord. You remind us to work out our salvation with fear and trembling for You are at work in us. You remind us to forget what lies behind and to strain forward to what lies ahead, being anxious for nothing, but taking everything to You in prayers and supplications. And You remind us we can do all things through You who strengthens us.

Thank You for these great, great reminders in Your Word. May we be doers of the Word and not hearers only as we apply these verses to our daily lives. Thank You for the Book of Philippians. In Jesus' name, amen.

MY THOUGHTS

FOUR DAYS IN COLOSSIANS

COLOSSIANS 1

Christ in You, the Hope of Glory

Today, we begin the Book of Colossians. Colossians is four chapters, one of the epistles of the New Testament. We will look at my English Standard Version Study Bible book introduction on this book.

During Paul's three-year ministry in Ephesus, a Colossian named Epaphras, probably in Ephesus, responded to Paul's gospel message. He then returned to his hometown and began sharing the good news of Jesus, which resulted in the birth of the Colossian church.

At the time of the writing of this letter, Epaphras was probably back in Rome with Paul. He may have shared the challenges of dangerous teachings that were threatening the church of Colossae. Paul writes the Colossians to respond to the threats and to encourage the believers in their growth in Christianity. But Paul never visited Colossae. The letter was probably written in 62 A.D. by Timothy, serving as Paul's secretary.

The theme of the letter is Christ. It is one of the Bible's most Christ-centered books. Christ is exalted as Lord over all creation, even the invisible realm. He secured redemption for His people and enabled us to participate with Him in His death, resurrection, and fullness. Our unity is in Him, the preeminent Christ. We are to press on to maturity in Christ by continuing to battle sin, pursuing holiness in Christ, and learning to live distinctly as Christians.

Is Christ in you? If so, is He changing the way you live your life? Please read or listen to Colossians 1.

COMMENTS

To help us through the Book of Colossians, I selected three of my personal Bible reading journals. I found one on Colossians that goes all the way back to 1986 when I was thirty-one years old. Then I selected one ten years later, in 1996, at forty-one years old, and the third one will be from 2006, at fifty-one years old. I was reading the New American Standard Version (NASB) in my daily quiet times in 1986 and 1996, and the English Standard Version in 2006. Three personal Bible reading journals from three different decades, ten years apart.

By the way, the first personal Bible reading journal I ever recorded was in 1983, so 1986 is very early in my journaling years. Looking back at my journal in 1986, I discovered I read Colossians 1 on three different days, breaking up this chapter into several different sections of verses. The first section was the first twelve verses of this chapter and I listed a few verses in my journal:

- Pray without ceasing, referring to verse 9.
- *Ask that you may be filled with the knowledge of His will in all spiritual wisdom and understanding, so that you (Allen) will walk in a manner worthy of the Lord, to please Him in all respects, bearing fruit in every good work and increasing in the knowledge of God* (vv. 9-10).

The next day, I read a hodgepodge of verses from scripture. I read Psalm 27, portions of Ephesians and Corinthians, along with Colossians 1:12-29. I noted in my journal, *"He is before all things and all things hold together in Him"* (v. 17).

Then I wrote, "Study on walk," and that is where I referred to some of those other verses concerning walking in Christ. Like Ephesians 4:1, *"Walk in a manner worthy of (your) calling"*; Galatians 5:16, *"Walk by the Spirit"*; 2 Corinthians 5:7, *"walk by faith, not by sight—"*. I was referring back to verse 10 of chapter 1 of Colossians where it says, *"Walk in a manner worthy of the Lord"*. So, I did a little study on "walk."

The next day I finished Colossians 1 by focusing on verses 19-29. I wrote, "Jesus is the fullness of forgiveness and peace comes through the blood of Jesus." Then I referred to verse 25, *"Of this church I was made a minister according to the stewardship from God bestowed on me for your benefit, so that I might fully carry out the preaching of the word of God."*

Ten years later, in 1996, when reading the New Testament that year, I read Colossians one chapter a day, and on Colossians 1, wrote, "Truth of gospel. Grace of God in truth," and then, *"ask that you may be filled with the knowledge of His will in all spiritual wisdom and understanding"* (v. 9).

> **Christ in you, the hope of glory.**
>
> **Col. 1:27**

Next, I referred to verse 17, *"in Him all things hold together."* And I quoted verse 27, *"Christ in you, the hope of glory."*

In 2006, another ten years later, I was reading the whole Bible, Old Testament passages each day and New Testament passages each day. On this day, I read some passages out of Isaiah, as well as Colossians 1. Concerning Colossians 1, I quoted the following verses:

- *Walk in a manner worthy of the Lord, to please Him in all respects, bearing fruit in every good work and increasing in the knowledge of God* (v. 10).
- *"He is the image of the invisible God"* (v. 15), not another good man or a prophet.
- *"Christ in you, the hope of glory"* (v. 27). This is a great truth. Jesus can dwell in us.

Those were my journal entries in 1986, 1996, and 2006 concerning Colossians 1. This is a great book, one of my favorite books in the Bible. In fact, one of my early memories was when I was in college and got in a Bible study. I did not know it was affiliated with The Navigators, but the guys who led the Bible study invited us to go to Glen Eyrie, the headquarters of The Navigators in Colorado Springs, Colorado. It is a beautiful facility. We sat in this big lodge and I remember one thing being taught in that study that weekend, *"Christ in you, the hope of glory"* (v. 27). I do not remember many sermons I hear or teachings I have listened to in my Christian life, but for some reason, that teaching still rings in my ears well over forty years later. It came right out of Colossians 1.

DIGGING DEEPER

Let's review a couple of the power verses in this chapter, starting with verse 10, *"so as to walk in a manner worthy of the Lord, fully pleasing to him: bearing fruit in every good work and increasing in the knowledge of God."* We could park right there for about a week and discuss the power of those phrases in this verse. Are you walking in a manner worthy of the Lord? Are you fully pleasing to Him? Are you bearing fruit and are you increasing in the knowledge of God? But we must move on.

Let's look at verse 15, *"He is the image of the invisible God"*. Yes, Jesus is the image of the invisible God. Verses 16 and 17 say, *"All things were created through him and for him. And he is before all things, and in him all things hold together."* That means Jesus was present in the creation.

Verse 19 says, *"For in him all the fullness of God was pleased to dwell,"* so Jesus was the image of the invisible God and in Him, the fullness of God dwelled.

Verse 20 says Jesus reconciled *"To himself all things, whether on earth or in heaven, making peace by the blood of his cross."* So, we are reconciled to Jesus, to God, through the cross of Christ and His blood alone. Verse 22 continues this thought, *"he has now reconciled in his body of flesh by his death, in order to present you holy and blameless and above reproach before him."* Jesus reconciled us through His death to present us holy and blameless before God.

But then, there is one of those "ifs" in the scriptures in verse 23, *"if indeed you continue in the faith, stable and steadfast, not shifting from the hope of the gospel that you heard"*. To be reconciled we must continue in the faith, we must be stable and steadfast in our beliefs.

We close with that great verse, verse 27, *"Christ in you, the hope of glory."* Paul calls it a mystery. He calls it God's riches in glory that Christ dwells within us. I do not know if I can truly comprehend what that means. And maybe that is why my mind stills go back to what I heard forty years ago when I first heard it at Glen Eyrie in that Navigator retreat, *"Christ in you, the hope of glory"* (v. 27).

Prayer

Father, we thank You for Colossians 1, that all of You, the fullness of You, came in the body of a man named Jesus Christ. He certainly was Your Son and God in the flesh, the image of You, the invisible God, the fullness of You, dwelling within Him. And through Him, we are reconciled to You because of the cross. Because of His death, burial, and resurrection, we now can say Christ is in us and we have the hope of glory.

I, for one, Lord, am thankful I cannot comprehend all these things. I am reminded in the Old Testament You say Your thoughts are higher than my thoughts, Your ways are higher than my ways. Though I may not be able to comprehend it, Lord, I can accept it. And I do.

Because I have the opportunity to have Christ dwelling within me, I want *"to walk in a manner worthy of the Lord, fully pleasing to (You): bearing fruit in every good work and increasing in the knowledge of God"* (v. 10). Thank You, thank You, thank You that Christ is in me, the hope of glory. Amen.

MY THOUGHTS

COLOSSIANS 2

Walk in Him

Today in Colossians 2, we will learn the fullness of God dwells in Jesus, His Son. We are also instructed to walk in Him. Are you walking in Jesus? Do people see that in you? Please read or listen to Colossians 2.

COMMENTS

In 1986, I read Colossians 2 on one day, and wrote in my personal Bible reading journal, "He is the fullness of the deity. We were dead in our sins but through His forgiveness gain eternal life. Jesus is all and in all. Don't get bogged down in religiosity, self-made religion."

Ten years later in 1996, I read Colossians 2 in one day, and wrote, "In Him. Walk in Him. Rooted and built up in Him. In Him dwells all the fullness of the godhead. You are complete in Him. In Him, circumcised."

Ten years later in 2006, reading the whole Bible that year, I read portions of Isaiah and portions of Colossians. Concerning chapter 2 of Colossians, I wrote, "In Jesus, all the fullness of deity dwells in bodily form." Then, "Our debt, sin nature, was nailed to the cross with Jesus." And that ends my journal entries on Colossians 2.

Early in chapter 2, Paul refers to the mystery in Christ as he did in chapter 1. In verses 2 and 3, he says, *"God's mystery, which is Christ, in whom are hidden all the treasures of wisdom and knowledge."* It is a mystery that in Christ are hidden all the treasures of wisdom and knowledge. If you need wisdom and knowledge in your life, you get it in Christ. I regularly pray for wisdom, knowledge, and understanding. These are found in the Word of God and in Jesus.

> **Therefore, as you received Christ Jesus the Lord, so walk in him.**
>
> **Col. 2:6**

Let's look at verse 6, *"Therefore, as you received Christ Jesus the Lord, so walk in him."* I presume most of you have received Christ. The question is are you walking in Him? We walk in Him by staying close to His Word, by understanding His precepts, His commandments, by gaining His wisdom and knowledge as we just read about in verse 2. So as a Christian, are you walking in Christ?

Verse 9 says, *"For in him the whole fullness of deity dwells bodily"*. Again, this is one of those concepts I cannot comprehend. The fullness of God, as we read in chapter 1, dwells in Jesus.

Now let's jump over to verses 13 and 14, *"And you, who were dead in your trespasses and the uncircumcision of your flesh, God made alive together with him, having forgiven us all our trespasses, by canceling the record of debt that stood against us with its legal demands. This he set aside, nailing it to the cross."*

That, friends, is the power of the gospel message. God has chosen to forgive us. Jesus canceled the record of our debt that stood against each one of us. Its legal demands are death on our part, but He set that aside, nailing it to the cross. Shout the Hallelujah! Your sin record has been nailed to the cross. It has been set aside by Jesus. Jesus has been given the authority to do this.

Look back at verse 10, *"and you have been filled in him, who is the head of all rule and authority."* Look at verse 15, *"He disarmed the rulers and authorities and put them to open shame, by triumphing over them"*. Yes, Jesus had the authority to cancel our record of debt with its legal demands. Hallelujah, Jesus! Verses like these remind us of the book introduction that said this book is all about Christ. It is all about Jesus in Colossians. Paul finishes the chapter by saying, let no one pass judgment on you anymore concerning religiosity.

DIGGING DEEPER

Remember, Paul was writing to the church of Colossae because they were facing some false teaching. We also face false teaching. Many of us get caught up in religion rather than the Word of God. Paul is freeing the church of Colossae from the rules and regulations of men; questions of food and drink, festivals, new moons, Sabbath, and worship of angels. He is saying, forget about all that stuff. The substance belongs to Christ. Hold fast to Jesus. Focus on the true gospel message, not all these distractions.

He reminds us in verses 20 and 21, when we accept Christ, we die to the elemental spirits of the world. We do not need to be subject to those kinds of regulations anymore; do not handle, do not taste, do not touch, according to human precepts and teachings.

He finishes the chapter with verse 23, *"These have indeed an appearance of wisdom in promoting self-made religion and asceticism and severity to the body, but they are of no value in stopping the indulgence of the flesh."* Paul is reminding us to keep the main thing the main thing. And the main thing is back in verses 13 and 14, *"And you, who were dead in your trespasses and the uncircumcision of your flesh, God made alive together with him, having forgiven us all our trespasses, by canceling the record of debt that stood against us with its legal demands. This he set aside, nailing it to the cross."*

That is the gospel. That is what we focus on. And when we receive that, when we accept that, we go back to verse 6, *"Therefore, as you received Christ Jesus the Lord, so walk in him."* Not in religiosity, not in self-made religion, but in Him. Let's pray.

Prayer

Lord, we thank You for the freedom of the gospel message of Jesus. We thank You that You canceled our debt, something we cannot do ourselves. But You did it, nailing it to the cross. You took the legal penalty we deserved, which was death, and You exchanged it for eternal life in You. All we can do is say thank You.

And then for those of us who have received You, we can walk in You as our token of thanksgiving for what You have done for us. Thank You for freeing us from self-made religion. Protect us from its tentacles of temptation. Keep us walking in You and You alone. Hallelujah. Amen.

MY THOUGHTS

COLOSSIANS 3

How Should Christians Live?

In Colossians 3, the question is, "How should Christians live?" Do you set your mind on earthly or heavenly things? Please read or listen to Colossians 3.

COMMENTS

In 1986, when I was thirty-one years old, I read Colossians 3 (NASB) over three days. I started with a summary of the first two verses, "Seek the things above, not the things of this world." The next day, I read 3:1-17, and wrote a lot about this:

- Die and let life be hidden with Christ in you. Die to old self. Allow Jesus to renew a new man in me.
- *Put on a heart of compassion* (v. 12).
- *Put on love* (v. 14).
- *Let the peace of Christ rule in your heart . . . and be thankful* (v. 15).
- *Let the word of Christ richly dwell within you . . . singing with thankfulness* (v. 16).
- *Whatever you do in word or deed, do all in the name of the Lord Jesus* (v. 17).

On the third day, I finished Colossians 3 with verses 18 through the end and wrote, "Family guidance," referring to verses 23 and 24. *"Whatever you do, do your work heartily, as for the Lord rather than for men, . . . It is the Lord Christ whom you serve."*

At forty-one years old, in 1996, I read Colossians 3 and wrote, *"Set your mind on the things above, not on the things that are on earth"* (v. 2). *"Put on a heart of compassion, kindness"* (v. 12).

At fifty-one years old, in the year 2006, I wrote, "I need this encouragement. *'Set your mind on things above, not on the things that are on earth. For you have died and your life is hidden with Christ in God'"* (vv. 2-3).

Then I wrote, "How should we Christians live? *'So, as those who have been chosen of God, holy and beloved, put on a heart of compassion kindness, humility, gentleness, and patience; bearing with one another, and forgiving each other, whoever has a complaint against anyone; just as the Lord forgave you, so also should you'"* (vv. 12-13).

> **Set your mind on the things above, not on the things that are on earth.**
>
> Col. 3:2

That ends my journal entries, but let's go back to the question I asked in 2006, how should we Christians live? *"Set your minds on things that are above, not on things that are on earth."* In the next several verses, he makes a distinction between earthly things and godly things. He says, *"Put to death therefore what is earthly in you: sexual immorality, impurity, passion, evil desire, covetousness"* (v. 5), *"But now you must put them all away: anger, wrath, malice, slander, and obscene talk . . . Do not lie to one another . . . (and) put off the old self with its practices"* (vv. 8-9) while putting on the new self. That is a long list of what is earthly.

Let's find out what he means by putting our minds on the things above. That list begins in verses 12-17:

> *compassionate hearts, kindness, humility, meekness, and patience, bearing with one another . . . forgiving each other . . . put on love which binds everything together in perfect harmony. And let the peace of Christ rule in your hearts . . . be thankful. Let the word of Christ dwell in you richly, teaching and admonishing one another in all wisdom, singing psalms and hymns and spiritual songs with*

thankfulness in your hearts . . . whatever you do, in word or deed, do everything
in the name of the Lord Jesus

Paul makes a pretty clear distinction between the things above and the things that are earthly. How are you doing with all that? Where is your mind? If you have a Bible, go back through those lists and see where your attention focuses. Are you taking Paul's advice to set your minds on the things above, not on the things on earth?

DIGGING DEEPER

As a practical application from today's lesson out of Colossians 3, take one of the things that put our minds above and think about that thing today. Maybe it is a compassionate heart. Maybe it is kindness or humility or meekness or patience. Maybe it is forgiveness. Maybe it is putting on love. Or maybe it is letting the peace of Christ rule in your heart. Or, lastly, maybe it is just being thankful. Pick one of those things and set your mind on that particular item today.

Also, as you think about the activities of your day, think about verse 17, *"And whatever you do, in word or deed, do everything in the name of the Lord Jesus"*. Is that how your day will go? Will you do everything in word or deed in the name of the Lord Jesus? How will you be an ambassador for Christ today? Why? Verses 23 and 24 say, *"Whatever you do, work heartily, as for the Lord and not for men, knowing that from the Lord you will receive the inheritance as your reward. You are serving the Lord Christ."*

Is that how you approach your day? Is that how you walk through your day? Will you do everything today heartily, as for the Lord and not for men? For *"You are serving the Lord Christ"* (v. 24).

Prayer

Heavenly Father, thank You for the challenge today in Colossians 3 to set our minds on the things above, not on the things on earth. Thanks for listing what is earthly and what things are above. Thanks for teaching us how to live life as a Christian.

Holy Spirit, help us today to do everything in word or deed in the name of the Lord Jesus, do everything heartily as for the Lord and not for men. Help us truly be ambassadors for Christ today. In the name of Jesus, we ask it. Amen.

MY THOUGHTS

COLOSSIANS 4

Fulfill Your Ministry

Today, we finish the Book of Colossians with chapter 4. Has God opened a door of ministry to you? Are you fulfilling it? Please read or listen to Colossians 4.

COMMENTS

In 1986, in the third journal I ever wrote, I wrote about Colossians 4 (NASB), "Pray that God may open a door for His Word, referring to verse 3. *'Let your speech always be . . . seasoned with salt'* (v. 6). *'Take heed to the ministry which you have received in the Lord, that you may fulfill it'"* (v. 17).

Ten years later, in 1996, I read Colossians 4 (NASB) on a Saturday morning which is usually when I go to a Gideons International prayer breakfast. I read the scriptures, but did not write any notes. Moving on to 2006, I was reading the whole Bible that year, reading Old Testament passages and New Testament passages each day. Concerning Colossians 4, I wrote, "My prayer is that God will open a door to us. A door for the Word, referring to verse 3."

I continued to write about verse 12, "I wish I *'May stand perfect and fully assured in all the will of God'"*. Then referring to verse 17, *"'Say to'* (Allen), *'Take heed to the ministry which you have received in the Lord, that you may fulfill it.'"* That ends my journal entries on Colossians 4.

As we look at chapter 4, let's not skip the first verse. It reminds us, we *"also have a Master in heaven."* Is that a reminder to us we serve a master much like a bondservant serves here on earth? We too serve a master who happens to be in heaven. Are you busy running your own life, or are you serving a master in heaven?

Verse 3 is a great verse. It says, *"At the same time, pray also for us, that God may open to us a door for the word."* I hope you will pray also for us, that God may open to us a door for the Word at the Ezra Project as we try to connect God's people to God's Word. As Paul asked those of the Colossian church to pray for him, I also ask you to pray for us.

> **Let your speech always be gracious, seasoned with salt.**
>
> **Col. 4:6**

Let's look at verse 6, *"Let your speech always be gracious, seasoned with salt"*. That verse might touch your heart. Are the words that come out of your mouth always gracious, seasoned with salt? I know I cannot say that. That verse challenges me greatly.

It reminds me of a verse in Ephesians 4:29 that also challenges me from time to time in my life. It says, *"Let no corrupting talk come out of your mouths, but only such as is good for building up, as fits the occasion, that it may give grace to those who hear."* Whoa! No corrupt talk, only words that are good for building up? Only words that give grace to those who hear?

The verse in Ephesians reminds us of the verses in James 3 about taming our tongue. James 3:5-10 says:

> *How great a forest is set ablaze by such a small fire! And the tongue is a fire, a world of unrighteousness. The tongue is set among our members, staining the whole body, setting on fire the entire course of life, and set on fire by hell. For every kind of beast and bird, of reptile and sea creature, can be tamed and has been tamed by mankind, but no human being can tame the tongue. It is a restless evil, full of deadly poison. With it we bless our Lord and Father, and with it we curse people who are made in the likeness of God. From the same mouth come blessing and cursing. My brothers, these things ought not to be so.*

DIGGING DEEPER

Today, your practical application may be to work on taming your tongue; to ask the Lord, to ask the Holy Spirit, to let your speech always be gracious, seasoned with salt. O, friends, I know it is really hard when we are just reading along in the scriptures, and suddenly it starts to talk to us personally. That is the power of God's Word. That is why we stay close to the Word. That is why we go back to Colossians 3:16, *"Let the word of Christ dwell in you richly, teaching and admonishing one another."* Yes, this passage may be teaching and admonishing each one of us about what comes out of our mouths.

At the end of Colossians 4, there are some pretty neat greetings that Paul makes to some of his friends. Verse 12 suggests to us that we should, *"stand mature and fully assured in all the will of God."* Are you maturing in your Christianity? Are you fully assured that you are in the will of God for your life?

Verse 17, *"See that you fulfill the ministry that you have received in the Lord."* Have you personally received a ministry from the Lord? If so, are you fulfilling it? If you do not know, if this is a question you have never pondered, maybe that is another practical application today. Ask the Lord what ministry He has for you. I do not believe God placed you on the earth just to sojourn in your own desires and your own will. I believe God creates every one of us for a purpose and a ministry. What is your purpose? What is your ministry? *"See that you fulfill the ministry that you have received in the Lord"* (v. 17).

Those words close Colossians 4. But let's go back to the beginning when we started this book. We said Paul wrote the Colossians to respond to threats and to encourage the believers in their growth in Christianity. I think we have seen plenty of things in this book that help us grow in our Christian faith.

Colossians is a Christ-centered book. In chapter 1, we were reminded in verses 16 and 17, *"all things were created through him and for him. And he is before all things, and in him all things hold together."* And in 1:19, *"For in him all the fullness of God was pleased to dwell"*. We were also reminded in Colossians 1:27, *"Christ in you, the hope of glory."*

In chapter 2, verse 6, *"Therefore, as you received Christ Jesus the Lord, so walk in him"*. To do so, in chapter 3, we were reminded to, *"Set your minds on things that are above, not on things that are on earth"* (v. 2). And Paul gave us a list of earthly things and things that are above. And he reminded us, *"Let the word of Christ dwell in you richly . . . And whatever you do, in word or deed, do everything in the name of the Lord Jesus"* (vv. 16-17).

Here in chapter 4, he reminds us to tame our tongue. To *"Let (our) speech always be gracious, seasoned with salt"* (v. 6), and we should, *"See that (we) fulfill the ministry that (we) have received in the Lord"* (v. 17). All those great concepts help us grow in our Christianity.

Prayer

Lord, that is our prayer as we finish the Book of Colossians. From dwelling in the Word of Christ richly, we will grow in our walk toward You and You will reveal a ministry to us and we will fulfill it in You.

Thank You for reminding us of who You are in this book and thank You for reminding us about who we are. Go with us as we move on to another book of Your Holy Bible. Thank You, Holy Spirit, for teaching us through the Book of Colossians. In Jesus' name, we pray. Amen.

MY THOUGHTS

FIVE DAYS IN 1 THESSALONIANS

1 THESSALONIANS 1

The Word of the Lord Sounded Forth

Today, we begin Paul's letter to the Thessalonians. We will look at my English Standard Version Study Bible book introduction to learn about 1 Thessalonians. The Apostle Paul wrote 1 Thessalonians from Corinth during his second missionary journey, around 50 A.D. Thessalonica was the capital of the Roman province of Macedonia. Because it was a harbor town, it was a flourishing city of trade and philosophy, with a population of over one hundred thousand people.

Paul, Timothy, and Silas all preached in the synagogue in Thessalonica to Jews and God-fearing Gentiles, and many converted to Christianity. Jewish opponents instigated a riot against Jason, Paul's host, forcing them all to leave Thessalonica prematurely. Paul was concerned for the new believers in Thessalonica, so he sent Timothy back there a few months later. Timothy and Paul met up in Corinth where Timothy updated Paul on the church.

Generally, the church was doing fine, but a few members had died, and because they did not understand the second coming, some thought those dead would miss it. That raised a second concern, the timing of the day of the Lord. What if they died, could they also miss the second coming?

They also did not expect the persecution of the church they were facing to last as long as it was lasting. Furthermore, they were disappointed Paul himself did not return to Thessalonica, sending Timothy instead. Finally, some of the new Christians were depending on wealthier Christians to provide for them rather than earning a living themselves. Paul composed 1 Thessalonians to address all those issues.

The most prominent theme of the letter is the second coming of Jesus. It is mentioned in every chapter of the book. Paul tells us how to prepare for the return of Christ: warn the lazy, comfort the frightened, care for the weak, be patient, and do something good for someone. The church in Thessalonica was the first Paul ever wrote a letter to. 1 Thessalonians is five chapters. We will take them one a day. Please read or listen to 1 Thessalonians 1.

COMMENTS

To help us through our study of 1 Thessalonians, I am going to do something different with my Bible reading journals. I found I read 1 Thessalonians three years in a row. So we are going to look at journals three years in a row: 1992, 1993, and 1994. I was thirty-seven, thirty-eight, and thirty-nine years old those years. In 1992, I read the New Testament, the next year I read various books, and in 1994, I also read various books of the Bible.

We begin with my journal entry from 1992. That year, I read 1 Thessalonians 1 and 2 on the same day. Concerning chapter 1, I wrote, "Paul was a pray-er." Then I wrote, "The Lord gave him time by imprisoning him. Help me be an example and sound forth the Word of the Lord, referring to verses 7 and 8."

The next year, 1993, I also read 1 Thessalonians (NASB) and wrote about chapter 1, *"'making mention of you in our prayers'* (v. 2). I need to pray more for people." And, *"'His choice of you'* (v. 4). God seeks us out. I need to go back to praying salvation for family members and friends." Then, *"'you turned to God from idols'* (v. 9). We need people to turn to God from their idols."

In 1994, when reading this chapter (NASB). I wrote, "Pray. Paul was a man of prayer. I need to do better." Then, *"For the word of the Lord has sounded forth from you"* (v. 8).

Let's look at 1 Thessalonians 1. Notice in the first verse, Paul writes, *"Paul, Silvanus, and Timothy",* so he writes as a team, not as an individual. I mentioned in the introduction, all three of these brothers preached in Thessalonica, so they are all writing back to the church.

In my journals, I mention Paul was a pray-er. Look at verse 2, *"constantly mentioning you in our prayers"*. Paul prayed for the church. He mentions in verse 5, the *"gospel came to (them) not only in word, but also in power and in the Holy Spirit and with full conviction."* Is that what the Word of God means to you? Is it in your life with power? Is it in your life with the Holy Spirit? Are you fully convicted to the Word and by the Word of God?

Look at what happened when they heard the Word of the Lord. Verse 7 says they became an example to others. Is that what happened to you when you heard the Word of the Lord? Have you become an example to others? Do others see Christianity in you?

Their impact was broad, *"For not only has the word of the Lord sounded forth from you in Macedonia and Achaia, but your faith in God has gone forth everywhere"* (v. 8). Friends, that is a challenge for us. It is a personal testimony.

> **Your faith in God has gone forth everywhere.**
> **1 Thess. 1:8**

What is our personal testimony? Is my walk with Christ sounding forth everywhere? If not, why not?

The words they heard from Paul, Silas, and Timothy were so impacting they turned away from the idols they served and committed to the true and living God. *"For they themselves report concerning us the kind of reception we had among you, and how you turned to God from idols to serve the living and true God"* (v. 9). Is that what people see in your life? Did they see a change? Did they see something happen when you became a Christian? For many of us, it is a long time ago. But some of you may be new Christians. Have people seen a difference? This chapter is a great testimony about the power of the gospel and how it should change our lives.

DIGGING DEEPER

Paul opens 1 Thessalonians very complimentary. Remember, they were run out of town quickly. They sent Timothy back, and Timothy reported the church was doing pretty good. How about you? What has been the impact of the gospel in your own life? When you heard it, did it change you dramatically? Did you receive the

Word of the Lord with power and in the Holy Spirit and with full conviction? And if you did when you became a Christian, has it faded?

I close with a story. I became a Christian at fifteen years old. I went to college and there started to learn more about my faith. I came home many times and visited with my parents. They were church goers. They raised me in the church. But the Word of the Lord was on me with power and in the Holy Spirit and with full conviction; a bit more than they could handle.

They finally said, "Would you please stop talking about this. Please don't ever bring your Bible into this home again. You are not a priest. You cannot teach us the Word of God." That is what this passage means. I was on fire for the Lord then, and sometimes when we are on fire for the Lord, we burn a few people.

I would rather be on fire for the Lord than be lukewarm. Sure, that fire has faded a bit over decades, but I am still excited to share my faith with other people. Are you? When was the first time, or the last time, you actually shared your faith with a non-believer? Is the Word of the Lord sounding forth from you? Let's pray.

Prayer

Father, the Word of God often convicts us. We thank You that these people in Thessalonica, when they heard the Word of the Lord, were excited and their testimony went forth all around them. Let it be so for us. May we be so excited about our relationship with You, we want to share it with others. Holy Spirit, give us the boldness to do so.

These people turn from idol worship to You. We have people all around us worshiping everything but You. Use us to turn them from idol worship towards You. The church in Thessalonica grew because people were excited about their relationship with You. Use us to grow Your kingdom here, as well. As we read through Thessalonians, may Your Word fall on us again with power and the Holy Spirit and with full conviction. In Jesus' name, we ask it. Amen.

MY THOUGHTS

1 THESSALONIANS 2

Entrusted with the Gospel

In 1 Thessalonians 2, Paul shares he, Silas, and Timothy were entrusted with the gospel. They shared it in Thessalonica and people converted to Christianity. Do you think you are entrusted with the gospel? Are you sharing it? Please read or listen to 1 Thessalonians 2.

COMMENTS

In 1992, I read 1 Thessalonians 1 and 2 on the same day. Concerning chapter 2, I wrote, "How to act: devoutly, uprightly, and blamelessly, referring to verse 10." Referring to verse 12, "Walk in a manner worthy of God." And related to verse 13, "Word of God, not word of men."

In looking in my journal in 1993, I have a confession to make. I noticed I read 1 Thessalonians 1 on a Friday and I read 1 Thessalonians 2 on a Monday. Did I really skip two days of daily Bible reading? Yes, I confess, I did miss a few days over four decades of Bible reading. These journals reveal this to me and you.

On Saturday mornings, I often go to a Gideon prayer breakfast where we read a portion of scripture. So I do get my daily Bible reading in when I go to a Gideon prayer breakfast. I indicated on this Saturday, I did enjoy a portion of God's Word that day. On Sunday, I actually gave a message in a church. I spoke in two services that Sunday morning, so I was in the Word in that way, but it does not appear I had a daily quiet time on that Sunday morning.

I confess these things so you can see I, too, miss a day or two once in a while. I hope that does not become an excuse for you, though. A good friend of mine once told me, "If you miss reading the scriptures on weekends, you miss a hundred days a year." I encourage you not to take weekends off. I do not anymore and I have not done so in decades.

Back to 1 Thessalonians 2. In 1993, I wrote, *"but just as we have been approved by God to be entrusted with the gospel so we speak'* (v. 4). Thank you, Lord, for entrusting me to speak. Help me never take it for granted or misuse the privilege." Next, I referred to verse 7, *"gentle among you'.* Then exhort, encourage, implore, referring to verse 11." And verse 13, "God's message, *'you accepted it not as the word of men, but for what it really is, the word of God'".*

On to 1994, I wrote, "Need to speak gospel amid opposition and with boldness, not as men pleasers but as God pleasers." Then I referred to verse 13, "A good verse to use in Gideon scripture distributions."

In chapter 2, Paul reminds the Thessalonians that as apostles, they were empowered by God to share what they shared when they were there. *"(A)s we have been approved by God to be entrusted with the gospel, so we speak, not to please man, but to please God who tests our hearts"* (v. 4). That verse is very important to me. I have the chance to stand in pulpits all over the world on behalf of The Gideons International and on behalf of the Ezra Project and share with people. I have been given the privilege to be entrusted with the gospel, so I speak.

> When you received the word of God, which you heard from us, you accepted it not as the word of men but as what it really is, the word of God.
>
> 1 Thess. 2:13

What a privilege, what an honor, even in these daily devotions, to speak to you. I have been entrusted with the Word of God, and I take it very seriously. As Paul, Silas, and Timothy shared the gospel, they did not seek glory from people, they were gentle among them. Like a nursing mother taking care of her own children, they were ready to share, not only the gospel, but themselves.

Through this chapter, we can see Paul, Silas, and Timothy poured themselves out to the people of Thessalonica. *"(H)ow holy and righteous and blameless was our conduct toward you believers . . . We exhorted each one of you and encouraged you and charged you to walk in a manner worthy of God"* (vv. 10, 12).

The people of Thessalonica received their message, *"when you received the word of God, which you heard from us, you accepted it not as the word of men but as what it really is, the word of God"* (v. 13). That is a powerful statement about what the Bible is; not the words of men, but the Word of God.

Paul closes the chapter by reminding them they were torn away from those in Thessalonica. They had to flee. In the introduction of this book, we were reminded the house of Jason, where Paul stayed, was ransacked and they were run out of town. He says, *"But since we were torn away from you"* (v. 17), so he reminds them of that circumstance and tells them they long to come back. But for some reason, Satan has hindered him from doing so.

DIGGING DEEPER

As we close chapter 2, let's think about a couple of things. You have been entrusted with the gospel. Oh, you may not preach in churches. You may not speak in front of crowds. But all of us who are Christians have been entrusted with the gospel. We get opportunities to speak, not to please men but to please God.

I do not know what your family is like. I do not know what your workplace is like. I do not know if you feel pressure when you try to share the gospel with somebody. I do not know any of those things, but I know you were entrusted with the gospel.

God tests our hearts. Are we willing to stand up for the Lord? If so, we do it as instructed in this chapter. Our conduct should be holy, righteous, and blameless. Sharing our faith does not have to be argumentative. We are to walk in a manner worthy of God, who calls you into His own kingdom and glory. So, for all of us who have been entrusted with the gospel, we are going to pray for boldness to share it with those around us, if God asks us to.

How did the church at Thessalonica grow? People shared their faith with others. Is your church growing? Are people in your church sharing their faith with others? Do you see people coming to Christ? Do you see new people visiting your church? Paul, Silas, and Timothy shared the gospel. That is why we get to read 1 Thessalonians today. Let's pray.

Prayer

Lord, we see in these first couple chapters of 1 Thessalonians, Paul, Silas, and Timothy shared the gospel, and they were run out of town for doing so. But that did not hinder them from sharing the gospel in the next town, and the next town, and going back to some of the very places they were run out of and sharing the gospel again and again.

Lord, many of us have become complacent. Some of us have never shared the gospel with someone else. So we pray for holy boldness, Lord. As we have been entrusted with Your gospel, so we speak. Holy Spirit, open doors around us so we can share what You have given to us.

Most of us care deeply about lost souls around us. Give us boldness to share our faith with someone today. Lord, as we do, remind us to be holy, righteous, and blameless before You and before those we share with. Make sure we walk in a manner worthy of the gospel we proclaim. Work through us, Lord, we do not want any glory. We want to turn the glory to You and we know that happens as You allow us to share the gospel with someone else. To God be the glory. In Jesus' name, we pray. Amen.

MY THOUGHTS

1 THESSALONIANS 3

Stand Firm

In 1 Thessalonians 3, Paul hears the Thessalonians are standing firm despite persecution. Have you suffered because of your faith? Can you stand firm? Have you? Please read or listen to 1 Thessalonians 3.

COMMENTS

For 1 Thessalonians, I selected journals three years in a row, 1992, 1993, and 1994, something different than I have done in other *Day by Day Through the Bible* daily devotions. I was thirty-seven, thirty-eight, and thirty-nine years old. It is interesting I read 1 and 2 Thessalonians in three consecutive years. I thought it might be interesting to see if the journal entries were all the same or if they were slightly different.

Here is my journal entry for 1 Thessalonians 3 from 1992, "Destined for affliction, referring to verse 3." Then referring to verses 5-8, "Those who stand firm give confidence to others."

In 1993 (NASB), I wrote, "Go, *'to strengthen and encourage you (in) your faith'*, referring to verse 2." Onto verse 8, *"we . . . live, if you stand firm"*. Then onto verse 13, "I would like my heart to be unblameable *'in holiness before our God and Father'*. Help me live to strengthen and encourage others so I can live because they stand firm."

In 1994 (NASB), I wrote, "Paul worried, did it stick? He couldn't get to the Thessalonians, so he sent Timothy. He hears back that they believe and they are growing in Christ. *'For now we really live, if you stand firm in the Lord'*" (v. 8).

> **For now we really live, if you stand firm in the Lord.**
>
> **1 Thess. 3:8**

Those three journal entries, from three years in a row, are pretty much the same with the similar emphasis on standing firm.

Let's look at chapter 3. Paul sent Timothy back to Thessalonica, *"to establish and exhort you in your faith"*, according to verse 2. As we saw in the book introduction, the Thessalonians were suffering continuing persecution for their faith in Jesus. They were probably hoping those afflictions would go away, but they had not.

In verses 3 and 4, Paul wrote, *"that no one be moved by these afflictions. For you yourselves know that we are destined for this. For when we were with you, we kept telling you beforehand that we were to suffer affliction"*. He relates those afflictions to *"the tempter"* (v. 5). When you became a Christian, when you accepted Jesus as your personal Savior, did you think your life was going to get better? Did you think you were going to be blessed? Did you think you were going to have the favor of God? Or did you understand you might suffer for your testimony for Christ?

I do not know about you, but I do not give the devil a lot of credit in my life. I want to live in verses like, *"greater is he that is in (me), than he that is in the world"* (1 John 4:4 KJV). But I do realize books like Thessalonians and other books in the scripture, remind us we can be, and will be, persecuted for our faith in Jesus.

Paul may have worried about them wilting under the afflictions, but he gets the good news from Timothy they have not. He says, *"For now we live, if you are standing fast in the Lord"* (v. 8).

Who led you to Jesus? How did you come to faith in Christ? If those who saw it happen saw you today, would they rejoice that you are standing fast, that you are standing firm in your faith in Christ?

When I became a Christian at fifteen years old, I was a lone ranger. I did not have any Christian friends. I was not in a youth group. All I had was the Word of

God. When I went to college, I was asked to get in a Bible study. The two guys leading the Bible Study, I eventually nicknamed "Peter" and "Paul". God used them to teach me things I did not know. He used them to keep me accountable in my walk with Christ. I was so young and dumb in the Lord; I think they never thought I would make it. That was four decades ago.

I do not stay in touch with "Peter" and "Paul". I do not see them. They live in different places. But I think if they saw my walk with Christ, they would feel like Paul. They would be excited, 1) I made it at all, and 2) I am still standing fast in the Lord. Those two guys had a huge influence in my life at that tender age of my Christian walk. Like Paul, Silas, and Timothy had on the church at Thessalonica, those two guys had that kind of influence in my life.

DIGGING DEEPER

How about you? Are you standing fast? Are you standing firm in your walk with the Lord? By this letter to the church in Thessalonica, Paul encourages them to keep going. Let's look at the last few verses of chapter 3, *"may the Lord make you increase and abound in love for one another and for all, as we do for you, so that he may establish your hearts blameless in holiness before our God and Father"* (vv. 12-13).

Are you increasing in your walk with the Lord? Are you abounding in love for one another and for all? Are you establishing your heart blameless and in holiness before God? Are you continuing to grow in your walk with Christ? These are questions worth pondering today.

You may ask, "How do I continue to grow? How do I continue to strengthen my walk with the Lord?" No surprise, I would say first, stay in the Word of God each and every day of your life. Why? Because that is where we hear from the Lord. Secondly, pray to the Lord each and every day. Those two things, reading the Bible and praying, give you an intimacy with God unmatched in anything else you can do on a daily basis.

Thirdly, get yourself in a Bible-believing church where you can be challenged, where you can grow in your faith in Christ. Fourth, surround yourself with some Christian friends, maybe in a home group, or maybe in a Bible study. Keep yourself connected to the body of Christ.

I believe those were the things the church in Thessalonica was doing. Those are the things we can do today. Let's pray.

Prayer

Father, some today might be suffering affliction. They may be suffering persecution for their faith in You. If so, we pray they would be strengthened by this passage and they would stand firm, hold fast, for You this day. Beyond just standing, Lord, I hope we continue to walk, walk toward You.

I pray, Lord, all of us would spend time each and every day in a portion of Your Word so we can hear from You. We would also lay our petitions at Your feet so You can hear from us and we can have intimacy with You.

Also, Lord, I pray for our churches. Strengthen our pastors and strengthen the preaching they do, that it would be truly of the Word and that we could grow thereby.

And lastly, Lord, surround us with some Christian friends, people who can hold us accountable, people who can help us grow in You. Keep us connected to You and the body of Christ. By doing so, we will grow in our walk with You and we will be pleasing in Your sight. So let it be written, so let it be done. In the name of Jesus, amen.

MY THOUGHTS

1 THESSALONIANS 4

The Will of God and the Rapture

I n 1 Thessalonians 4, Paul answers questions about the coming of the Lord, commonly referred to as the rapture. He also comments on the will of God. Do you wonder about the rapture, or the will of God? Please read or listen to 1 Thessalonians 4.

COMMENTS

In 1992, when I read 1 Thessalonians chapter 4 (NASB), I wrote concerning verses 1 and 10, *"excel still more."* Then concerning verses 3-17, "The will of God: sanctification, stay away from sexual immorality." Then concerning verse 11, "Make it your ambition to lead a quiet life and attend to your own business and work with your hands." Then, lastly, "We are going to be always with the Lord!"

One year later, in 1993 (NASB), I wrote, *"'excel still more',* referring to verse 1." Then referring to verse 3, *"this is the will of God, your sanctification; that is, that you abstain from sexual immorality."* And verse 7, *"For God has not called us for the purpose of impurity, but in sanctification."*

Then concerning verse 8, "Consequently, *'he who rejects this'* (sanctification), *'is not rejecting man but the God who gives His Holy Spirit to you.'"* I continued to write, "So God wants us sanctified. Part of that is sexual purity. Those who reject that notion are rejecting God. We have a lot of that going on today." Next, I wrote about verse 10, *"excel still more".* I finished with verses 11 and 12, *"'lead a quiet life',* work, *'behave properly',* don't be in need."

One more year later, in 1994 (NASB), I wrote, *"'excel still more'* (v. 1). In what? Walk and please God, sexual morality, sanctification, love one another, lead a quiet life, attend to your own business."

Let's take a look at chapter 4. I find a little humor in the first phrase of verse 1, *"Finally, then, brothers".* That is the beginning of chapter 4. There is all of chapters 4 and 5 left! It reminds me of when I hear preachers say, "In closing," and they go on and on.

Some Christians ask, "What is the will of God for my life?" Here is an example of the will of God for your life:

For this is the will of God, your sanctification: that you abstain from sexual immorality; that each one of you know how to control his own body in holiness and honor, not in the passion of lust like the Gentiles who do not know God; that no one transgress and wrong his brother in this matter, because the Lord is an avenger in all these things, as we told you beforehand and solemnly warned you. For God has not called us for impurity, but in holiness. Therefore whoever disregards this, disregards not man but God, who gives his Holy Spirit to you (vv. 3-8).

> For this is the will of God, your sanctification.
>
> 1 Thess. 4:3

There are several aspects of what the will of God is for our lives right here in these verses. Let's go back over this list. Let's start with sanctification. I looked in my English Standard Version Study Bible for a definition of sanctification. I did not find one, so I asked Siri on my Apple smartphone. Here is what she had to say, "Sanctification means set apart or declare holy; consecrate; free from sin; purify." Not bad, Siri.

Sanctification is the will of God for our lives. So is abstaining from sexual immorality. So is controlling our own body so we do not cave in to the passions of lust. The will of God is also that we do not wrong our brothers, or our neighbors. And the will of God is holiness. Sometimes we ask questions we do not want answers to. Those are some pretty tall orders of what the will of God is for our lives.

Next, Paul covers brotherly love. And brotherly love is also part of the will of God for our lives. He describes it by saying, do it more and more and he lists how, *"to aspire to live quietly, and to mind your own affairs, and to work with your hands, as we instructed you so that you may walk properly before outsiders and be dependent on no one"* (vv. 11-12).

Remember in our book introduction, part of the concern the church had was some people were not working. They were depending on wealthier Christians, and they were not making their own living. Paul addresses that right here. He makes it pretty clear. Work with your hands. Depend on no one.

Then he goes on to address one of their other concerns about those people who died. Did they miss the second coming? He answers their question very clearly, *"But we do not want you to be uninformed, brothers, about those who are asleep"* (in other words, those who have died), *"that you may not grieve as others do who have no hope. For since we believe that Jesus died and rose again, even so, through Jesus, God will bring with him those who have fallen asleep"* (vv. 13-14).

He continues to answer that question, but he also answers the second question, what about those of us who are alive now? Have we missed the second coming? Let's go on with some famous verses in scripture. It is not Paul's opinion. He heard this from the Lord:

> *For this we declare to you by a word from the Lord, that we who are alive, who are left until the coming of the Lord, will not precede those who have fallen asleep. For the Lord himself will descend from heaven with a cry of command, with the voice of an archangel, and with the sound of the trumpet of God. And the dead in Christ will rise first. Then we who are alive, who are left, will be caught up together with them in the clouds to meet the Lord in the air, and so we will always be with the Lord* (vv. 15-17).

That answers the questions of the Thessalonians. Nobody has missed the second coming. Nobody has missed the day of the Lord, dead or alive. The word "rapture" does not appear in scripture, but this is a passage most refer to when talking about the rapture. It is that time when the Lord Himself will descend from heaven. We will hear the voice of an archangel. We will hear the sound of the trumpet. The dead in Christ will rise, and anybody who is still alive will be caught up with them in the air forever to be with the Lord.

DIGGING DEEPER

Paul answers the questions of the Thessalonians. He answers our questions too about how things will end here on earth. He finishes the chapter with these words, *"Therefore encourage one another with these words"* (v. 18). I hope you are encouraged by what we read in 1 Thessalonians 4. Whether we die or whether we are here when the Lord comes back, either way, we are going to be caught up together with them in the clouds to meet the Lord in the air and so we will always be with the Lord. That is eternal life.

Prayer

Lord, we thank You for the day of the Lord. We thank You for the rapture. We thank You that You are the King of kings and Lord of lords. You said You would come back and You will.

We thank You that as You encouraged the Thessalonians with these words, we also can be very encouraged with these words. Thank You for encouraging us as we spend time in Your Word. We give You the praise and the glory. You deserve it all. Amen.

MY THOUGHTS

1 THESSALONIANS 5

Our To-Do List

Today, we finish 1 Thessalonians with chapter 5, all about the day of the Lord. Jesus will come as a thief in the night. Before that day, we are to encourage and build up one another. Paul closes the letter with a few instructions, a Christian "to-do" list. When you master it, let me know. Please read or listen to 1 Thessalonians 5.

COMMENTS

We will take a last look into my journals when I was thirty-seven, thirty-eight, and thirty-nine years old in 1992, 1993, and 1994. On 1 Thessalonians 5, in 1992 (NASB), I wrote, "Be sons of light and of the day. Our deeds can be exposed and that's okay, referring to verses 5-8." Referring to verse 9, I wrote, "Destined for salvation," and verse 11, "'*encourage . . . and build up one another.*' Verses 11-15, help people. Verse 16, '*Rejoice always*'". Then, "My spirit is often not in the rejoicing mood. '*Pray without ceasing*'" (v. 17). I finished with, "My prayer life is not what it ought to be."

One year later, in 1993 (NASB), I wrote, "We are not people of the dark, but rather people of the light. Therefore, although Jesus may come as a thief in the night, we being of the light and sober in spirit should not be surprised, overtaken, when He comes. '*Therefore encourage one another and build up one another*'" (v. 11).

One year later in 1994 (NASB), I wrote, "Peace and safety. People are concerned about dying. Help me understand and help people find peace and safety in Christ." I referred to verse 11, *"encourage and build up one another'.* Appreciate those over me. Rejoice, pray, give thanks, hold fast to that which is good. *'Faithful is He who calls you, and He also will bring it to pass'"* (v. 24).

Amazing, in all my journals, I failed to write one thing about the day of the Lord. So let's go back through the final chapter of 1 Thessalonians. Remember, they were concerned about the second coming. They were concerned some missed it, so Paul is writing and saying they really do not need to hear about this. They know enough. But he does go on to say in verse 2, *"For you yourselves are fully aware that the day of the Lord will come like a thief in the night."*

The next verse goes on to say, some people would look at that and be afraid, but he says because you are children of the light, not darkness, there is no need to be afraid of that night. Verse 4, *"But you are not in darkness, brothers, for that day to surprise you like a thief."* In other words, for us, there is no fear of the day of the Lord. Verses 9 and 10 say, *"For God has not destined us for wrath, but to obtain salvation through our Lord Jesus Christ, who died for us so that whether we are awake or asleep we might live with him."*

Paul sets the hearts of the Thessalonians at ease with these comforting words about the day of the Lord, *"Therefore encourage one another and build one another up, just as you are doing"* (v. 11).

> **See that no one repays anyone evil for evil, but always seek to do good to one another and to everyone.**
>
> **1 Thess. 5:15**

Paul shares about leadership. *"(R)espect those who labor among you and are over you in the Lord and admonish you, and to esteem them very highly in love because of their work"* (vv. 12-13). He goes on to say. *"See that no one repays anyone evil for evil, but always seek to do good to one another and to everyone"* (v. 15).

How about this? *"Rejoice always, pray without ceasing"* (vv. 16-17). I wrote in my journal I don't always have a rejoicing attitude and my prayer life certainly needs improvement.

Paul continues, *"Do not quench the Spirit. Do not despise prophecies, but test everything; hold fast what is good. Abstain from every form of evil"* (vv. 19-22).

We can spend a lot of time on the laundry list of things we should be like. How are you doing with rejoicing always or praying without ceasing or giving thanks in all circumstances? In my flesh, I probably cannot accomplish much of that, but thank God we have the Holy Spirit to help us.

If that is not enough, how about verse 23? *"Now may the God of peace himself sanctify you completely, and may your whole spirit and soul and body be kept blameless at the coming of our Lord Jesus Christ."* In my lifetime, I have described myself in many ways, but I have never described myself as blameless. I'm giggling now because verse 24 tells us how to do all this. *"He who calls you is faithful; he will surely do it."* I wish it was that easy! But on a serious note, I have experienced the fact that *"He who calls you is faithful; he will surely do it"* (v. 24). This ministry, the Ezra Project, is a great example of just that. He called me to do this and He has been faithful to do it.

Paul wrote to the Thessalonians to answer a bunch of questions they had as an early Christian church. He probably thought he did a pretty good job answering those questions; however, he needed to write again, so he wrote 2 Thessalonians.

DIGGING DEEPER

What is our practical application from this last chapter in 1 Thessalonians? Well, it is a pretty tall order, as we have already seen:

- *respect those who labor among you* (v. 12)
- *Be at peace among yourselves* (v. 13)
- *admonish the idle* (v. 12)
- *encourage the fainthearted* (v. 14)
- *help the weak* (v. 14)
- *be patient with them all* (v. 14)
- *See that no one repays anyone evil for evil* (v. 15)
- *always seek to do good to one another and to everyone* (v. 15)

- *Rejoice always* (v. 16)
- *pray without ceasing* (v. 17)
- *give thanks in all circumstances* (v. 18)
- *Do not quench the Spirit* (v. 19)
- *Do not despise prophecies* (v. 20)
- *test everything* (v. 21)
- *hold fast what is good* (v. 21)
- *Abstain from every form of evil* (v. 22)

How are you doing so far?

Lastly, keep your whole spirit, soul, and body blameless. When you get all that done, let me know. Contact me at the Ezra Project and tell me you have this list mastered. When you do, I cannot wait to meet you! Verse 25 closes with, *"Brothers, pray for us",* and I am going to do that right now.

Prayer

Lord, we had a little fun with the end of this book, but You are serious about holiness. All these would be qualities of being holy, living a holy life. But, Lord, in our human strength, we cannot do it. Thank You for the gift of the Holy Spirit that can at least help us on the path toward these things.

We thank You as You close this book with this promise, that *"He who calls you is faithful; he will surely do it"* (v. 24). You are faithful, so help us with all these qualities in our lives. As we see improvement in any of these areas, may we give You the praise and the glory. As You shine us up, may we be an encouragement to one another and build each other up in You. Hallelujah, amen.

MY THOUGHTS

THREE DAYS IN 2 THESSALONIANS

2 THESSALONIANS 1

Persevere

Today, we begin 2 Thessalonians. We will look at my English Standard Version Study Bible book introduction as we look at 2 Thessalonians. As in 1 Thessalonians, Paul is the writer of 2 Thessalonians. 2 Thessalonians was probably written shortly after 1 Thessalonians, from Corinth, in about 50-51 A.D., because Paul had received a report that the situation in Thessalonica had taken a surprising turn.

The church had accepted the strange claim that the day of the Lord had already come. As a result, they were shaken and frightened. They were also suffering persecution, which may have contributed to their confusion about the end times.

Paul wrote 2 Thessalonians to reassure those terrified by the thought the day of the Lord had come, that it certainly had not. He also addressed some of the lingering issues of his first letter, persecution, and some still refusing to work.

The overriding theme of 2 Thessalonians is the second coming of Jesus, much like the first letter. 2 Thessalonians is the only book in the Bible written to correct a misunderstanding of a previous book, 1 Thessalonians. Paul also gives a graphic and frightening view of Jesus's return and a very clear statement about what makes hell so horrific. Heaven is real, but so is hell. Please read or listen to 2 Thessalonians 1.

COMMENTS

To help us through 2 Thessalonians, this short little book, I selected the three journals we used in 1 Thessalonians, 1992, 1993, and 1994. Let's see if there are differences in reading the same book three years in a row.

Let's start with my journal entry from 1992 (NASB), "The Thessalonian example, big faith, according to verse 3. Growing love for each other, again according to verse 3. Perseverance in persecution, verse 4. *'(W)orthy of the kingdom of God'*" (v. 5). I finished with, "For me, count me worthy, fulfill goodness, work in faith, and power."

The next year, 1993, while looking at the journal, I discovered something very interesting. On the weekend I was reading 2 Thessalonians, I was at a men's retreat in Fairplay, Colorado. By looking at the notes in my journal, this was the weekend of the first message of the Ezra Project, ever.

I was asked by a friend to speak at a men's retreat. I told him, "No, I don't speak at men's retreats." He persisted, and I ended up speaking. I remember, in the preparation ahead of time, wondering what in the world I would share with a bunch of men. I got some advice from a friend who did speak at men's retreats. He suggested sharing about being husbands and sharing about being fathers. But his real advice was to share something really, really important to me. Because the Word of God was really, really important to me, I developed the first "Ezra Project message" for this retreat in 1993.

This was before the Ezra Project even existed; it started in 2002. Looking back on some notes leading up to that weekend, I had one note that said, "For Sword Ministries," my own ministry of the Word of God. So it was not even called the Ezra Project. It had no name. It was Sword because the Word of God is sharper than any two-edged sword. Another note I wrote leading up to the retreat was, "For each man attending the men's retreat, for their needs and expectations, for an anointing on me as I share with them, for God's will at the retreat."

On Saturday, I made this note about Friday night, "Nineteen men are here. Lord, You were easy on me for this humble beginning. Last night went well. I spoke for about forty minutes on 'Seek: Seeking God through His Word.' I shared my testimony and my journals, had discussion and had a time of prayer afterwards. Brought ten journals, gave away seven. Have three left. Today is 'Find'."

Then I wrote my prayer, "For the nineteen men here that God's will be done in each life here. That these men would become daily Bible readers. That their needs will be met here at this retreat." Yes, this was the precursor message to the Ezra Project which started almost ten years later. This retreat was 1993; the Ezra Project started in 2002.

On that day, I read 2 Thessalonians (NASB), the whole book in one day, all three chapters. I summarized the whole book in this journal entry, *"'stand firm and hold to the traditions which you were taught'* (2:15) because there will be deluding influence so

> **Stand firm and hold to the traditions which you were taught.**
>
> **2 Thess. 2:15**

that they may believe what is fake. Work so we won't be a burden to others. And live a disciplined life. *'(D)o not grow weary of doing good'"* (3:13).

The next year, 1994, I read the first chapter of 2 Thessalonians (NASB) on one day and wrote, *"'give thanks . . . because your faith is greatly enlarged'* (v. 3), you love one another, persevere in the midst of persecutions." Then, "There will be a righteous judgment. God will repay those who affect us. He will deal out retribution to those who do not know God and to those who do not obey the gospel. The penalty will be eternal destruction."

Let's take a look at 2 Thessalonians 1. We notice in the very first verse, like in 1 Thessalonians, Paul takes a team approach to writing this letter saying, *"Paul, Sylvanus, and Timothy"* all of whom had visited and preached in Thessalonica.

Paul begins with a compliment in verse 3, *"We ought always to give thanks to God for you, brothers, as is right, because your faith is growing abundantly, and the love of every one of you for one another is increasing."* Could that be said about your Christianity? Is your faith growing abundantly and your love for everyone increasing? Growing faith and increasing love should be evidence of our Christianity, just like they were for the church at Thessalonica.

He goes on to compliment them for their steadfastness and their faith, in spite of persecutions and afflictions they were enduring. Again, can that be said of your Christianity? Though you may have faced persecutions, you may have faced afflictions, were you steadfast? Did you endure? In verse 5, Paul tells them they are considered worthy of the kingdom of God because they persevered through suffering and persecution.

He addresses that persecution we learned about in the introduction of this book. He says God will repay those who are persecuting them with a mighty hand, *"in flaming fire, inflicting vengeance on those who do not know God and on those who do not obey the gospel of our Lord Jesus. They will suffer the punishment of eternal destruction"* (vv. 8-9).

We conclude chapter 1 with this powerful encouragement, *"so that the name of our Lord Jesus may be glorified in you, and you in him, according to the grace of our God and the Lord Jesus Christ"* (v. 12).

DIGGING DEEPER

Does your Christian life glorify the Lord? Let's close with a couple of applications from this short chapter:

- Grow in your faith
- Increase in love for people
- Stand steadfast in persecution and affliction

Does your Christian life give glory to God in all you do and say?

Prayer

Father, it is good to see what Paul sees in the Thessalonica church, growth and maturity. He sees them growing in their faith, growing in their love, standing firm against persecution and affliction, and glorifying You in their lives. May we, as Christians, never be stagnant but always be growing in the same way.

Holy Spirit grow us up in You. May those around us, 1) know we are Christians, 2) see our faith growing, 3) see our love increasing, 4) see us stand firm against persecution and affliction, and finally, 5) glorify You in all we do. Help us, Holy Spirit, do these things. In Jesus' name, amen.

MY THOUGHTS

The Man of Lawlessness, the Antichrist

In 2 Thessalonians 2. Paul answers questions about the day of the Lord. He reminds us not to be quickly shaken or alarmed. The day of the Lord cannot come until the son of destruction exalts himself. Will you recognize him, or be deceived? Please read or listen to 2 Thessalonians 2.

COMMENTS

In 1992, I read 2 Thessalonians 2 and 3 (NASB) on the same day. Concerning chapter 2, I wrote, "Jesus will slay the lawless one with the breath of his mouth. That's power. There will be no fight, no struggle. Jesus by his word will end Satan." Then I wrote concerning verse 15, *"stand firm and hold to the traditions which you were taught"*.

In 1993, at that men's retreat, I read all of 2 Thessalonians (NASB) on one day. I summarized it yesterday, but I will summarize it again today. Concerning 2 Thessalonians, I wrote, *"stand firm and hold to the traditions which you were taught'* (v. 15) because there will be *'a deluding influence so that they will believe what is false'* (v. 11). Work so we won't be a burden to others."

In 1994, the third year in a row, I read 2 Thessalonians 2 (NASB). I wrote, "The Thessalonians thought they had missed the second coming. Paul says it can't happen until antichrist sits in the temple. Jesus *'will slay him with the breath of his mouth'* (v. 8). The power of the word of God. Why do people perish? *'(B)ecause they did not receive the love of the truth so as to be saved'"* (v. 10). Then I wrote, *"stand firm and hold to the traditions which you were taught'"* (v. 15).

In chapter 2, Paul addresses the concern the Thessalonians raised about missing the day of the Lord. First, he calms them down. He says, do not be *"quickly shaken . . . or alarmed"* (v. 2), by either what you heard or read. Then he says, *"Let no one deceive you . . . For that day will not come"* (v. 3). Then he describes when and why they have not missed the day of the Lord.

In verse 3, Paul refers to the *"man of lawlessness"* who was also referred to in other places as "antichrist." This lawless one has to appear first before the day of the Lord. Paul is saying that has not occurred yet. He tells him what this antichrist will be like. He will exalt himself *"against every so-called god or object of worship, so that he takes his seat in the temple of God, proclaiming himself to be God"* (v. 4).

Paul reminds them he talked about this with them when he was there, and that the antichrist cannot reign because there is a restrainer right now. He cannot reign until the restrainer releases him for his time. My English Standard Version Study Bible footnote says this about the restrainer, "Scholarly theories on the identity of this restrainer include the Roman Empire/Emperor, the Holy Spirit, and the archangel Michael" (p. 2318). I am going with the Holy Spirit.

The footnote goes on to say, "The restrainer functions to make sure that the man of lawlessness is revealed in his time and not before" (p. 2318). Again, I am going with the Holy Spirit on this. I believe the Holy Spirit is restraining the lawless one from taking power and claiming to be God. Praise God for the Holy Spirit.

> But the Helper, the Holy Spirit, whom the Father will send in my name, he will teach you all things and bring to your remembrance all that I have said to you.
>
> John 14:26

The Holy Spirit, the restrainer, was promised by Jesus. Go to John 14:16-17, *"And I will ask the Father, and he will give you another Helper, to be with you forever, even the Spirit of truth, whom the world cannot receive, because it neither sees him nor knows him. You know him, for he dwells with you and will be in you.* " Dropping down to verse 26, John says, *"But the Helper, the Holy Spirit, whom the Father will send in my name, he will teach you all things and bring to your remembrance all that I have said to you."*

The promise of this restrainer is again mentioned in Acts 1:

So when they had come together, they asked him, "Lord, will you at this time restore the kingdom to Israel?" He said to them, "It is not for you to know times or seasons that the Father has fixed by his own authority. But you will receive power when the Holy Spirit has come upon you, and you will be my witnesses in Jerusalem and in all Judea and Samaria, and to the end of the earth" (vv. 6-8).

It is the power of the Holy Spirit in our world today that restrains the lawless one, the antichrist, from assuming power and taking over the temple of God. But let's not be confused. The lawless one is working in our world today. In this chapter, verse 7 tells us that: *"The mystery of lawlessness is already at work."* He just is not bold enough to proclaim himself as God yet.

Paul warns the Thessalonians, and he warns us, we need to be on guard against the powers of the enemy:

The coming of the lawless one is by the activity of Satan with all power and false signs and wonders, and with all wicked deception for those who are perishing, because they refused to love the truth and so be saved. Therefore God sends them a strong delusion, so that they may believe what is false, in order that all may be condemned who did not believe the truth but had pleasure in unrighteousness (vv. 9-12).

If you think this refers only to unbelievers, let's think again. Jesus warns us, even the elect can be deceived by the power of delusion of the lawless one. Matthew 24:22-24, says *"And if those days had not been cut short, no human being would be saved. But for the sake of the elect those days will be cut short. Then if anyone says to you, 'Look, here is the Christ!' or 'There he is!' do not believe it. For false christs and false prophets will arise and perform great signs and wonders, so as to lead astray, if possible, even the elect."* Let's not cut Satan short. He comes with power, false signs and wonders, wicked deception, and strong delusion.

DIGGING DEEPER

How do you shield yourself from the enemy's attacks, from these delusions, from wicked deception? Paul tells us right here, *"love the truth"* (v. 10). Believe in the truth. Those who refuse to love the truth are the ones who are going to have a problem.

And where do we find truth? John 17:17 says, *"Sanctify them in the truth; thy word is truth."* Stay in the Word, stay close to the Word of God. It is always our defense against the attacks of the enemy.

Look at 2 Thessalonians 2:13, *"But we ought always to give thanks to God for you, brothers beloved by the Lord, because God chose you as the firstfruits to be saved"*. Through what? *"(T)hrough sanctification by the Spirit and belief in the truth"* (v. 13).

When these attacks come, this wicked deception, strong delusion, *"So then, brothers, stand firm and hold to the traditions that you were taught by us, either by our spoken word or by our letter"* (v. 15). Those letters make up the Bible today, so hang on to the truth. *"(S)tand firm and hold to the traditions that you were taught"* (v. 15) through the scriptures.

Prayer

Father, thank You for the scriptures that remind us the day of the Lord has not yet come; but it will. We thank You for the restrainer, the Holy Spirit, keeping Satan away from his time of proclaiming himself as God. That day will come. If it comes in our day, Lord, may we be strong enough to stand on your truth and not be deceived by the enemy.

Thank You for Your truth, Your Word is truth. Holy Spirit, continue to stir in us a desire for Your truth. We ask it, in Jesus' name. Amen.

MY THOUGHTS

Should Christians Help the Poor?

Today, we finish 2 Thessalonians with chapter 3. Paul finishes his second letter by seeking prayer and warning against idleness. *"If anyone is not willing to work, let him not eat"* (v. 10) or *"do not grow weary in doing good"* (v. 13). Which is it when it comes to the poor? Please read or listen to 2 Thessalonians 3.

COMMENTS

In 1992, at thirty-seven years old, concerning 2 Thessalonians 3 (NASB), I wrote in my personal Bible reading journal, "We still need to pray that *'the word of the Lord may spread rapidly and be glorified'''* (v. 1). Then I wrote, "Separate from sinners, referring to verses 6 and 14." And I wrote in capital letters, "WORK, referring to verses 8, and 10-13."

In 1993, at thirty-eight years old, I read all of 2 Thessalonians (NASB) two days in a row, making journal entries on both days. I wrote on the first day, "Do not grow weary in good work. Don't act like a busybody, undisciplined life. Work is part of the blessing of life. Do it and do it well." The next day, when I read those same chapters all over again, concerning chapter 3, I wrote, "And live a disciplined life. *'(D)o not grow weary of doing good'''* (v. 15). So, kind of the same themes on both those days.

In 1994, the third year in a row, at thirty-nine years old, I read 2 Thessalonians 3, and wrote, "Not all men have faith, but the Lord is faithful." Then I referred to verses 6-15, "Takes aim at those who are lazy. They have no discipline. They won't work, but they want a handout from the church. Don't associate with such people. But don't tire of doing good (feeding and taking care of them, is that what doing good is?). Admonish them as brothers, not enemies." Then I wrote a question, "How can one do both? Not feed the poor and feed the poor." That ends my journal entries on 2 Thessalonians 3.

Let's look at chapter 3. I love the first verse. It is an Ezra Project verse, *"Finally, brothers, pray for us, that the word of the Lord may speed ahead and be honored"*. We have not used that verse as a theme verse for a year of the Ezra Project, but we may, as it draws my attention today. *"(P)ray for us, that the word of the Lord may speed ahead and be honored"* (v. 1).

> **But the Lord is faithful. He will establish you and guard you against the evil one.**
>
> **2 Thess. 3:3**

On to verse 3, *"But the Lord is faithful. He will establish you and guard you against the evil one."* Praise God. We get a challenge in verse 5, *"May the Lord direct your hearts to the love of God and to the steadfastness of Christ."* May He direct our hearts accordingly.

Then Paul takes on one of the other concerns of the Thessalonians, those who were idle or those who would not work anymore. I wrote in my journal he tells us to separate ourselves from sinners. He does here in verse 6, *"Now we command you, brothers, in the name of our Lord Jesus Christ that you keep away from any brother who is walking in idleness and not in accord with the tradition that you received from us."*

Let's look at my English Standard Version Study Bible footnote on this verse:

Paul strongly commands the community as a whole to discipline by disassociation those who are not working but are depending on others for a living. The community is to **keep away from** these idlers, which probably means excommunicating them. Paul takes the sin of these people seriously, but at this point he still regards them as "brothers." **In idleness** means "in an undisciplined, irresponsible, or disorderly manner." These people are shirking their obligation to work. This behavior was **not in accord with the tradition** passed on by the missionaries regarding the necessity of working for one's keep (p. 2319).

Like in Thessalonica, we still have able-bodied people who simply choose not to work. What is a Christian to do? Paul tells them to go to work, *"Now such persons we command and encourage in the Lord Jesus Christ to do their work quietly and to earn their own living"* (v. 12). Right before that, is a verse many of us are familiar with, *"If anyone is not willing to work, let him not eat"* (v. 10). Paul takes a pretty hard stand against those who are capable of working and simply choose not to.

But in the very next verse, Paul says, *"do not grow weary in doing good"* (v. 13). Many of us would consider doing good, helping those in need. I wrote about that when I wrote a question in my 1994 Journal, "But don't tire in doing good. Isn't feeding and taking care of them, doing good?" Let's get some help from my English Standard Version Study Bible once again. The footnote on verse 13 says, "The community as a whole, particularly wealthier members exploited by the idle, might **grow weary in doing good,** but Paul calls on them to continue being charitable, albeit only to those who are deserving" (p. 2319).

Scripture is making a distinction. There is a difference between people who can work but will not and those who cannot work and need help. Certainly, part of Christianity is helping those in need. Paul goes on to say, *"If anyone does not obey what we say in this letter, take note of that person, and have nothing to do with him, that he may be ashamed"* (v. 14).

Again, a footnote helps me understand this verse:

Paul believes it is very possible that some will ignore his warning and continue in their idle ways, so he instructs the community as a whole to **take note of** such people and **have nothing to do with** them. The purpose of this disassociation is so that the stubbornly insubordinate brothers will be ashamed, repent, and be restored to the community. Church discipline must always aim at renewing discipleship (p. 2319).

Some of us might refer to this as "tough love," but we are to keep a right heart as verse 15 reminds us, *"Do not regard him as an enemy, but warn him as a brother."*

DIGGING DEEPER

This discussion in chapter 3 about idleness, or those who can work but will not work, is very, very helpful as an application today about how we as Christians ought to live. This chapter makes it very clear we are to help those who are in need; but, we are not to make a way, we are not to accommodate, those who can work and simply choose not to.

If we are bold enough, we are to *"encourage (those people) in the Lord Jesus Christ to do their work quietly and to earn their own living"* (v. 12). We are not to regard them as enemies, but as brothers. Our goal should be to restore them to fellowship in the body and reconcile their own economic well-being. I have never served on a benevolence committee in a church, so I cannot say how churches handle these delicate issues. But hopefully, we get some guidance from 2 Thessalonians 3.

As we close this short book, we are reminded of the two major issues it covered. People thought they missed the day of the Lord, and they had some people that chose not to work. Paul addresses both issues very clearly in his letter back to the Thessalonians.

Prayer

I close with chapter 3 verse 1, *"pray for us"*, the Ezra Project, *"that the word of the Lord may speed ahead and be honored"*. Would you consider praying for us that we can spread the Word of God with honor through *Day by Day Through the Bible*, ADDBIBLE, and through the Ezra Project, by connecting God's people to God's Word? To God be the glory. In Jesus' name, we ask it. Amen.

MY THOUGHTS

SIX DAYS IN 1 TIMOTHY

1 TIMOTHY 1

Love from a Pure Heart

Today, we begin the Book of 1 Timothy. I often refer to my English Standard Version Study Bible book introductions when I introduce a new book. I will do so again here. 1 Timothy was written by Paul in the mid-60s A.D, possibly after his first imprisonment in Rome at the close of the Book of Acts. Tradition states that Paul may have been released after a few years, did further mission work, and was imprisoned a second time. He was executed under Nero in 68 A.D.

Paul wrote 1 Timothy to advise Timothy about issues arising at the church of Ephesus. Paul left Timothy in Ephesus so he wrote him some instructions about how Christians should behave. False teachers are the primary problem Paul addresses, but he also wants Christian behavior grounded in the gospel.

The theme of 1 Timothy is the gospel leads to the practical, visible change in the lives of those who believe it. In 1 Timothy, we can look for the most explicit teaching in the Bible, that there is one God, one mediator between Him and men, the Lord Jesus Christ. We will see that in chapter 2. We will find a list of qualifications for church leadership in chapter 3. And how to live a blameless life in chapter 6. Please read or listen to 1 Timothy 1.

COMMENTS

I am not a preacher, I am not a pastor, I am just a guy who reads his Bible every day and wants to see what God has to say to me. I have journaled my daily Bible reading for over thirty-five years, and for 1 and 2 Timothy I chose journals from 1992, 2002, and 2012, ten years apart. I learned about journaling in my English class in my high school years, but I did not do much of it until 1983 when I started journaling my time in God's Word. I have done so ever since. What I share is what I wrote down after I read a chapter of scripture and what I received from the Lord. That is what I will share with you concerning 1 Timothy 1.

In 1992, I wrote in my journal, "Goal of instruction, *'love from a pure heart and a good conscience and a sincere faith'*" (v. 5 NASB). Then I wrote, "Thanks for putting me into service, referring to verse 12." And then a reference to verse 14, "Grace of God more than abundant."

My journal in 2002 indicates I was in Thailand when reading 1 Timothy. At that time, I was serving in The Gideons International on the International Extension Committee. Part of my responsibility was to visit several countries in Asia and the South Pacific. What does it take to get to Thailand from Denver, Colorado? I wrote, "Lost October 31st in the air. Had a good trip. Left at 7:45 p.m., Wednesday, October 30th from Denver to San Francisco. Left there at 11:45 p.m. for Hong Kong. Fifteen-hour flight, arrived 6:00 a.m., Friday, November 1st. Left at 9 a.m. to Bangkok, arrived 10:45 a.m., about twenty-seven hours later."

> **The aim of our charge is love that issues from a pure heart and a good conscience and a sincere faith.**
>
> **1 Tim. 1:5**

From Bangkok, I wrote about 1 Timothy 1 (NASB), "Love comes *from a pure heart and a good conscience and a sincere faith'*" (v. 5). Then, *"I thank Christ Jesus our Lord, who has strengthened me, because He considered me faithful, putting me into service"* (v. 12). Pretty much the same verses I quoted in 1992.

In 2012, I wrote, "Stay in Ephesus to challenge false teachers. We don't shy away from false doctrine. We confront it and challenge it. But we do it in love. The law, the Old Testament, is good. The law defines sin in the first chapter, verses 9 and 10. Without the law, how would sin, disobedience, be defined? God lays out his standard of conduct. Those who are just, already live within the parameters of the law. Homosexuality is clearly sexually immoral, included in a long list of undesirable behaviors."

Then I quoted verse 12, *"'I thank him who has given me strength, Christ Jesus our Lord, because he judged me faithful, appointing me to his service'. This is true for me too.* He gives us mercy, grace, faith, and love. Jesus came into the world to save sinners. Thank You, Jesus, for saving me."

DIGGING DEEPER

Paul opens up 1 Timothy with saying, *"The aim of our charge is love that issues from a pure heart and a good conscience and a sincere faith"* (v. 5). Paul also reminds Timothy, and us, Christ Jesus came into the world to save sinners and we can be saved by His mercy. Have you been saved by His mercy? If so, does your heart issue love from a good conscience and a sincere faith?

Paul gives God all the glory, "To the King of the ages, immortal, invisible, the only God, be honor and glory forever and ever. Amen" (v. 17). Do you give God all the glory for your salvation and your heart of love? What a great place to start 1 Timothy.

Prayer

Father, we thank You that Your aim is love. And You came into this world to save sinners. And by receiving Your mercy, we too can be saved and have eternal life with You. You do deserve all the glory. *"To the King of the ages, immortal, invisible, the only God, be honor and glory forever and ever. Amen"* (v. 17).

MY THOUGHTS

1 TIMOTHY 2

One Way Jesus

Today, we are in 1 Timothy 2. Christians are accused of saying there is only one way to heaven. Do you agree? Please read or listen to 1 Timothy 2.

COMMENTS

This is a short, but power-packed chapter. We begin with my journal in 2012, "Pray for all people. Pray also for people in high positions that life might be quiet and peaceful. Life is hardly described today as quiet and peaceful. It is hectic, overwhelming, too busy, noisy. God *'desires for all to be saved'* (v. 4). How? One God, one way to Him, Jesus, referring to verses 5 and 6. This is not Christian doctrine, it is biblical doctrine. God is exclusive. One way to heaven. Roles of women in the church. Controversial." Really? No kidding! We will cover that topic later.

My journal entry in 2002 (NASB) was from Bangkok, Thailand, "God wants *'all men to be saved and to come to the knowledge of the truth'* (v. 4). There's only one way that will happen, through Jesus Christ. Many believe there are several ways to God. Christians believe there's only one way, through Jesus, *'one mediator . . . between God and men'"* (v. 5).

From my journal in 1992, let's see what I had to say about some of these controversial issues in this chapter. I wrote, "Pray. Pray for all men, for those in authority, so we can lead a tranquil and quiet life in godliness and dignity. Tranquil. What a forgotten word! There is not much tranquility in the world today, at least not where I live. People are going a hundred miles an hour and burning out at that pace."

Let's step aside from the journal for a moment because I wrote that twenty-five years ago. The pace of life in twenty-five years has been turbocharged. Who would say you live a tranquil life? Who would say your life is peaceful and quiet? Maybe it is because we forgot the next phrase in verse 2, *"godly and dignified in every way."*

Our lives do not depend on those in high authority, kings or those in high positions, but if they were godly and they were dignified in every way, our lives might be more peaceful and quiet. But the same holds true for us. Is your life godly? Is it dignified? Or are you just running with the herd? Maybe this passage will remind you to take some time to think about what it would take to actually live a peaceful, quiet, tranquil life. It may mean making some changes, not keeping up with those around you. Verse 3 says, *"This is good, and it is pleasing in the sight of God our Savior."* Is the pace of your life good and is it pleasing in the sight of God your Savior?

I continue with my journal entry in 1992, "God desires that all would be saved, however, He won't force us. We have the choice to stay unsaved." Then I wrote, "One God, *'the man Jesus Christ'"* (v. 5). Then, "Men should pray."

I continued, "Women should reflect godliness, be submissive, and not be over men. Why? Because that's what the Word of God says. Like other situations in life, we can't have everyone with authority. God has selected men to lead and women to receive instruction with submissiveness. If men would lead, women would be more likely to follow. But because most men won't lead, women fill the gap." Remember that was a journal entry twenty-five years ago, 1992.

DIGGING DEEPER

First, let's talk about God's desire, then we will talk about men and women. 1 Timothy 2 is a very clear gospel message. Verses 3-6 say, *"God our Savior, who desires all people to be saved and to come to the knowledge of the truth. For there is one God, and there is one mediator between God and men, the man Christ Jesus, who gave himself as a ransom for all".* Let's not think about our own philosophies, let's not think about what our churches teach, let's think about what the Word of God says right here. The passage clearly says God *"desires all people to be saved"* (v. 4).

> For there is one God, and there is one mediator between God and men, the man Christ Jesus, who gave himself as a ransom for all.
>
> 1 Tim. 2:5-6

He says how that happens. One God, one mediator, Christ Jesus, who gave Himself so we could be saved. That is why Christians are labeled "one-way Christians." There is no other way to be saved than through Jesus Christ. That is what the Word of God says, not what I say, not what your pastor says, not what your church teaches. It is what the Word of God says. Acts 4:12, says, *"And there is salvation in no one else, for there is no other name under heaven given among men by which we must be saved."* That name is Jesus Christ.

As I wrote in my journal in '92, "God desires that all would be saved, however, He won't force us. We have the choice to stay unsaved." So, today, you can choose to believe what we heard and read, or you can choose to reject it. But God's Word is clear: He loves you and He desires that you be saved.

Now let's cover men and women in the church. Again, let's not worry about what we think. Let's just read what the Word of God says. Let's look at verses 12 and 13, *"I do not permit a woman to teach or to exercise authority over a man; rather, she is to remain quiet. For Adam was formed first, then Eve."* This is about creative order, about how God created men and women. Let's go back to where that happened in Genesis 2:7, *"then the Lord God formed the man of dust from the ground and breathed into his nostrils the breath of life, and the man became a living creature."*

In Genesis 2:18, the Word continues, *"Then the Lord God said, 'It is not good that the man should be alone; I will make him a helper fit for him.'"* Verses 21 and 22 continue, *"So the Lord God caused a deep sleep to fall upon the man, and while he slept took one of his ribs and closed up its place with flesh. And the rib that the Lord God had taken from the man he made into a woman."*

Verse 23 says, *"Then the man said, 'This at last is bone of my bones and flesh of my flesh; she shall be called Woman, because she was taken out of Man.'"* In Genesis 3, when sin enters the world, God says this to Eve, *"Your desire shall be for your husband, but he shall rule over you"* (v. 16). My English Standard Version Study Bible footnote on this verse is pretty clear:

> **Your desire shall be for your husband, and he shall rule over you.** These words from the Lord indicate that there will be an ongoing struggle between the woman and the man for leadership in the marriage relationship. The leadership role of the husband and the complementary relationship between husband and wife that were ordained by God before the fall have now been deeply damaged and distorted by sin. This especially takes the form of inordinate desire (on the part of the wife) and domineering rule (on the part of the husband) . . . The ongoing result of Adam and Eve's original sin of rebellion against God will have disastrous consequences for their relationship: (1) Eve will have the sinful "desire" to oppose Adam and to assert leadership over him, reversing God's plan for Adam's leadership in marriage. But (2) Adam will also abandon his God-given, pre-fall role of leading, guarding, and caring for his wife, replacing this with his own sinful, distorted desire to "rule" over Eve. Thus one of the most tragic results of Adam and Eve's rebellion against God is an ongoing, damaging conflict between husband and wife in marriage, driven by the sinful behavior of both in rebellion against their respective God-given roles and responsibilities in marriage (p. 56).

I understand biblical teaching on this issue may not be popular today, but it is still biblical teaching. The passage in Genesis refers to creative order. There is a passage in 1 Corinthians 11:3 that refers to spiritual headship, *"But I want you to understand that the head of every man is Christ, the head of a wife is her husband, and the head of Christ is God."* The passage in 1 Timothy 2 stirs up two very, very important biblical truths. There is creative order and there is spiritual headship. Those are biblical views.

As we close out 1 Timothy 2, let's not get lost in the controversy about the role of men and women, but let's focus on God's love. The most important verse to me in this chapter is, *"God our Savior, who desires all people to be saved and to come to the knowledge of the truth. For there is one God, and there is one mediator between God and men, the man Christ Jesus, who gave himself as a ransom for all"* (vv. 3-6).

Prayer

Lord, we can get stirred up about the culture of our day, the role of men and women, but in this chapter, You remind us to, first of all, pray for all people, including those in high positions who have leadership over us.

But most importantly, Lord, You remind us You desire all people be saved. Help us, Lord, to do all we can to make sure that happens by sharing our faith with others. Remind us to tell people about Jesus. Remind us to share that most famous verse in all the Bible, John 3:16, *"For God so loved the world that he gave his only Son that whoever believes in him should not perish, but have eternal life."* That is Your desire, Lord, and we thank You for loving and caring for us so much that You gave Your only Son that we can be saved. Hallelujah! Thank You. In Jesus' name, amen.

MY THOUGHTS

1 TIMOTHY 3

Leadership

Today, we are in 1 Timothy 3. Paul outlines for young Timothy characteristics of leadership. Are you a leader? Do you follow biblical characteristics of leadership in your home, workplace, or church? Please read or listen to 1 Timothy 3.

COMMENTS

In my personal Bible reading journal in 1992, I wrote, "Leadership in the church begins at home. Whether bishop, overseer, or deacon, a man's household must be in order before he can lead in God's house."

Ten years later, in 2002, I wrote pretty much the same thing. "The first place to be a Christian is in my own home. I must follow biblical principles with my wife, children, home, business, etc., before I can be considered for leadership outside the home. We should take heed to lead our families before we lead our churches, schools, communities, etc. We would have more success if we had stronger families." By the way, that entry was from Bangkok, Thailand, where I was serving on behalf of The Gideons International, visiting Gideon camps in Thailand.

In 2012, another ten years later, I wrote, "Leadership. Paul lists many qualities of character that should be observable of one aspiring to leadership. One key is how you manage your own household. Another is reputation in the community. Leadership also should have first been tested and proven. Leadership in the church of God is serious business."

DIGGING DEEPER

The theme of 1 Timothy 3 is pretty obvious: leadership. What are some characteristics of Christian leadership? As we read through the list Paul enumerates, think about how you measure up with these characteristics:

- **Above reproach**. You may wonder what reproach means, so I asked my smartphone, I asked Siri. A couple of words came up, disapproval and disappointment. The term "above reproach" probably means you have not disappointed people, or you have not been disapproved by people based on your behavior, you have not been accused of anything, or you have not been rebuked for some kind of behavior. Are you above reproach?
- **Husband of one wife.** I am going to skip the meaning of this and go to the next one.
- **Sober-minded.** It means clear thinking.
- **Self-controlled.** It can mean self-controlled physically, self-controlled mentally, and self-controlled spiritually.
- **Respectable.** You respect others and others respect you.
- **Hospitable.** Do you welcome people into your home? Do you actually take care of people?
- **Able to teach.** If we are going to be leaders, can we instruct others?
- **Not a drunkard.** That is a pretty obvious qualification of leadership; however, we know of way too many politicians, way too many people in leadership, way too many business folks, who have a little too much to drink.

- **Not violent, but gentle; not quarrelsome**. A leader cannot be argumentative, violent, or out of control.
- **Not a lover of money.** That does not mean a leader cannot have money, but he cannot have a love for money.
- **Manage your own household.** This perspective is not just your own, but the perspective of your spouse and your children. *"(F)or if someone does not know how to manage his own household, how will he care for God's church?"* (v. 5). A training ground for leadership is our own homes.

> For if someone does not know how to manage his own household, how will he care for God's church?
>
> 1 Tim. 3:5

- **Not a recent convert.** That makes sense to most of us. If you are going to lead in the church, you probably should have been a Christian for at least some period of time.
- **Well thought of by outsiders.** A good leader would have a good reputation.

The list goes on concerning Deacons:
- **Dignified.** I, again, asked my smartphone, Siri, what dignified means and 'she' said, "Having or showing a composed or serious manner that is worthy of respect." Are you serious? Are you composed?
- **Not double-tongued.** You cannot say one thing and do another. You cannot speak out of both sides of your mouth. This list ought to be read to politicians, business leaders, school educators, even those who wear the cloth.
- **Not addicted to much wine.** We covered this above with regard to drunkards.
- **Not greedy for dishonest gain.** In other words, you ought to have a good work ethic.
- **Hold the mystery of the faith with a clear conscience.** You need to be a good Christian and you need to stand for what you believe.

- **Be tested first.** You rise to leadership by being tested in smaller things until you rise to bigger things. The testing ground is oftentimes our own homes.

That is quite a list. How do I measure up? How do you measure up?

Paul outlines to Timothy in chapter 3, the characteristics of leadership so he can choose leaders for the church at Ephesus. Why is good leadership so important in the church? Paul gives us the answer, the church is *the household of God . . . a pillar and buttress of the truth*" (v. 15). O, that churches would reflect this today. Some do, and some do not. For those who do not reflect this, it may be because they do not follow these qualifications for leadership in the church.

Prayer

Father, we thank You for this list Paul delineates for Christian leadership in Your churches. We pray our churches today would reflect these qualifications in their leadership. Especially that Christian leaders would hold the mystery of the faith with a clear conscience.

Lord, bless those in Christian leadership today. May we represent the household of God and truly be a buttress for truth in our world today. God bless Christian leadership. In Jesus' name, we pray. Amen.

MY THOUGHTS

1 TIMOTHY 4

Living a Godly Life

In 1 Timothy 4, Paul describes godly living. Are you a good example of living a godly life? Are you an ambassador for this thing called Christianity? Please read or listen to 1 Timothy 4.

COMMENTS

In 1992, I was thirty-seven years old, when I wrote in my journal (NASB), "Strong words from Paul. *'Seared in their own conscience as with a branding iron'* (v. 2), *'nourished on the words of the faith'* (v. 6). A good place to eat." Then I quoted verse 7, *"'discipline yourself for the purpose of godliness'.* Discipline is a lost art. People are not willing to work at or for something. If it isn't easy or free or quick, it isn't worth the effort. Self-discipline, marriage, children, so much is suffering because there is so little discipline anymore."

Then I wrote, "Public reading of the Word is so necessary in our country today. Lord, how can I be part of this mission field?" Lastly, quoting verse 15, *"be absorbed in (spiritual gifts), so that your progress will be evident to all."*

In 2002, at forty-seven years old, I was in Bangkok, Thailand. I wrote a little bit about being in Thailand, "Spoke in a church yesterday pastored by a man from Georgia. It was a good church and he was very supportive of the Gideons. It's wonderful to hear worship in other languages, to see the body of Christ in another country." I wrote about 1 Timothy 4, "Set an example for the believers in speech, in life, in love, in faith, and in purity. Devote yourself to the public reading of scripture, to preaching, and to teaching. God calls us to be exemplary. People are watching how Christians live. What are they seeing?"

In 2012, at fifty-seven years old, I wrote, "In later times, people will be deceived by deceitful spirits and teachings of demons and liars. It is hard to say or believe that religions other than Christianity are demonic, but that is what is claimed here. Why we pray before meals." I cited verses 4 and 5. Then I referred to verses 7 and 8, "Exercise is of some value. But more valuable is training in godliness." Then I quote verse 10, "'*Savior of all people, especially of those who believe.'* What does that mean?" Finally, I referred to verse 12, "Be an example of Christianity in speech, conduct, love, faith, and purity. Practice these things. Immerse yourself in them to grow and be an example for others."

DIGGING DEEPER

1 Timothy 3 was about the qualities of leadership. This chapter gets more personal. It gives us instructions about how to live a godly life. Let's see how Paul instructs Timothy and, thereby, instructs us today. He says in verse 6, "*If you put these things before the brothers, you will be a good servant of Christ Jesus*".

He starts with, "*being trained in the words of the faith and of the good doctrine*" (v. 6). Yes, we need to be trained "*in the words of the faith and of the good doctrine*" which comes from the Word of God. That is why the Ezra Project produces ADDBIBLE and *Day by Day Through the Bible*, so Christians can stay close to the Word of God; a key part of godly living.

Paul goes on to say to Timothy, "*Have nothing to do with irreverent, silly myths. Rather train yourself for godliness*" (v. 7). For us, he is telling us we do not need to be focused on the ways of the world. We need to stay focused on the ways of the Word.

Training in godliness takes work; it takes effort, like physical exercise. Paul says, *"while bodily training is of some value, godliness is of value in every way"* (v. 8). Do you spend more time focused on your body or on your spirit?

Next, he reminds Timothy that we have *"our hope set on the living God, who is the Savior of all people"* (v. 10). Setting our hope on the living God is a major part of living a godly life. Paul instructs Timothy to command and teach these things. You may not be a teacher in that regard, but we are all to share in our sphere of influence the truths of the gospel, and our relationship with Jesus.

Then he tells Timothy, *"set the believers an example in speech, in conduct, in love, in faith, in purity"* (v. 12). Is that what people see in your life? I said in one of my journals, "People are watching." What do they see when they observe Christians? Are you an example *"in speech, in conduct, in love, in faith, in purity"* (v. 12) to those around you? The term is used in scripture; *"we are ambassadors for Christ"* (2 Cor. 5:20). How do people see Jesus if they see me or you?

Paul also tells Timothy, *"Do not neglect the gift you have"* (v. 14). We all have gifts. We all have different gifts. We are not to neglect the gifts God has given us to further His kingdom. What is your gift? What gift has God given you to further His kingdom?

> **Practice these things, immerse yourself in them, so that all may see your progress. Keep a close watch on yourself and on the teaching.**
>
> **1 Tim. 4:15-16**

Paul finishes by reminding Timothy all this takes work, *"Practice these things, immerse yourself in them, so that all may see your progress. Keep a close watch on yourself and on the teaching. Persist in this, for by so doing you will save both yourself and your hearers"* (vv. 15-16).

Christianity is not a spectator sport. It takes work. We are to keep practicing. We are to immerse ourselves in our faith. We are to keep a close watch on ourselves. We are to persist. Why? Paul says, *"for by so doing you will save both yourself and your hearers"* (v. 16).

Godly behavior takes work, it takes practice, it takes persistence. I know I am still a work in progress. Are you? I hope so because Paul starts this chapter with a serious warning. He says, *"in later times some will depart from the faith by devoting themselves to deceitful spirits and teachings of demons, through the insincerity of liars whose consciences are seared"* (vv. 1-2).

Surely, we are in these later times. Many have departed from the faith. Many are being wooed away from biblical Christianity by deceitful spirits, the teachings of demons, and lies. To keep that from happening to you, Paul says, *"devote yourself to the public reading of Scripture, to exhortation, to teaching"* (v. 13). In other words, stay in the Word of God. Keep a close watch on yourself and on the teaching.

Prayer

Lord, keep us close to the fire, so our flame does not go out. Thanks for the reminder that I do not arrive in Christianity, rather it is a continuing journey. It takes practice and it takes persistence. And though I understand I am not saved by my works, I also understand others can be saved through my works.

You call me to be an example *"in speech, in conduct, in love, in faith, in purity"* (v. 12). Lord, forgive me when I fail in those things. Strengthen me so I can be a better example of Christianity for You. In Your name, we pray. Amen.

MY THOUGHTS

1 TIMOTHY 5

Take Care

In 1 Timothy 5, Paul instructs Timothy to take care of the elderly and church leaders. Are you caring for elderly parents at this time or preparing to do so? Does your church take care of the pastor and his team? Please read or listen to 1 Timothy 5.

COMMENTS

My 1992 journal says, "I have responsibility to provide for my own family. Thank You for blessing me with provision so far." Then I wrote, "Do nothing in a spirit of partiality."

In 2002, from Bangkok, Thailand, I wrote, "Yesterday, I was driven to Chonburi. A guy took me to a seaport restaurant with fresh seafood and to a Thai beach. Food was great, beach was nice." I wrote about 1 Timothy 5, "Verses 4-8 relate to us now about Dad. The family is to care for parents. My sister and brothers should read this. We all need to practice it." Then I wrote about verse 22, "Do not share in the sins of others. The sins of some men are obvious, reaching a place of judgement ahead of them. The sins of others trail behind them, referring to verse 24." I finished with, "Walk worthy." 2002 was probably a time where we were taking care of my father after my mom died. That was the reference in the journal about my dad and my siblings.

In 2012, I wrote, "Encourage rather than rebuke people. Caring for the elderly, especially widows, is first the responsibility of the family. If no family, then the responsibility of the church. The church was the center of the community back then. It was the gathering place. There was no government to step into the responsibility. Imagine today's churches, rather than the government, caring for the elderly."

DIGGING DEEPER

> But if anyone does not provide for his relatives, and especially for members of his household, he has denied the faith and is worse than an unbeliever.
>
> 1 Tim. 5:8

A couple of my journals had entries about taking care of the elderly. Let's go back and read what this passage says, *"But if a widow has children or grandchildren, let them first learn to show godliness to their own household and to make some return to their parents, for this is pleasing in the sight of God"* (v. 4). Children, even grandchildren, are to take care of the elderly. Verse 8 goes on to say, *"But if anyone does not provide for his relatives, and especially for members of his household, he has denied the faith and is worse than an unbeliever."*

I have some personal experience with this. I lived about sixty miles, or an hour away, from my parents. My mom went in for a heart procedure one time and got complications and never came out. So we never had to "care" for my mom. After that, my father was alone. I remember committing to drive to Colorado Springs from Denver about twice a week to see my dad. I tried to go once during the week and once on the weekend. I did not make it every week, but I did the best I could. I kept doing it when my father was placed in a care facility.

My other family members were very loving and caring, as well. At the time, none of us lived in Colorado Springs, so it was not as if we could take care of him ourselves. Looking back, I think our family fulfilled the requirements of these verses. If you have an elderly parent right now, hopefully this will be a reminder that you should be caring for your parents. And surely, that looks different for each of us.

Another interesting concept in this chapter is caring for our shepherds or our pastors. Let's look at verses 17 and 18, *"Let the elders who rule well be considered worthy of double honor, especially those who labor in preaching and teaching. For the Scripture says, 'You shall not muzzle an ox when it treads out the grain,' and 'The laborer deserves his wages.'"*

These verses remind us to honor those in leadership in our churches. They remind us to pay our pastors as well as we can. It is too bad so many pastors who serve in our churches seem to have to take an oath of poverty to do so. These verses say, *"Let the elders who rule well be considered worthy of double honor"* (v. 17), and *"The laborer deserves his wages"* (v. 18). Let's take care of those in Christian leadership. Let's take care of our pastors.

Lastly, Paul reminds Timothy, once again, to, *"keep yourself pure"* (v. 22). Is purity something you think about as a Christian? Do you think you have an obligation to keep yourself pure? As people see us at work, at school, or in our neighborhood, and they know we are Christians, do they see us as pure? How are you reflecting Jesus Christ?

Prayer

Lord, these are challenges from 1 Timothy 5. First, to take care of the elderly. Second, to take care of our pastors. And third, to take care of ourselves. Lord, we recognize we are humans and we fail. We ask You to forgive us when we fail and strengthen us so we can do better so when people see us, they actually see a reflection of You. Holy Spirit continue to purify us from the inside out. We ask for it, in Jesus' name. Amen.

MY THOUGHTS

1 TIMOTHY 6

Fight the Good Fight of Faith

Today brings us to the close of 1 Timothy with chapter 6. Paul reminds young Timothy to guard what has been entrusted to him, to fight the good fight of faith. What has been entrusted to you? Do you guard it and fight for it? Please read or listen to 1 Timothy 6.

COMMENTS

We are going to finish 1 Timothy with journal entries from 1992, 2002, and 2012, all ten years apart. In 1992, all I wrote was, "1 Timothy 6." I did not write any notes about it, but at least I did read it on that day.

In 2002, I was still in Thailand. I wrote from Bangkok, "Leaving here today for Buriram to organize another new Gideon camp. Will stay in an orphanage with a Texas Gideon." I was in Thailand on a Gideon International trip. I was visiting Gideon camps and found out there was a guy from Texas who had an orphanage in Thailand. I was on my way to Buriram to start a new camp and see this Texas/Thai Gideon.

I wrote about the last chapter of 1 Timothy, "Godliness with contentment is great gain. People who want to get rich fall into temptation and often ruin themselves and others. Be careful what we love, godliness or money. Do not put hope in money, put it in God. Guard what has been entrusted to my care: Terry, family, Area 11 of the Gideons, and the Ezra Project."

Interesting, I wrote about having the Ezra Project in my care, because 2002 was the year I started this ministry. When I was writing this journal, it was a mere six months old. Let's go back to the day I started the Ezra Project and see what my journal entry was in 2002. On April 1, 2002, I wrote, "The first day of the rest of my life! Today I begin a dream, a passion, to work on the Ezra Project full-time. What a way to begin the day after Easter. Praise God for this marvelous opportunity." That is my journal entry the day I started the Ezra Project in 2002. Over the years, God has certainly blessed and preserved the desire of my heart to connect God's people to God's Word.

In 2012, I broke up the chapter into smaller, bite-sized pieces. These entries are from two different days. The first day. I read verses 1-10. The second day, I read verse 11 through the end of the chapter. I wrote, "There are so many today who teach a different doctrine than the sound words of Jesus Christ and godliness in churches, homes, and communities, and it causes quarrels, envy, dissention, slander, constant friction between people. There is no honor, no trust, very little truth in anything today: church, business, government. Imagine the contentment possible if we could agree and follow the teachings of Jesus." I continued to write, "The desire to be rich, or the love of money, creates temptation. How we handle temptation determines whether we fall into a snare, senseless and harmless desires, and ruin."

That was day one, let's looks at day two, the rest of the chapter, "I have been introduced from time-to-time as a 'man of God.' The first time it stunned me. But if I am one, I am to follow Paul's advice: flee the entrapment of wealth and *'Pursue righteousness, godliness, faith, love, steadfastness, gentleness'* (v. 11) keeping the commandments *'unstained and free from reproach'* (v. 14). I am to guard the deposits entrusted to me, the call to spread a passion for God's Word." I finished by writing, "Avoid contradictions to what has been entrusted to me. Don't swerve."

DIGGING DEEPER

Let's summarize some principles in this last chapter of 1 Timothy. Paul tells Timothy, *"If anyone teaches a different doctrine and does not agree with the sound words of our Lord Jesus Christ and the teaching that accords with godliness, he is puffed up with conceit and understands nothing"* (vv. 3-4). That is pretty straight forward. Those who are teaching a different doctrine, those who are not teaching the sound words of our Lord Jesus Christ, understand nothing. Unfortunately, there are many out there today in this category. Paul says they cause controversy. They quarrel about words, which produce *"envy, dissension, slander, evil suspicions, and constant friction among people"* (vv. 4-5). We have plenty of that today.

Paul goes on to a second, very important principle in verse 6. He says there is great gain in godliness and contentment. He reminds us, *"we brought nothing into the world, and we cannot take anything out of the world"* (v. 7). Godliness brings contentment.

He goes on to say, *"But those who desire to be rich fall into temptation"* (v. 9). *"For the love of money is a root of all kinds of evils"* (v. 10). Money is not the root of all evil. The love of money is the root of all evil. Being rich or being wealthy is not sinful. In fact, it is often a blessing from the Lord. But our focus should be on godliness, not money or wealth. Godliness brings contentment.

Then Paul reminds Timothy: *"Fight the good fight of the faith"* (v. 12). *"To keep the commandment unstained and free from reproach"* (v. 14). And lastly, he says to Timothy, *"Guard the deposit entrusted to you"* (v. 20).

As we close 1 Timothy, take these last couple of instructions to heart. *"Fight the good fight of the faith"* (v. 12), *"keep the commandment unstained and free from reproach"* (v. 14), and *"guard the deposit entrusted to you"* (v. 20).

> **Guard the deposit entrusted to you.**
>
> **1 Tim. 6:20**

Whatever God has entrusted to you to build the kingdom here on earth, Paul says guard it, and he warns us not to swerve from our faith.

1 Timothy is about combatting false teaching. It is about solid ground of how Christians should behave. And it is about practical, visible changes in the lives of those who believe the gospel. We learned there is one God, one mediator between Him and men, the Lord Jesus Christ. We learned a list of qualifications for Christian leadership. We learned how to live a blameless life in Christ. Surely, we thank the Lord for this short book. But there is a second book Paul writes to Timothy, and it contains the last words Paul ever wrote to Timothy, and to us.

Prayer

Father, we thank You for the instruction from Your Word. Though sometimes it may be uncomfortable in our culture today, we appreciate biblical truth. As You reminded Timothy to keep the commandments, may we guard what is entrusted to us. Holy Spirit, help us do that so people see Jesus in us like they saw Jesus in Timothy. Guide and direct our steps. In Your name, we pray. Amen.

MY THOUGHTS

FOUR DAYS IN 2 TIMOTHY

2 TIMOTHY 1

Fan the Flame

Today, we begin 2 Timothy. It is a short book, only four chapters. Let's look at a little background before we begin. Paul wrote 2 Timothy, most likely, during his second imprisonment in Rome, somewhere between 64 and 68 A.D. It is his last letter. It is a very personal letter to his close friend and co-laborer, Timothy. He calls on Timothy to stand firm and continue in faithfulness. 2 Timothy is a clear call for perseverance in the gospel despite suffering. Anticipating his death soon, he passes the baton of faith and the gospel to Timothy. This letter is a farewell.

As we get into 2 Timothy, let's look for things like: all scripture is breathed out by God, in chapter 3; preach the Word, in chapter 4; a description of what we can expect the world to be like in the last days, in chapter 3, a far more accurate account than any Hollywood movie we see today. Please read or listen to the eighteen verses of 2 Timothy 1.

COMMENTS

To help us through 2 Timothy, I selected three Bible reading journals; the same ones used on 1 Timothy. We will use a journal from 1992, the second one from 2002, ten years later, and the third one from 2012, another ten years later. These are my personal Bible reading journals. Each day I read the Bible, I jot down what I sense the Lord says to me. I have been doing so for over thirty-five years. Let's take a look at 2 Timothy 1, through the eyes of my personal Bible reading journals.

In 1992, I just wrote one line, *"kindle afresh the gift of God which is in (me)"* (v. 6 NASB). We could probably camp right there on just that phrase alone out of this chapter, but we will look at some other journal entries.

In 2002, I wrote, *"'kindle afresh the gift of God, which is in you'* (v. 6 NASB). Do not be ashamed to testify about our Lord, referring to verses 6-8. Help me be strong for You, Lord. Help me to mentor, pass on, Christianity, to a few close men."

> **Kindle afresh the gift of God, which is in you.**
>
> **2 Tim. 1:6**

In 2012, I read 2 Timothy at a slower pace, so I have journal entries from two days. On the first ten verses, I wrote, "Know who you are. Paul knew who he was, *'an apostle of Christ . . . by the will of God'* (v. 1). He served God with a clear conscience. Paul prayed. He reminds Timothy to know who he is, *'I am reminded of your sincere faith . . . fan into flame the gift of God, which is in you'* (vv. 5-6). I continued to write, "'God will help fan His gift into a flame with His *spirit not of fear but of power and love and self-control'* (v. 7). God calls us to *'a holy calling . . . because of his own purpose and grace'"* (v. 9).

The next day, I continued in 2 Timothy 1 with the last verses from 10-18, "Jesus Christ *'abolished death and brought life and immortality'* (v. 10). No one else can this be said about. No other religious figure claims this." I continued, "Though Paul is in a Roman jail, he is not ashamed of his Christ because he knows *'whom I have believed'"* (v. 12). Then I quoted verse 14, *"'guard the good deposit entrusted to you.'* God has gifted each of us. We are to guard what He has entrusted to us. He told Timothy the same thing, referring to 1 Timothy 6:20."

DIGGING DEEPER

Who are you in Christ? Paul knew who he was, *"Paul, an apostle of Christ Jesus by the will of God according to the promise of the life that is in Christ Jesus"* (v. 1). Paul knows who he is.

He goes a little bit farther in verse 3 when he says he serves God *"with a clear conscience"*. Then he reminds Timothy who he is, *"I am reminded of your sincere faith, a faith that dwelt first in your grandmother Lois and your mother Eunice and now, I am sure, dwells in you as well"* (v. 5). Timothy had a heritage of Christianity. Maybe you do, too. Maybe you grew up in a Christian home. Or maybe you are a first-generation Christian. Who are you in Christ?

Then Paul reminds Timothy he has a gift. We each have been gifted by God. He tells Timothy not to sit on that gift, but to fan it into a flame. How about you? Are you sitting on your gift or is your gift from God burning before others?

In verse 8, he tells Timothy, *"Therefore do not be ashamed of the testimony about our Lord, nor of me his prisoner, but share in suffering for the gospel by the power of God."* Good words for you and me as well. Do not be ashamed of your testimony for Christ; share it in the power of God.

Paul goes on to say, *"I am not ashamed, for I know whom I have believed, and I am convinced that he is able to guard until that day what has been entrusted to me"* (v. 12). There is no reason to hide our Christianity, if we know who we believe in and we are convinced He can guard us with what He entrusts us with.

I love what Paul shares next. He tells Timothy, *"Follow the pattern of the sound words that you have heard from me, in the faith and love that are in Christ Jesus. By the Holy Spirit who dwells within us, guard the good deposit entrusted to you"* (vv. 13-14). He tells Timothy, and he is telling us, follow God's Word and stand in our faith and in the love of Jesus. Trust the Holy Spirit and share that good deposit He has entrusted in us.

What has God entrusted you with? What may He be asking you to fan into a flame after reading this chapter? Think about your gifting. Do you have a burning passion, something in your heart you want to share? Remember, Paul said he could not refrain from preaching the gospel. It was a passion in him. What are you passionate about? What has God entrusted you with? Do not let that flame go out. Fan that flame, not in *"a spirit . . . of fear but of power and love and self-control"* (v. 7). Do not be ashamed to share what God has entrusted you with.

Prayer

Lord, give us the power, give us the boldness to share what You have entrusted in us. Each one of us may have a different message or a different gift, but we are to share it with those around us. That is what Paul is telling young Timothy. That is what You may be telling us today. Lord, we thank You for trusting us with something You want us to share with others. Give us the courage to do so. We ask it, in Jesus' name. Amen.

MY THOUGHTS

2 TIMOTHY 2

Christian Character

In 2 Timothy 2, Paul shares with Timothy virtues of Christian character. Do you wonder what God wants from you as a believer? Please read or listen to the twenty-six verses of 2 Timothy 2.

COMMENTS

In 1992, I wrote, "He remains faithful even when we become faithless. Also, handle accurately the word of truth. *'(A)void worldly and empty chatter, for it will lead to further ungodliness'*" (v. 16).

In 2002, I wrote, "Don't quarrel. Correctly handle the word of truth. Avoid godless chatter. Don't have anything to do with foolish and stupid arguments. Do not quarrel. Be kind to everyone. Gently instruct. Let God bring them to their senses." I wrote a prayer after that journal entry, "O, that I would never quarrel again. O, that I would subdue anger forevermore. O, that I would be kind to everyone all the time. Lord, change me. Strengthen me to do well at this. Help me be peaceful, trusting You in all things." I probably have made a little bit of progress on some of those things, but certainly have more work to do.

In 2012, I broke up 2 Timothy 2 in two sections on two different days. The first day was verses 1-13. The second day was verses 14-26. Let's go over those two journal entries. First, "Pass on faith by staying the course. Stay focused. Play by the rules. Work hard. Remember Jesus. That is who we are passing on. But, if we deny Him, He also will deny us, referring to verse 12."

The next day, I finished the chapter, "A great theme verse for life, *'Do your best to present yourself to God as one approved, a worker who has no need to be ashamed, rightly handling the word of truth'* (v. 15). Avoid irreverent babble and don't swerve from the truth. *'(B)e a vessel for honorable use, set apart as holy'* (v. 21), with a pure heart. The Lord's servants are not quarrelsome but kind to everyone."

After this journal entry, I wrote a similar prayer that I wrote ten years before, "Almighty God, approve me as a worker for You. Always help me rightly divide the word of truth. Guard my mouth, my heart, to avoid irreverent babble and be kind to everyone."

DIGGING DEEPER

Let's look at the instructions Paul gave young Timothy and thereby, also gives us today. He first tells Timothy to, *"be strengthen by the grace that is in Christ Jesus"* (v. 1). Next, he tells Timothy to pass on to faithful men that which he has learned from Paul. He then tells Timothy to, *"Share in suffering as a good soldier of Christ Jesus"* (v. 3). And he tells Timothy to compete according to the rules.

He tells Timothy, *"Think over what I say, for the Lord will give you understanding in everything"* (v. 7). Maybe you are being instructed to think over the things we are hearing in 2 Timothy 2 and the Lord will give you understanding.

Then he tells Timothy, *"Remember Jesus Christ"* (v. 8). Is Jesus on your mind on a regular, daily basis? And he tells Timothy to *"Remind them of these things"* (v. 14). Remind them of what? Remind them the Word of God is not bound. Remind them if we have died with Him, we will also live with Him. If we endure, we will also reign with Him. If we deny Him, he will also deny us. If we are faithless, He remains faithful for He cannot deny Himself.

Paul told Timothy to remind the Corinthians of those things. He reminds us of those things as we hear them in this chapter. Next, he tells Timothy, *"Do your best to present yourself to God as one approved, a worker who has no need to be ashamed, rightly handling the word of truth"* (v. 15). I mentioned in one of my journals that is a great theme verse for life. Are you doing your best for the Lord?

> Do your best to present yourself to God as one approved, a worker who has no need to be ashamed, rightly handling the word of truth.
>
> 2 Tim. 2:15

Then he tells Timothy, *"Avoid irreverent babble"* (v. 16). I wrote in my journal I need to do this, and you may need to as well. We probably all engage in a lot of chatter, a lot of irreverent babble, that goes nowhere. What Paul says is, *"it will lead people into more and more ungodliness"* (v. 16). Avoid irreverent babble.

Next, Paul tells Timothy, flee from youthful passions. And what do we replace youthful passions with? Paul tells us, *"So flee youthful passions and pursue righteousness, faith, love, and peace, along with those who call on the Lord from a pure heart"* (v. 22).

Next, Paul tells Timothy, *"Have nothing to do with foolish, ignorant controversies; you know that they breed quarrels"* (v. 23). I know I need to do this, and you may need to do this, as well. There are many discussions I get into that just breed controversy; they breed quarrels. I know in my life, I am trying to refrain from engaging in those kind of discussions.

Paul finishes out the chapter by telling Timothy, *"And the Lord's servant must not be quarrelsome but kind to everyone, able to teach, patiently enduring evil, correcting his opponents with gentleness. God may perhaps grant them repentance leading to a knowledge of the truth, and they may come to their senses and escape from the snare of the devil, after being captured by him to do his will"* (vv. 24-26).

Are you one of the Lord's servants? Let's close this chapter by going over these last instructions. We are not to be quarrelsome. We are to be kind. We should be able to teach. We should patiently endure evil. We should be able to correct our opponents with gentleness. Why? Because *"God may . . . grant them repentance leading them to a knowledge of the truth . . . they may come to their senses and escape the snare of the devil"* (vv. 25-26). That is worth helping people do.

Prayer

Lord, may You use us to do these things. There is a laundry list here of many things You instructed Timothy to do that You are telling us to do as well. This is basically an outline of Christian character. If I need to go back over this, will You guide me to review this daily devotion again? Or will You remind me to read this chapter on my own and think through these things?

Lord, help me correct, help me improve my own Christian character, so You may use me to lead someone else to Your truth. Also, You may use me to get someone out of the snare of the devil. Lord, let it be so, and we will give You the praise. In Jesus' name, amen.

MY THOUGHTS

2 TIMOTHY 3

The Last Days

2 Timothy 3 is one of my favorite chapters in the Bible. Do you wonder what the last days will be like? Please read or listen to the seventeen verses of 2 Timothy 3.

COMMENTS

Here we go with some insightful journal entries from 1992, 2002, and 2012. We begin with the first one in 1992, "We must be in the last days because we have all these problems, referring to verses 1-9. Children disobedient to parents. Ungrateful. Lovers of money. Savings and Loan scandal. Lovers of pleasure rather than lovers of God. AIDS. Abortion. A form of godliness, religion without Christ. Always learning but never to come to the knowledge of the truth. Going on all over our country. *'But they will not make further progress'* (v. 9 NASB). Amen. Stop them, Lord. But you, follow my teaching. Yes, Lord."

Back in 1992, I was saying we must be in last days because we have all the problems listed in the first nine verses of this chapter. It is over twenty-five years later. These problems are more evident today than then.

Let's see if it gets any better in 2002, "Godly living is not easy living. Paul suffered greatly. Many have for the cause of Christ. If Christianity is not the only way, why suffer? If everybody's going to make it anyway, who cares about doctrine, manner of life, etc. Christianity would be no threat to anyone then. So why persecute it? Because it shines truth in darkness, and darkness doesn't like light." That was profound, wasn't it?

In 2012, I divided up this chapter, so I read the first nine verses on one day and the rest of the chapter the second day. I wrote, "I wonder if every generation since Paul and Timothy saw these characteristics. We certainly would say these verses apply to us today; there is information overload, but little knowledge of the truth. Paul calls fake teaching folly. We have much of it today."

On the second day, I wrote, "What if someone followed me around? What kind of Christianity would they see? How is my teaching, my conduct, my aim in life, my faith, my patience, my love, my steadfastness? What is Christianity like?" I quoted verse 12, *"All who desire to live a godly life in Christ Jesus will be persecuted."* I wrote, "All will be, while evil people get away with their behavior. Life is not fair." I continued to write, "Scripture unveils salvation through faith in Christ Jesus. All scripture is God-breathed. It is His Word, not the words of men."

DIGGING DEEPER

I mentioned in the introduction to the Book of 2 Timothy, there would be a description of the last days and it would be more true than anything we see in Hollywood movies. Here it is in the first nine verses of this chapter. Let's review what Paul says the

> **Always learning and never able to arrive at a knowledge of the truth.**
>
> **2 Tim. 3:7**

condition of the world will be like in the last days. As I go through this list, mentally check them off if you think they are applicable today, *"For people will be lovers of self, lovers of money, proud, arrogant, abusive, disobedient to their parents, ungrateful, unholy, heartless, unappeasable, slanderous, without self-control, brutal, not loving good, treacherous, reckless, swollen with conceit, lovers of pleasure rather than lovers of God, having the appearancl e of godliness, but denying its power"* (vv. 2-5).

How did you do? I put a mental check mark on every one of those things. And there is one more, *"always learning and never able to arrive at a knowledge of the truth"* (v. 7). We are in the information age. There is more knowledge, more access to information on our smartphones than ever in the history of the world. We can ask Google anything. But does Google really have the answers to life? Paul's warning is clear. In the last days, we will always be learning, but never able to arrive at the knowledge of the truth.

I offer you a challenge today. Spend more time in the truth. And where is that? In God's Word, not Google. We can have knowledge of the truth. John 17:17 (KJV) says, *"Sanctify them through thy truth; thy word is truth."* How do we know God's Word is truth? This chapter declares it, *"All Scripture is breathed out by God"* (v. 16). That means the Bible, from cover to cover, is God's Word. Because it is God's Word, it is *"profitable for teaching, for reproof, for correction, and for training in righteousness, that the man of God may be complete, equipped for every good work"* (vv. 16-17).

If you are concerned about the last days, if you are concerned about knowledge, but without knowledge of the truth; if you want to be trained in righteousness; if you want to be equipped for every good work in this life, then spend time in God's Word each and every day.

Prayer

Yes, Lord, we may be in the last days. We see the evidence by the characteristics described by Paul all around us. But you also tell us, right here, we can know truth. We thank You that You loved us enough to provide truth, Your Word. Holy Spirit, draw us into it each and every day of our lives. And as You do, teach us, train us, in righteousness. Equip us for every good work. Thank You. In Jesus' name, we pray. Amen.

TRUTH IN THE LAST DAYS

If you believe in the last days the world is going to need truth, God's Word, join the Ezra Project in making that possible. These *Day by Day Through the Bible* devotions may outlive all of us. Maybe God will use them as a beacon of truth in the last days, whenever they may be. But, they will need to be available. Invest in the last days. Visit ezraproject.net to make sure they will be.

MY THOUGHTS

2 TIMOTHY 4

Preach the Word

Today, we finish the Book of 2 Timothy. These are Paul's last words to young Timothy. He passed on the baton of sharing the gospel. Do you share the gospel? Are you passing it on to the next generation? Please read or listen to the twenty-two verses of 2 Timothy 4.

COMMENTS

We will look at entries from my personal Bible reading journals from 1992, 2002, and 2012, for the last time on 2 Timothy. In 1992, I wrote, "Paul encourages young Timothy as a companion and friend. Preach the Word. Be sober. Endure. Do. Fulfill your ministry."

In 2002, I wrote, *"For the time will come when they will not endure sound doctrine; . . . and will turn their ears away from the truth'* (vv. 3-4 NASB). So before that, and even during that, preach the Word. I love the Ezra Project. Lord, help me with it."

In 2012, I read 2 Timothy more slowly, reading verses 1-8 on the first day and 9-22 on the second day. On the first day, I wrote, "Jesus judges the living and the dead, no other. He will come again. Preach the Word, not about the Word, not around the Word, not a new version—a politically correct interpretation of the Word.

Preach the Word, God's Word. Why? Because the time is coming, and now is, when people will not endure sound teaching, the Word. People will turn from listening to the truth and prefer myths or fables. *'But as for you, . . . fulfill your ministry'* (v. 5). Me too. Paul realizes his time is up. I wonder if I will know that. There are rewards in heaven. I hope I can earn a crown of righteousness too. For I, too, have *'loved his appearing'"* (v. 8).

My second entry, "People. Some in love with the present world, while some are useful to God in ministry. Some do ministry great harm. The Lord repays for their deeds, not me. Ministry can be lonely, referring to verse 16. But God is with us. Stay on task. God is in control and will bring us through it all safely home. Lord, be with my spirit and give me Your grace."

DIGGING DEEPER

Let's go back to the very beginning of this chapter:

I charge you in the presence of God and of Christ Jesus, who is to judge the living and the dead, and by his appearing and his kingdom: preach the word; be ready in season and out of season; reprove, rebuke, and exhort, with complete patience and teaching. For the time is coming when people will not endure sound teaching, but having itching ears they will accumulate for themselves teachers to suit their own passions, and will turn away from listening to the truth and wander off into myths. As for you, always be sober-minded, endure suffering, do the work of an evangelist, fulfill your ministry (vv. 1-5).

> For the time is coming when people will not endure sound teaching, but having itching ears they will accumulate for themselves teachers to suit their own passions, and will turn away from listening to the truth and wander off into myths.
>
> 2 Tim. 4:3-4

What great words for the days and times we live in. First, they state categorically that Jesus is to judge the living and the dead. What an important reality in our day today. People need to understand this. Jesus Christ is going to judge the living and the dead. Therefore, it is our responsibility to tell them.

Paul says it this way, *"preach the word; be ready in season and out of season"* (v. 2). I have never believed that is only for pastors or preachers. At the time, Timothy was a young man, so take those words to heart. We are all to preach the Word and be ready in season and out of season. Why? Because *"The time is coming when people will not endure sound teaching"* (v. 3). We can see that all around us today. There is a lack of biblical teaching in our churches. We see people accumulating for themselves teachers to suit their own passions. We see many turning away from the truth, more interested in myths or fables. If you are a biblical Christian, it is your responsibility to be ready, in season and out of season, to preach the Word or share the truth of God's Word. Paul tells Timothy, he tells us, do the work of an evangelist, *"fulfill your ministry"* (v. 5).

In the introduction of this book, we said this was a farewell address; these are Paul's last words. He says so in verses 6 and 7, *"For I am already being poured out as a drink offering, and the time of my departure has come. I have fought the good fight, I have finished the race, I have kept the faith."* What a declaration of a life well lived. Will that be your declaration in your farewell address? Will you be able to say, *"I have fought the good fight, I have finished the race, I have kept the faith"* (v. 7)? May we all finish strong for the Lord.

Paul passed the baton of spreading the gospel to Timothy. Timothy spread it to others. Hopefully, in your life, you grabbed the baton and are spreading the gospel to those around you.

Prayer

Lord, we thank You for the Book of 2 Timothy. We thank You for the personal communication between Paul and his beloved friend and co-worker, Timothy. We thank You for the reminder to fan the flame of gifts You entrust us with, to present ourselves as a worker, approved by You, not ashamed of the Word of God.

We thank You for the understanding that all scripture is breathed out by God. And by it, we can be *"equipped for every good work"* (3:17). And we thank You for that description of the last days. We see it all around us. May You find us faithful in the days we live.

Lord, help us finish strong. May You find us doing the work of an evangelist, which is just sharing Jesus with others. May You find we have *"kept the faith"* (4:7). Thank You, Almighty God, for Your Word seared into our hearts. Amen.

MY THOUGHTS

THREE DAYS IN TITUS

TITUS 1

Church Leadership Qualifications

Today, we begin the Book of Titus. Titus is one of the shortest of the New Testament books, only three chapters and only forty-six verses. It was written by Paul to his co-worker Titus in about the mid-sixties, A.D. Titus was not Jewish; he was a Greek taught and nurtured by Paul.

Paul went to the Island of Crete and established new churches. He left Titus with those new churches. Like in many other locations where Paul founded new churches, false teaching followed. The letter back to Titus deals with the false teachers, but includes much, much more:

- the link between faith and practice, and belief and behavior
- a description of elders or leadership in the church
- proper Christian living
- a portrait of a healthy church
- proper leadership
- proper handling of error
- proper Christian living
- the gospel as a proper source of godliness

Paul covers much in only forty-six verses in a curt, businesslike manner. Please read or listen to Titus 1.

COMMENTS

I will be referring to three of my personal Bible reading journals as we go through Titus. The first one is from 1995, when I was forty years old. The next one is from 2008, when I was fifty-three years old. The third one is from 2013, five years later. I try to select journals in different decades; here we are in the nineties, the 00's, and the 0-teens. Let's look at Titus 1.

My Bible reading journal in 1995 is going to be one of these very sparse versions. On Titus 1 (NASB), I referred to some verses, *"God, who cannot lie"* (v. 2). "Qualifications of elders, referring to verses 6-9, and to be a leader, one must hold fast the faithful Word, referring to verse 9." That is all I wrote in 1995.

In 2008, I was much wiser! I wrote, "Titus 1. God cannot lie. Church leaders need to be above reproach. Church teaching should come from *'holding fast the faithful word'* (v. 9 NASB). Beware of deceivers. They profess to know God, but by their deeds they deny Him."

In 2013, I actually read the whole Book of Titus first and then broke it down into chapters. Here is my overview of the whole Book of Titus. "Read the whole book. Paul's similar theme. There are false teachers Titus must stand against. Paul proclaims truth, others come in and dispute it or revert it back to old practices of Judaism. Titus' job is to stand against false teachers. We have the same today. False teaching in the church. We need pastors and others to stand for biblical truth."

The next day, I read the first chapter again and wrote, "How would I describe myself like Paul does in verse 1? Who am I?" I continued, "God never lies. He manifests his promises in His Word, proclaimed accurately by those called or entrusted with it. I have been humbly entrusted with awesome responsibilities in Ezra and as one of the top three elected Gideons in The Gideons International. I take it very seriously. I have been elected to a place of high leadership in The Gideons and meet most of the qualifications listed by Paul. The questionable one is my children being believers. I must be able to *'hold firm to the trustworthy word as taught, so that he may be able to give instruction'* (v. 9). I am to be an encouragement to others. We are to love, but

Paul has some hard words. We are to rebuke those who contradict truth and silence false teachers rebuking them sharply. People *'profess to know God, but they deny Him by their works'"* (v. 16).

DIGGING DEEPER

Let's start this review of chapter 1 with what I referred to in my last journal; how would you describe yourself to someone? Paul describes himself as *"a servant of God and an apostle of Jesus Christ"* (v. 1). How do people see you? Do they see you as a servant of God and a spokesman, or ambassador, for Jesus Christ?

Next, I referred to this phrase in each of my journals, "God who never lies." Mentally, we may affirm that but think about what it really means. If God never lies, and we believe the Bible is God's Word, then the Bible cannot lie. It has to be correct, it has to be true; therefore, the whole Word of God is believable.

> If God never lies, and we believe the Bible is God's Word, then the Bible cannot lie.

We will finish chapter 1 by looking at the meat of the chapter, the qualifications of elders. Titus was left in Crete, according to Paul, *"so that you might put what remained into order, and appoint elders in every town as I directed you"* (v. 5). These verses are referred to by many churches in looking for its volunteer leadership.

The first qualification is to be above reproach. I refer to my footnote in my English Standard Version Study Bible. Above reproach means, "There should be no legitimate accusation that could be brought against the elder that would bring disrepute on the gospel or the church; his life should be seen as worthy of imitation" (p. 2348).

The next qualification is the husband of one wife. I believe that indicates elders are male. For example, it does not say, "or the wife of one husband."

The next qualification is his children are believers. That qualification is a little tougher because no father can guarantee the conversion of his own children. In 1

Timothy 3, the verse that refers to this qualification says only that children must be well behaved, not that their conversion is a requirement for their father to be an overseer.

The list goes on, *"He must not be arrogant, or quick-tempered or a drunkard or violent or greedy for gain, but hospitable, a lover of good, self-controlled, upright, holy, and disciplined"* (vv. 7-8). Verse 9 concludes the list of characteristics, *"He must hold firm to the trustworthy word as taught, so that he may be able to give instruction in sound doctrine and also to rebuke those who contradict it."*

An elder of a church must be a man of the Word, meaning you have to be in it, hopefully each and every day. Secondly, you have to know it so well you can teach it. Lastly, you need to know the Word so well you can rebuke those who contradict it.

According to Paul, those are the characteristics Titus was to look for as he appointed elders, or overseers, of all new churches in Crete. Characteristics of leadership within our churches is to be taken very seriously. The descriptions of an elder or overseer listed by Paul seem almost impossible to fulfil. Yet, churches need people they can look up to, people who they can model their behavior after, people who know the Word, can teach the Word, and hold people accountable to the truth of God's Word.

If you are in a leadership position in a church or a Christian organization, I encourage you to go back and look at Titus 1 and these qualifications of leadership. Pray them through. Ask God to strengthen your weaknesses and get you into the Word of God on a daily basis.

Prayer

Lord, we thank You we serve a God who never lies. We read a Bible we can trust and You have qualifications for leaders in the church You established. You are the one that said, the gates of hell will never prevail against the church, referring to Matthew 16:18.

We thank You that You have leaders in our churches who can be models for Christian behavior. They are close to us. They also know and can instruct us in the Word of God. We give You thanks for leaders in our churches today. In the name of Jesus, we pray. Amen.

MY THOUGHTS

TITUS 2

Being Different

Titus 2 covers many ways Christians should be different than the world. Do people see Christian virtues in you? Please read or listen to Titus 2.

COMMENTS

In 1999, I had a couple of one-line summaries, "Speak the things which are fitting for sound doctrine." Then I referred to verses 2, 6, and 8, "Old men and young men." Lastly, "Chapter 2 is a great men's chapter."

In 2008 I wrote, *"speak the things which are fitting for sound doctrine'* (v. 1 NASB). Where do we get sound doctrine? The Bible. Act in ways so that the Word of God will not be dishonored so nothing bad can be said about us. Deny ungodliness and worldly desires."

In 2013, I wrote, *"But as for you'* (v. 1). We need to be different than what is in the world." I continued, "As an older man, I am to be dignified, sound in my faith, and in love. Older women are to be reverent in behavior and teach young women to be godly wives and mothers. We should all be models of good works with integrity and sound speech. We represent Jesus. There needs to be a difference in our behavior."

Paul starts chapter 2 with the phrase, *"But as for you"* (v. 1). Let's go back to the end of chapter 1 to see what he is contrasting here. In 1:10-11, Paul says, *"For there are many who are insubordinate, empty talkers and deceivers, especially those of the circumcision party. They must be silenced, since they are upsetting whole families by teaching for shameful gain what they ought not to teach."* He continues, *"To the pure, all things are pure, but to the defiled and unbelieving, nothing is pure; but both their minds and their consciences are defiled. They profess to know God, but they deny him by their works. They are detestable, disobedient, unfit for any good work"* (1:15-16).

Chapter 2 continues, *"But as for you"* (v. 1). Of course, Paul is talking to Titus. The *"But as for you"* (v. 1) applies to us today too. As Christians, are we noticeably different in our behavior? Paul gives us some examples for older men and older women here in chapter 2.

DIGGING DEEPER

How are we to be different as Christians? He says, *"Older men are to be sober-minded, dignified, self-controlled, sound in faith, in love, and in steadfastness"* (v. 2). I am not sure where the line gets drawn between younger men and older men; but I supposed at my current age, in my 60's, I am an older man. Am I sober-minded, dignified, self-controlled, sound in faith, in love, and steadfast? Lord, let it be so.

Paul goes on to address younger men. *"Likewise, urge the younger men to be self-controlled. Show yourself in all respects to be a model of good works, and in your teaching show integrity, dignity, and sound speech that cannot be condemned"* (vv. 6-8). Regardless of our age, we are to be men of integrity, faith, love, dignity, and self-control.

Paul also addresses women. *"Older women likewise are to be reverent in behavior, not slanderers or slaves to much wine. They are to teach what is good, and so train the young women to love their husbands and children, to be*

> **Do you exemplify biblical, godly character to those around you?**

self-controlled, pure, working at home, kind, and submissive to their own husbands, that the word of God may not be reviled" (vv. 3-5). Older women have the responsibility to train up younger women.

Why act this way? Why be different than the world? *"For the grace of God has appeared, bringing salvation for all people, training us to renounce ungodliness and worldly passions, and to live self-controlled, upright, and godly lives in the present age"* (vv. 11-12). People around us should see the difference salvation makes in a life.

Do people see these characteristics in you? Whether you are an older person or a younger person, do you exemplify biblical, godly character to those around you? From Titus 2, I encourage you to take an inventory of not only what you believe, but how you behave.

Prayer

Father, help us to line up our behavior with our beliefs. Help us represent You well here in our sojourn on the earth. By Your grace, You have brought salvation for all people. May people see Jesus in us through our behavior.

And if we are failing, where we are failing, Lord, help us renounce ungodliness and worldly passions and live a self-controlled Christian life in You. Holy Spirit, help us live godly lives while we wait for our blessed hope, the appearing of the glory of our great God and Savior, Jesus Christ, in whose name, we pray. Amen.

INSIGHTS

The Ezra Project was founded in 2002 to connect God's people to God's Word. We have a passion for the Word of God, and a heart-felt desire to see Christians live lives according to biblical principles. For the first fourteen years of the Ezra Project, we spoke in churches, encouraging folks to come back to the habit of daily Bible reading.

In 2016, God reshaped our ministry outreach with ADDBIBLE, audio daily devotions, available directly to the Christian community. We hope you will explore the ADDBIBLE app and share it with your circle of friends and family.

In 2019, we took the ADDBIBLE transcripts and reshaped them into *Day by Day Through the Bible,* a series of written daily devotions according to various authors, Solomon, John, Paul, and more. We hope you are being blessed with *Day by Day.*

To learn more about the Ezra Project mission and resources, visit our website, ezraproject.net. We believe connecting God's people to God's Word is one of the greatest needs in our churches today. We hope you agree and will prayerfully consider passing on the Ezra Project to those you want to enjoy God's Word. Thank you.

MY THOUGHTS

TITUS 3

Salvation by the Father, Son, and Holy Spirit

Today we will finish this short Book of Titus. How are we saved? Did you know each person of the Trinity is involved in your salvation? Please read or listen to Titus 3.

COMMENTS

My journal, in 1995, had a one-line summary, "Do good deeds." Yes, that could be a summary for this chapter, but let's look at it more deeply with my other two journals.

In 2008, I wrote, "Christians are to be subject to rulers and authorities, and considerate to all people. God saves us, *'not on the basis of deeds . . . but according to His mercy, by the washing of regeneration and renewing by the Holy Spirit, whom He poured out upon us richly through Jesus Christ our Savior'* (vv. 5-6 NASB). Every part of the Trinity is involved in my salvation. Christians are to learn to engage in good deeds to meet pressing needs so they will not be unfruitful."

In 2013, I wandered through this chapter with various notes. "We are *'to be submissive to rulers and authorities'* (v. 1). In other words, we should not be the one stirring up trouble. Submissive and obedient? Those are tough on most of us. We should treat all people with dignity, respect, honor. I don't think very often of what I would be like without being a Christian. Surely, it would not be a pretty picture."

Then I wrote, "The gospel is summarized in verses 4-7, *'he saved us'* (v. 5). God acts first. Not by works, we cannot save ourselves, *'but according to his own mercy'* (v. 5). His motive, His reasons, His way. *'(J)ustified by his grace'* (v. 7). Again, it's Him, not us. It's always through Jesus Christ. No other person, no other way." I finished with, "Devoted themselves to good works. That's what our people need to display. See that they lack nothing. How people sent out from the church should be cared for."

DIGGING DEEPER

Paul finishes his instructions to Titus with a laundry list of how Christians are to live. Let's look at this check list and see how we are doing.

In the first verse of chapter 3, Paul reminds us to be submissive and obedient to rulers and authorities. Submissive and obedient. I bet most of us do not like those two words and do not do very well with those two words in our Christian character. Submissive and obedient can apply to various things. Most often we probably think of government authorities here. In more than one place in the scripture, we are reminded to be submissive to government authorities.

The reference to rulers and authorities could also apply to our church leadership. It can also apply to our work-a-day world; the bosses we work with each and every day. And it can apply to our families. For the most part, most of us are under authority for most aspects of our lives. The question is, do we have a submissive and obedient heart to those in authority over us?

That one was fun enough, let's look at a couple more. Paul goes on *"to speak evil of no one, to avoid quarrelling"* (v. 2). Wow! How are we doing with that one? Speak evil of no one and avoid quarrelling? Fortunately, he goes on to tell us how we could do that, *"to be gentle, and to show perfect courtesy toward all people"* (v. 2). I suppose, if we spent more time being gentle and more time being courteous, we would spend less time speaking evil of others and quarrelling with them.

Paul goes on to say, *"those who have believed in God may be careful to devote themselves to good works. These things are excellent and profitable for people"* (v. 8). As we devote ourselves to good works, we will be gentle and courteous to people and that will cause us to avoid speaking evil and quarrelling with people.

> If we spent more time being gentle and more time being courteous, we would spend less time speaking evil of others and quarrelling with them.

Though we are to devote ourselves to good works, verses 4-7 put those good works into perspective:

But when the goodness and loving kindness of God our Savior appeared, he saved us, not because of works done by us in righteousness, but according to his own mercy, by the washing of regeneration and renewal of the Holy Spirit, whom he poured out on us richly through Jesus Christ our Savior, so that being justified by his grace we might become heirs according to the hope of eternal life.

There is the good news. There is the gospel in just a couple of verses. We are not saved by our good works. Though we are to devote ourselves to do good works, we are not saved because of works done in righteousness. He saves us.

Let's finish with verses 4-7, *"the goodness and loving kindness of God"* (v. 4). God the Father is at work in our salvation because of His goodness and because of His love. The Holy Spirit shows up, *"by the washing of regeneration and renewal of the Holy Spirit"* (v. 5). So the Holy Spirit is involved in our salvation by regeneration, washing, and renewal. In verses 6 and 7, Jesus Christ our Savior shows up. Verse 7 says, *"so that being justified by his grace we might become heirs according to the hope of eternal life."* Salvation is dependent on Jesus our Savior and His grace. So, we are saved by the Triune God. God the Father, God the Son, God the Holy Spirit, all having a role in our salvation experience.

As we finish the Book of Titus, let's be reminded of some things we learned. We learned there is a link between our faith and our practice, and our belief and our behavior. We saw a description of the elders and how to properly live this Christian life, the portrait of a healthy church, and how to deflect false teaching by holding firm to the Word of God.

Prayer

Lord, we thank You for the Book of Titus. Thank you for the challenge to line up my beliefs with my behavior and to line up what I practice with my faith. Strengthen me, Lord, to be a better witness for You. Holy Spirit, help my walk in this life be more consistent with what I believe. Might my testimony be pleasing in Your sight. In Jesus' name, we pray. Amen.

MY THOUGHTS

ONE DAY IN PHILEMON

Does Your Conversion Matter?

Today, we will look at the one-chapter book of Philemon. You find it between Titus and Hebrews in the New Testament. My English Standard Version Study Bible book introduction says this about Philemon, "Philemon was a wealthy slaveholding Christian who lived in Colossae about 100 miles inland from Ephesus" (p. 2353). He may have heard the gospel while Paul was in Ephesus and was saved. One of his slaves, Onesimus, fled to Rome and somehow, he encounters the Apostle Paul in Rome. He, too, becomes a Christian and a helper to Paul. As much as Paul may have wanted to keep Onesimus around, he knew of the fugitive slave's severed relationship to his master and it needed to be addressed.

Paul writes Philemon to encourage him to understand the transformation Onesimus went through and receive him back, not just as a slave, but as a beloved brother. The elements in Paul's letter helped lay the foundation for the abolition of slavery. Paul probably wrote Philemon from Rome about the same time he wrote Colossians and Ephesians, around 62 A.D. All three letters were delivered by Tychicus and Onesimus.

Have you been converted? Does your conversion matter? Philemon is only one chapter, twenty-five versus. Please read or listen to the letter of Paul to Philemon.

COMMENTS

To guide us through this very short book, I will use two of my personal Bible reading journals, ten years apart, one from 1986, one of the very first journals I ever wrote, then 1996.

In 1986, I wrote, *"refresh my heart in Christ."* The full verse is, *"Yes, brother, let me benefit from you in the Lord; refresh my heart in Christ"* (v. 20 NASB). "Be a benefit to others. Be refreshing. Beautiful. I love it."

Ten years later, in 1996, I wrote, *"that the sharing of your faith may become effective"* (v. 6 NKJV). Then, *"'let me have joy from you in the Lord; refresh my heart in the Lord',* referring to verse 20."

The conversion of Philemon has obviously taken root:

I thank my God always when I remember you in my prayers, because I hear of your love and of the faith that you have toward the Lord Jesus and for all the saints, and I pray that the sharing of your faith may become effective for the full knowledge of every good thing that is in us for the sake of Christ. For I have derived much joy and comfort from your love, my brother, because the hearts of the saints have been refreshed through you (vv. 4-7).

> **Did people recognize you as a Christ-follower right off the bat? Were the hearts of those around you refreshed through you and your new testimony for the Lord?**

That is a powerful testimony of a new convert in Christ. Even Paul has heard about his conversion. Philemon has been refreshing to the brothers and sisters around him and has been sharing his faith. Paul encourages him to do more sharing of his faith and become effective for the Lord.

Is that what happened to you when you became a Christian? Did people recognize you as a Christ-follower right off the bat? Were the hearts of those around you refreshed through you and your new testimony for the Lord? Did you start sharing your faith, your conversion, your love for the Lord for the sake of Christ? Hopefully, that is what your conversion looked like. Or, if it has not happened to you yet, that could be what it will look like when you do decide to receive Jesus as your Lord and Savior.

Paul then encourages Philemon to accept Onesimus back, not only as a slave but as a brother in the Lord, because of his conversion to Christ. Paul even infers maybe he left Philemon so he could be converted, *"For this perhaps is why he was parted from you for a while, that you might have him back forever, no longer as a slave but more than a slave, as a beloved brother"* (vv. 15-16).

Philemon was changed once he heard the gospel of Christ. Now Paul is letting him know his slave was also changed when he heard the gospel of Christ. They now can have a new relationship as brothers in the Lord. Regardless of what your status is, rich or poor, a business owner or a worker, once you are in Christ, you are a new creature. Old things pass away, all things become new. You are now a beloved brother, both in flesh and in the Lord.

As such, we should become a benefit to others. We should be refreshing people's hearts in Christ. That is what Paul says he wants from Philemon, *"Yes, brother, I want some benefit from you in the Lord. Refresh my heart in Christ"* (v. 20).

DIGGING DEEPER

Are you a refreshing spirit because you are in Christ? That can be our application out of this very short one-chapter book in the New Testament. Your conversion to Christ should matter. People around you should know it. They should see it in how you live out your life. They should also receive joy and comfort and be refreshed in Christ in your presence. And you should be sharing your faith for the sake of Christ so others can have what you have.

Those are powerful life applications from this little book tucked between Titus and Hebrews. We have seen two people significantly affected by their conversions to Christ, Philemon and Onesimus. What about you? Have you been significantly changed because of your conversion to Christ?

Prayer

Lord, we thank You Paul wrote this book to Philemon. We thank You for the effect of conversions on these two people, Philemon and Onesimus. It challenges us to think about our own conversion. First, thank You for converting me in You. May I be a testimony to those around me because I have been converted to Jesus Christ.

Help me, Lord, to bring joy, comfort, and refreshment to those You put in my path. Holy Spirit, help me be bold enough to share my conversion with others so they can come to full knowledge of You, the Lord Jesus Christ. Please help me let the Jesus in me come out to those around me. In Your name, we ask it. Amen.

MY THOUGHTS

ABOUT THE AUTHOR

Allen J. Huth is the Founder and President of the Ezra Project. The Ezra Project's mission is to re-connect God's people to God's Word.

At age fifteen, Allen was in a tragic car accident. God saved his life physically and spiritually that day. That night, he started reading the Bible. Allen has been a daily Bible reader for over fifty years. He started keeping journals of what God was showing him through His Word in 1983 and continues doing so today.

He is a former member of the staff of the Colorado state legislature, a former vice president of the Colorado Association of Commerce and Industry, and was a partner in a business consulting firm, when God called him to start the Ezra Project in 2002.

Allen has been an active volunteer in The Gideons International for over forty years. He served as the international president, international vice president, and international treasurer.

He has spoken in churches, banquets, and conferences in nearly forty countries including Australia, Belgium, Brazil, Chile, Egypt, India, Indonesia, Kenya, Korea, Germany, Norway, Singapore, Cambodia, Papua New Guinea, Romania, South Africa, Thailand, and the People's Republic of China.

Allen and his wife, Terry, have been married over forty-five years. They have three adult children and five grandchildren.

Besides *Day by Day Through the Bible: The Writing of Paul*, Allen has authored *Day by Day Through the Bible: The Writing of Solomon*, and *Day by Day Through the Bible: The Writing of John*. He also wrote the *Chronological Bible Reading Journal*, the *Trio Bible Reading Journal*, and *12 Practical Principles of Leadership According to Ezra*. Find his works at *ezraproject.net*.